HOW TO USE FRENCH VERBS

HOW TO USE FRENCH VERBS

By Laura W. Fleder
Department of French and Romance Philology
Columbia University

Diane Wolfe Levy
Assistant Professor
Department of French
State University of New York at Albany

Barron's Educational Series Inc.
WOODBURY, NEW YORK

All inquiries should be addressed to:
Barron's Educational Series, Inc.
113 Crossways Park Drive
Woodbury, New York 11797

Library of Congress Catalog Card No. 75-22441

Library of Congress Cataloging in Publication Data

Fleder, Laura W.
  How to use French verbs.

  1. French language—Verb. I. Levy, Diane Wolfe,
joint author. II. Title.
PC2271.F55   445   75-22441
ISBN 0-8120-0599-6

International Standard Book No. 0-8120-0599-6

PRINTED IN THE UNITED STATES OF AMERICA

2 3 4 5 6 7 8 9 10 11 M 9 8 7

Table of Contents

Introduction

This book is intended to help students over two of the toughest hurdles in learning French: the use of prepositions and pronouns with verbs.

Prepositions are troublesome because they are governed by usage, not by systematic rules. No grammar rule will tell you, for example, why "J'essaye *de* finir mon travail" (I am trying to finish my work) uses *de* rather than some other preposition or no preposition at all. The use of *de* is completely arbitrary. Moreover, the use of prepositions is not consistent from one language to another. The student cannot rely on English usage as a model for his French sentence. In English, you wait *for* the bus; in French, "vous attendez l'autobus"—no preposition. Even more perplexing problems arise because many verbs can have different meanings with different prepositions.

Compare: Je réponds *à* Georges.   I answer George.
and: Je réponds *de* Georges.   I vouch for George.

The VERB LIST of this book helps you with this problem area. It lists 1500 verbs, the various prepositions each verb can take, and the meaning of each verb-preposition combination.

The second problem area, pronoun use, is tackled in the REVIEW and VERB CATEGORIES sections. Pronouns do follow systematic rules, but their usage is tricky: there are many more pronouns in French than in English and each pronoun in French has a very specific function. The REVIEW provides the basic concepts and rules necessary for understanding and using pronouns: it defines direct and indirect objects and explains the various types of personal pronouns. The REVIEW also outlines the basic verbal structures: the difference between transitive and intransitive verbs, the use of reflexive verbs, the rules for using *être* and *avoir* in compound tenses, the agreement of the past participle in compound tenses, and the use of infinitives. The REVIEW identifies and explains the various elements of verb usage. The VERB CATEGORIES section shows how to put these verbs and pronouns into use.

How to use this book

The VERB LIST goes hand in hand with the VERB CATEGORIES section. Suppose, for example, that you want to use the verb *penser* in the sentence, "I am thinking about my sister." How do you know what preposition to use after the verb, if any at all?

1. Check in the VERB LIST. You will find the following entry:

penser

1. _____ à Qn ou Qch (to think about . . .) III
2. _____ Qch de Qn ou Qch (to think . . . of, about . . . ; in questions, to have an opinion about . . . Ex: *Que pensez-vous du nouveau professeur?* What do you think of the new professor?) VI
3. _____ *Inf.* (to intend to . . . ; to think that . . . Ex: *Il pense pouvoir le faire.* He thinks that he can do it.) VII-A
4. _____ à *Inf.* (to think about, to consider ---*ing*) VIII-A

The first entry, "penser à Qn ou Qch," is what you need: You can substitute "ma soeur" for "quelqu'un" and you have, "Je pense à ma soeur."

2. Suppose you want to substitute a pronoun for "ma soeur," to say, "I am thinking about her." If you are not sure which pronoun to use or how to incorporate it in the sentence, turn back to the Category indicated by the roman numeral after the definition. You will find Category III (p. 44): VERBS WHICH TAKE À BEFORE A NOUN BUT WHICH CANNOT USE AN INDIRECT OBJECT PRONOUN TO SUBSTITUTE FOR THAT NOUN. You find that **penser** does not work like most verbs which take *à*, such as *parler, e.g.,* "Je parle *à ma soeur*" → "Je *lui* parle." Category III tells you that when the noun is a person, you keep the preposition *à* and replace the noun with a *tonic pronoun*. The category gives you an example of this type of substitution:

Je m'habitue *à mon nouveau patron.*	I'm getting used to *my new boss.*
Je m'habitue *à lui.*	I'm getting used to *him.*

Using the example as a model, make the same kind of substitution:

Je pense *à ma soeur.*	I'm thinking *about my sister.*
Je pense *à elle.*	I'm thinking *about her.*

3. If you are unsure of a grammatical term used in the Category entry, such as "tonic pronoun" or "indirect object pronoun," check in the REVIEW for a more detailed definition and explanation.

This book serves students at all levels of proficiency. Advanced students can use the VERB LIST exclusively, as a quick reference to check the preposition required by a verb. The less advanced student can use the VERB LIST along with the VERB CATEGORIES section to find out how to make a pronoun substitution. Beginners will need the REVIEW in addition to the VERB CATEGORIES as a reference for terms and as a basic grammar and guide to verb usage. In short, this book will show you step-by-step, **How to Use French Verbs.**

PART ONE

Review

A.   Verbs: Basic Concepts

There are two kinds of verbs: Intransitive and Transitive.

Intransitive Verbs

Intransitive verbs do not take a direct or indirect object. This means that the subject of the verb directs no action at another person or thing. Most intransitive verbs are complete in themselves:

Je pars.	I am leaving.
Il dort.	He is sleeping.
Nous travaillons.	We are working.

SUBJECT $\xrightarrow{\text{VERB}}$

Some intransitive verbs do take a noun after the verb: this noun is called a predicate noun.* The predicate noun is not, however, the object of the verb. The predicate noun is always the same person or thing as the subject, and the verb serves as a kind of equal sign, linking the subject to the predicate noun:

Mon frère est *médecin.*   My brother is a *doctor.*

$$\text{SUBJECT} \xrightarrow[=]{\textbf{VERB}} \text{PREDICATE NOUN.}$$

Intransitive verbs can also take a predicate adjective after the verb. The predicate adjective simply modifies the subject of the sentence. The verb acts as a link between the subject and the predicate adjective which describes it.

Vous semblez *fatigué.*   You seem *tired.*

$$\text{SUBJECT} \xrightarrow{\textbf{VERB}} \text{PREDICATE ADJECTIVE.}$$

The most common intransitive verbs which take predicate nouns and adjectives are *devenir* (to become), *être* (to be), *paraître* (to seem, to look), *rester* (to remain), *se montrer* (to appear), *se sentir* (to feel), and *sembler* (to seem).

---

*The term *predicate* refers to the "verb" part of the sentence and includes the verb and anything which completes the sense of the verb.

SUBJECT	PREDICATE	
We	walked.	
(*subject*)	(*verb*)	
The boys	walked	to the store.
(*subject*)	(*verb*)	(*adverbial phrase*)
Einstein	was	a genius.
(*subject*)	(*verb*)	(*predicate noun*)

Transitive Verbs

Transitive verbs can take a direct object, an indirect object, or both a direct object AND an indirect object.

1. *Transitive verbs which take a direct object*

A noun is a direct object if it receives the action of the verb directly, without the help of a preposition.

J'ouvre *la porte*.	I open *the door*.
Je vois *mes amis*.	I see *my friends*.
Elle amène *sa fille* chez le dentiste.	She takes *her daughter* to the dentist.

$$\text{SUBJECT} \xrightarrow{\textbf{VERB}} \textbf{DIRECT OBJECT.}$$

The direct object always answers the questions "What?" or "Whom?"

J'ouvre *la porte*.	(What do I open?)
Je vois *mes amis*.	(Whom do I see?)

Be careful not to confuse the direct object, which answers the questions "What?" or "Whom?" with nouns telling "Where", "When", "How", or "Why". In the following sentences, there are NO direct objects. The phrases *au Mexique* and *avant le professeur* are simply adverbial phrases telling "Where" and "When".

Je vais au Mexique.	I am going to Mexico.
Les élèves arrivent avant le professeur.	The students arrive before the teacher.

Many verbs can be either transitive or intransitive, depending on how they are used.

(*Intransitive*)	Elle écrit bien.	She writes well.
(*Transitive*)	Elle écrit une lettre.	She is writing a letter.
(*Intransitive*)	La cheminée fume.	The chimney is smoking.
(*Transitive*)	Il fume des cigares.	He smokes cigars.

2. *Transitive verbs which take an indirect object*

In English, an indirect object is rarely used without a direct object (see Section 3 on following page).

In French, an indirect object is a noun that is linked to the verb by the preposition *à*.

Je parle à *Jean*.	I speak to John.
J'écris à *ma mère*.	I write to my mother.
Nous obéissons à *la loi*.	We obey the law.*

$$\text{SUBJECT} \xrightarrow{\quad\text{VERB}\quad} \text{à} \longrightarrow \text{INDIRECT OBJECT.}$$

Many verbs in French take prepositions other than *à* before a noun (for example, *se moquer de*—to make fun of; *lutter avec*—to struggle with; *protester contre*—to protest against). The nouns following these prepositions are not technically indirect objects. Only nouns following the preposition *à* are indirect objects in French; and only these nouns can be replaced by indirect object pronouns.

---

*Note that the French verb *obéir* takes an indirect object, whereas the English verb *to obey* takes a direct object.

3. *Transitive verbs which take a direct* AND *an indirect object*

While the direct object receives the action of the verb, the indirect object can be said to "receive" the direct object.

In English, an indirect object is commonly used with a direct object. It is a noun or pronoun placed between the verb and the direct object. The indirect object answers the question "To whom?" or "For whom?"

She brought *him* the book.	Elle *lui* a apporté le livre.
I loaned *my friend* ten dollars.	J'ai prêté dix dollars à *mon ami.*

In French, the indirect object can be used alone—as in the examples in Section 2 above—or with a direct object. It is most often linked to a direct object.

J'ai posé + *une question* + à *l'agent.*
        (*direct object*)   (*indirect object*)
I asked the policeman a question.

J'ai envoyé + *une lettre* + à *mon sénateur.*
        (*direct object*)   (*indirect object*)
I sent my senator a letter.

SUBJECT $\xrightarrow{\text{VERB}}$ **DIRECT OBJECT** ⌐ à ↳**INDIRECT OBJECT.**

4. *Reflexive verbs*

A reflexive verb takes a pronoun object which "reflects" back to the subject of the sentence; that is, the subject and the object of the verb's action are the same person or thing. In English, the reflexive pronoun (*myself, himself, yourself, etc.*) is usually only implied.

Je *me* lave.	I get washed. ("I wash *my-self*.")
Nous *nous* dépêchons.	We are hurrying. ("We hurry *ourselves*.")
Il *se* couche.	He goes to bed. ("He puts *himself* to bed.")

SUBJECT	REFLEXIVE PRONOUN	VERB

The French reflexive pronouns are:

SINGULAR	PLURAL
me	nous
te	vous
se (masculine & feminine)	se (masculine & feminine)

These pronouns may be direct or indirect objects, depending on whether or not the verb takes the preposition *à*.

Il *se* réveille.	He wakes up. ("He wakes *himself*.")
	se = direct object
Elle *se* parle.	She talks to *herself*.
	se = indirect object

In the plural, the reflexive pronoun can have a reciprocal sense, meaning "each other."

Ils *se* regardent tendrement.	They look at *each other* tenderly.
Elles *se* parlent tous les jours.	They talk to *each other* every day.

The context of the sentence tells you whether the pronoun has a reciprocal or a reflexive meaning. In the above two sentences, for example, *"Ils se regardent"* and *"Elles se parlent"* could conceivably mean "They look at themselves" and "They talk to themselves"; but in light of the context, these latter meanings seem very unlikely.*

Reflexive verbs are often used in French where the passive form is used in English:

Cela *ne se fait pas* en bonne société.	That *isn't done* in polite company.
Ce médicament *se vend* à la pharmacie.	That medicine *is sold* at the pharmacy.

Most transitive verbs can be reflexive or not, depending on whether the object of the verb is the same person or thing as the subject.

Je lave ma robe.	I wash my dress.
Je *me* lave.	I wash (*myself*).
Elle habille sa fille.	She dresses her daughter.
Elle *s'*habille.	She gets dressed. ("She dresses *herself*.")

Some verbs, however, are ALWAYS reflexive, even though the action of the verb is directed at someone or something other than the subject. For these verbs the reflexive pronoun has no true reflexive or reciprocal meaning.

---

*In order to avoid ambiguity, and if the meaning intended is "at each other," or "to each other," the following can be added to make the thought clear: *l'un l'autre* in the first sentence or *l'une à l'autre* in the second sentence.

Il *se* moque de son petit frère.	He makes fun of his little brother.
Je ne *me* souviens pas de votre nom.	I don't remember your name.
Elle *s'*aperçoit de son erreur.	She realizes her error.

Position of Reflexive Pronouns

Reflexive pronouns, like other personal pronouns, normally **precede** the verb:

Il *se* lève.	He gets up.
Il ne *se* lève pas.	He doesn't get up.
Se lève-t-il?*	Is he getting up?
Ne *se* lève-t-il pas?	Isn't he getting up?

In compound tenses, the reflexive pronoun **precedes** the AUXILIARY verb:

Il *s'*est levé.	He got up.
Il ne *s'*est pas levé.	He didn't get up.
*S'*est-il levé?	Did he get up?
Ne *s'*est-il pas levé?	Didn't he get up?

---

*Be careful of the position of the subject pronoun and the reflexive pronoun in questions using the inverted form: The reflexive pronoun keeps its position directly preceding the verb and the subject pronoun swings around *after* the verb. The verb and the subject pronoun are then joined with a hyphen:

[Tu] *te* leves.	[Vous] *vous* levez.
Te lèves-[tu]?	*Vous* levez-[vous]?

EXCEPTION: Note the following changes that occur in the affirmative imperative (command form):

(1) The reflexive pronoun goes AFTER the verb.
(2) The stressed pronoun *toi* replaces *te*.

Levez-*vous!*	Get up!
Lève-*toi!*	Get up! (familiar)
Levons-*nous!*	Let's get up!

There is no change in the negative imperative form. The reflexive pronoun remains **in front** of the verb:

Ne *vous* levez pas!	Don't get up!
Ne *te* lève pas!	Don't get up! (familiar)
Ne *nous* levons pas!	Let's not get up!

Use of Auxiliary Verbs AVOIR and ÊTRE in Compound Tenses

1. Verbs conjugated with AVOIR

Most verbs in French are conjugated with AVOIR in compound tenses:

Avez-vous reçu ma lettre?	Did you receive my letter?
Ils *ont* acheté une nouvelle maison.	They bought a new house.

2. Verbs conjugated with ÊTRE

All Reflexive Verbs

Elle s'*est* couchée tard.	She went to bed late.
Nous nous *sommes* promenés aujourd'hui.	We went for a walk today.

The Following Verbs:

aller	to go
venir	to come
entrer	to enter, go in
sortir	to go out
arriver	to arrive
partir	to leave
revenir	to come back
retourner	to return, go back
rentrer	to go in again, go back
monter	to go up
descendre	to go down
tomber	to fall
passer	to go by, pass by
rester	to remain
devenir	to become
naître	to be born
mourir	to die

Thinking of these verbs as "verbs of movement" is a handy way to remember them. NOTE, however, that while all these verbs which take **être** are verbs of movement (literal or figurative), not all verbs of movement take **être**. There are many verbs of movement that do NOT take **être**. For example, *courir* (to run) and *marcher* (to walk) take **avoir**.

J'*ai* marché à l'école.	I walked to school.
Nous *avons* couru pour attraper l'autobus.	We ran to catch the bus.

The verbs of movement which take **être** are all intransitive verbs—that is, they do not take a direct or indirect object. Five of these verbs—*monter, descendre, sortir, rentrer,* and *passer*—can also be used in a transitive sense and take a direct object. When they take a direct object, they are conjugated with **avoir**. Compare the following examples:

1. Il *est* monté au premier étage.

   He went up to the second floor.

   Le porteur *a* monté les valises.

   The porter took the suitcases up.

2. Je *suis* descendu à la gare St-Lazare.

   I got off at the St. Lazare station.

   J'*ai* descendu l'escalier en vitesse.

   I went down the stairs quickly.

3. Elle *est* sortie à huit heures.

   She went out at eight o'clock.

   Elle *a* sorti un livre de la bibliothèque.

   She took a book out of the library.

4. Il *est* rentré tôt.

   He came home early.

   Il *a* rentré les chaises avant la pluie.

   He took in the chairs before the rain.

5. Je *suis* passé chez vous cet après-midi.

   I came by your house this afternoon.

   J'*ai* passé un examen de biologie ce matin.

   I took a biology exam this morning.

Agreement of the Past Participle in Compound Tenses

AGREEMENT WITH SUBJECT	—	VERBS CONJUGATED WITH **ÊTRE**
AGREEMENT WITH PRECEDING DIRECT OBJECT	—	ALL VERBS CONJUGATED WITH **AVOIR** AND ALL REFLEXIVE VERBS

1. The past participle of verbs conjugated with *être* agrees in gender and number with the SUBJECT.

Il est sorti.	He went out.
Ils sont sortis.	They went out.
Elle est allée en classe.	She went to class.
Elles sont allées en classe.	They went to class.

2. The past participle of verbs conjugated with *avoir* agrees in gender and number with the DIRECT OBJECT, if the direct object PRECEDES the verb.

Study the following examples:

(a) Quelle robe avez-vous *portée*   What dress did you
      hier soir?   wear last night?

AGREEMENT: The past participle agrees with the PRECEDING direct object, which is feminine singular.

(b) Les légumes que j'ai *achetés*   The vegetables that I
      sont délicieux.   bought are delicious.

AGREEMENT: The past participle agrees with the PRECEDING direct object, the relative pronoun *que,* whose antecedent is *les légumes. Les légumes* is masculine plural.

(c) Où sont mes clés?   Where are my keys?
      Je les ai *perdues!*   I've lost them!

AGREEMENT: The past participle agrees with the PRECEDING direct object pronoun *les; les s*tands for *les clés,* which is feminine plural.

BUT:

(d) J'ai *acheté* des⎡légumes⎤   I bought some vegetables
     au supermarché.   at the supermarket.

NO AGREEMENT: The direct object comes AFTER the verb.

NOTE: The past participle **does not agree** with **en** when **en** is the PRECEDING direct object:

Avez-vous acheté des disques?   Did you buy any records?
Oui, j'en ai *acheté.*   Yes, I bought some.

3. The past participle of reflexive verbs agrees with the DIRECT OBJECT, if the direct object PRECEDES the verb.

(a) Jeanne⎡s⎤'est *levée* de   Jeanne got up early.
     bonne heure.

AGREEMENT: The past participle agrees with the PRECEDING direct object, *se; se,* like the subject, is feminine singular.

(b) Les enfants⎡se⎤sont *lavés.*   The children got washed.
                           ("washed themselves")

AGREEMENT: The past participle agrees with the PRECEDING direct object, *se; se,* like the subject, is masculine plural.

BUT:

(c) Les enfants se sont *lavé*   The children washed
     les mains.   their hands.

NO AGREEMENT: The direct object (*les mains*) comes AFTER the verb. When a reflexive verb is followed by a noun direct object, the reflexive pronoun is considered to be the indirect object.

(d) Elles se sont *parlé* au They talked to each other
téléphone. on the telephone.

NO AGREEMENT: There is no direct object in this sentence. The reflexive pronoun *se* is an indirect object: the verb *parler* takes the preposition *à*.*

B. Verbs and Pronouns

Introduction to Pronouns

A pronoun is a word that is used to replace a noun. It can perform all the functions that nouns perform: subject, direct object, indirect object, or object of a preposition. Pronouns are less specific than nouns, but we usually use these "shorthand" forms within a context which avoids confusion. You wouldn't say "*He* came" or "I saw *her* yesterday" or "I put *it* there" if you didn't know who, or where, or what you were talking about.

The general pronouns we use to substitute for persons or things are called personal pronouns. They change form depending on their function. In English, there are only two forms: one for subject pronouns and one for object pronouns. For example, we say "*She* is ready" (subject); "I spoke to *her*" (object); "Where are *they*?" (subject); "The letter is for *them*" (object).

---

*If you are not sure whether a verb takes a direct or an indirect object, check the verb in the **VERB LIST**.

The Personal Pronouns

English Personal Pronouns

SUBJECT	OBJECT
I	me
you	you
he, she, it	him, her, it
we	us
you	you
they	them

The object form of English pronouns is used for all objects—direct, indirect, or object of a preposition:

I heard *them*. (*direct object*)

I brought *them* some wine. (*indirect object*)

I spoke with *them*. (*object of a preposition*)

In French, however, there is a special form for each kind of object pronoun:

I heard *them*.   Je *les* ai entendus.

I brought *them* some wine.   Je *leur* ai apporté du vin.

I spoke with *them*.   J'ai parlé avec *eux*.

French Personal Pronouns

SUBJECT	DIRECT OBJECT	INDIRECT OBJECT	TONIC OR STRESSED PRONOUNS (OBJECT OF PREPOSITION)
je	me	me	moi
tu	te	te	toi
il, elle, on	le, la (se)	lui (se)	lui, elle
nous	nous	nous	nous
vous	vous	vous	vous
ils, elles	les (se)	leur (se)	eux, elles

Notice that although some forms are identical, the context clearly determines what kind of pronoun you are dealing with:

Nous partons. (*subject*) — *We* are leaving.

Il est venu avec *nous*. (*object of preposition*) — He came with *us*.

Elle *lui* parle. (*indirect object*) — She is speaking *to him*.

Elle parle de *lui*. (*object of preposition*) — She is speaking about *him*.

Subject Pronouns

Subject pronouns represent persons or things. They generally precede the verb.

Il can mean "he" or "it" and *elle* can mean "she" or "it", depending on whether the noun replaced by the pronoun is a person or a thing.

Voilà ma petite soeur.	There is my little sister.
Elle a neuf ans.	*She* is nine.
Voilà ma voiture.	There is my car.
Elle est neuve.	*It's* new.

On is an indefinite subject pronoun which has various meanings in English. The most common are the vague or indefinite "you" or "they". Other translations for *on* are "one" or "people".

On ne devrait pas parler pendant un concert.	You (*one*) shouldn't talk during a concert.
On le dit très riche.	They (*people*) say he's very rich.

On is also used as a substitute for *nous* in spoken French:

Si *on* allait au cinéma?	Shall *we* go to the movies?
On s'est disputé hier.	*We* had a quarrel yesterday.

French people generally avoid using the passive form. *On* is often used as an active subject where a passive would be used in English.

Ici *on* parle français.	French *is spoken* here.
On a libéré le prisonnier.	The prisoner *was freed*.

Direct Object Pronouns

Direct object pronouns represent either persons or things. Unlike noun direct objects, which follow the verb, pronoun direct objects PRECEDE the verb in French, except in the affirmative imperative (command form).

Il connaît *cette femme.*	He knows *that woman.*
Il *la* connaît.	He knows *her.*
Il ferme *la porte.*	He is closing *the door.*
Il *la* ferme.	He is closing *it.*
Fermez *la porte.*	Close *the door.*
Fermez-*la.*	Close *it.*

Le can mean "him" or "it" and *la* can mean "her" or "it", depending on whether the noun replaced by the pronoun is a person or a thing.

Indirect Object Pronouns

Indirect object pronouns are used to substitute for persons, animals, or animate objects, and ONLY when the preposition following the verb is *à*.* Unlike noun indirect objects, which follow the verb, pronoun indirect objects PRECEDE the verb in French except in the affirmative imperative (command form). The indirect object pronoun replaces both the preposition *à* and the noun group following it.

---

*See p. 43 for a list of verbs which take direct objects in English and indirect objects in French.

Il a téléphoné *à son amie.*	He called *his girlfriend.*
Il *lui* a téléphoné.	He called *her.*
Ecrivez *à vos parents.*	Write *to your parents.*
Ecrivez-*leur.*	Write *to them.*
Le médecin *me* défend de fumer.	The doctor forbids *me* to smoke.
Elle parle *à ses plantes* tous les jours!	She talks *to her plants* every day!
Elle *leur* parle tous les jours!	She talks *to them* every day!

Tonic Pronouns

Tonic, or stressed pronouns, have several functions. They are used:

1. after prepositions
2. for emphasis, to reinforce a subject, direct object or indirect object
3. after *c'est* or *ce sont*
4. in a compound subject, direct object, or indirect object
5. in comparisons
6. when there is no verb in the sentence

1. After Prepositions

Since indirect object pronouns are used only when a verb takes the preposition *à*, a different set of pronouns is used with other prepositions: *the tonic pronouns.*

Like the indirect object pronouns, *tonic pronouns* used as the object of a preposition replace nouns representing people, animals, or animate objects. Tonic pronouns are placed AFTER the preposition, just like the noun they replace.

On s'est révolté contre *le dictateur.*	They rebelled against *the dictator.*
On s'est révolté contre *lui.*	They rebelled against *him.*
Il compte sur *ses amis.*	He is counting on *his friends.*
Il compte sur *eux.*	He is counting on *them.*

2. For Emphasis

In English, subject or object pronouns can be stressed by the inflection of the voice. For example, you could say "You invited *him*?!" or "*I* did it!" In French, however, *tonic pronouns* are added to the sentence for emphasis. They are used in addition to the unstressed subject or object.* The tonic pronoun can be added at the beginning or at the end of the sentence.

---

*All tonic pronouns except *moi* and *toi* can be used alone as an *emphatic* subject, without a subject pronoun:

Lui ne parle jamais.	*He* never speaks.
Il ne parle jamais, *lui.*	*He* never speaks.

Tu l'as invité, *lui*?	You invited *him*?
Je l'ai fait, *moi*!	*I* did it!
Moi, j'y vais tous les jours.	*I* go there every day.

3. After *C'est* or *Ce Sont*

The subject or object can also be stressed by using the expression *c'est* or *ce sont* + tonic pronoun. *C'est* is used with *moi, toi, lui, elle, nous* and *vous*. *Ce sont* is used only with the pronouns *eux* and *elles*. This construction is often followed by a relative clause.

C'est Pierre qui téléphone?	Is it Peter calling?
Oui, c'est *lui*.	Yes, it's *he*.
C'est *lui* que j'ai vu.	I saw *him*.
C'est *moi* qui ai raison et ce sont *eux* qui ont tort!	*I'm* right and *they're* wrong!

4. *In Compound Subjects and Objects*

Tonic pronouns are used in compound subjects, direct objects or indirect objects:

Georges et *lui* viennent demain.	George and *he* are coming tomorrow.

They are also used to make a subject or object more explicit:

Nous restons à la maison,   We are staying at home,
     elle et *moi*.   *she* and *I*.

5. In Comparisons

Tonic pronouns (NOT subject pronouns) are used as the second element of a comparison in French:

Tu es plus aimable qu'*eux*.   You are nicer than *they*.

Il mange moins vite que   He eats less quickly than
     nous.   *we*.

6. When There Is No Verb

Tonic pronouns are used in sentences where the verb is merely implied:

Qui est là? *Moi*. (*C'est moi*.)   Who's there? *Me*.

Tu n'aimes pas l'art   You don't like modern
     moderne? *Lui* non plus.   art? Neither does *he*.

The Adverbial Pronouns Y and En

As we have seen above, indirect object pronouns and tonic pronouns are used only to represent people, animals, or animate objects. What pronoun do you use if the indirect object or the object of a preposition is a THING? The adverbial pronouns **y** and **en** are used in this case:

Je réponds *à la question.*   I answer *the question.*

J'*y* réponds.   I answer *it.*

Elle se souvient *de l'adresse.*   She remembers *the address.*

Elle s'*en* souvient.   She remembers *it.*

These useful pronouns have other functions as well. They can help you out of many awkward grammatical situations. Read on!

The Adverbial Pronoun Y

The pronoun **y** has two major functions. It can replace:

1.   *à* + noun (thing)
2.   a prepositional phrase of location

1. *À* + noun (thing)

Y is used as an indirect object pronoun to substitute for THINGS. Like indirect object pronouns used to substitute for people, **y** replaces both the preposition *à* and the noun group following it. **Y** normally precedes the verb, except in affirmative imperative sentences:

Nous obéissons *à la loi*.	We obey *the law*.
Nous *y* obéissons.	We obey *it*.

Pensez *à ce problème*!	Think about *this problem*!
Pensez-*y*!	Think about *it*!

2. *Prepositional Phrases of Location*

Y is also used as a pronoun of place. It can replace any prepositional phrase of location or position (except those using the preposition *de*) when the noun following the preposition is a THING. In this case, **y** means "there."

J'ai laissé les clés *dans la voiture*.	I left the keys *in the car*.
J'*y* ai laissé les clés.	I left the keys *there*.

Nous allons *à Moscou*.	We are going *to Moscow*.
Nous *y* allons.	We are going *there*.

Va *à la poste*!	Go *to the post office*!
Vas-*y*!	Go *there*!

Il a jeté des cailloux *contre la fenêtre*.	He threw some pebbles *at the window*.
Il *y* a jeté des cailloux.	He threw some pebbles *(there) at it*.

The Adverbial Pronoun En

The various uses of **en** are not hard to remember if you keep in mind that this pronoun is usually associated in some way with the preposition *de*. You can use **en** to replace the word or group of words following:

1. a partitive article (*du, de la, de l', des, de, d'*)
2. an expression of quantity (*beaucoup de, trop de, etc.*)
3. The preposition *de*

1. Partitive Articles

When the noun direct object of a verb is introduced by a partitive article, *you cannot replace the noun direct object with a direct object pronoun.* **En** is used to replace the partitive article AND the direct object, PERSON or THING. **En** normally precedes the verb.

Il connaît *des gens importants.*	He knows *some important people.*
Il *en* connaît.	He knows *some* (people).
Je veux *du gâteau.*	I want *some cake.*
J'*en* veux.	I want *some.*

but:

Elle gronde *les enfants.*	She scolds *the children.*
Elle *les* gronde.	She scolds *them.*
J'ai perdu *ma montre!*	I've lost *my watch!*
Je *l'*ai perdue!	I've lost *it!*

2. *Expressions of Quantity*

Similarly, you cannot replace the noun direct object of a verb with a direct object pronoun when the noun direct object is introduced by an expression of quantity. **En** is used to replace the direct object, PERSON or THING. Notice that **en** normally precedes the verb, while the word of quantity stays after the verb.

Ce médecin a guéri *beaucoup de malades.*	This doctor has cured *many patients.*
Ce médecin *en* a guéri *beaucoup.*	This doctor has cured *many (of them).*
J'ai *tant de travail!*	I have *so much work!*
J'*en* ai *tant!*	I have *so much! (of it)*
Elle a *trois enfants.*	She has *three children.*
Elle *en* a *trois.*	She has *three (of them).*
Le chef a mis *trop de sel* dans la soupe.	The chef put *too much salt* in the soup.
Le chef *en* a mis *trop* dans la soupe.	The chef put *too much (of it)* in the soup.

The same sequence is used with certain indefinite pronouns like *quelques-uns, quelques-unes* (some, a few); *plusieurs* (several); *certains, certaines* (certain ones); and *aucun, aucune* (none).

Il a invité *quelques amis.*	He invited *a few friends.*
Il *en* a invité *quelques-uns.*	He invited *a few (of them).*

J'ai cassé *plusieurs verres.*	I broke *several glasses.*
J'*en* ai cassé *plusieurs.*	I broke *several (of them).*

3. The Preposition de

A. Many verbs* take the preposition *de* before a noun. **En** can replace *de* + noun when the noun following *de* is a THING:

Elle a besoin *d'argent.*	She needs (*some*) *money.*
Elle *en* a besoin.	She needs *some.*

Je me moque *de l'examen.*	I don't care about *the test.*
Je m'*en* moque.	I don't care about *it.*

When the noun following *de* is a PERSON, keep *de* and replace the noun with a *tonic pronoun.*

Je me méfie *de cet homme.*	I don't trust *that man.*
Je me méfie *de lui.*	I don't trust *him.*

B. *De* can introduce a prepositional phrase modifying an adjective. **En** replaces *de* + noun when the noun following *de* is a THING.

Nous sommes contents *de notre progrès.*	We are happy with *our progress.*
Nous *en* sommes contents.	We are happy with *it.*

---

*And verbal expressions such as *avoir besoin de, avoir envie de, avoir peur de.*

Il était surpris *de votre réponse*.	He was surprised by *your answer*.
Il *en* était surpris.	He was surprised by *it*.

When the noun following *de* is a PERSON, keep *de* and replace the noun with a *tonic pronoun*.

Il est fier *de son fils*.	He is proud of *his son*.
Il est fier *de lui*.	He is proud of *him*.

C. *De* can introduce a prepositional phrase modifying a noun. **En** replaces *de* + noun when the noun following *de* is a THING.

Il a mangé la moitié *du gâteau*.	He ate half *of the cake*.
Il *en* a mangé la moitié.	He ate half (*of it*).
J'ai oublié la fin *de l'histoire*.	I've forgotten the end *of the story*.
J'*en* ai oublié la fin.	I've forgotten the end (*of it*).

When the noun following *de* is a PERSON, *de* + noun is usually replaced by a *possessive adjective*.

Sais-tu le nom *de cette femme*?	Do you know *that woman's* name?
Sais-tu *son* nom?	Do you know *her* name?

Je n'aime pas les films *de cet acteur-là.*	I don't like *that actor's* films.
Je n'aime pas *ses* films.	I don't like *his* films.

D. *De* is sometimes used as a preposition of place, meaning "from." **En** can be used to replace *de* + the noun of place, and means "from there."

Il est arrivé *de Paris* ce matin.	He arrived *from Paris* this morning.
Il *en* est arrivé ce matin.	He arrived (*from there*) this morning.
Elle vient *du bureau.*	She is coming *from the office.*
Elle *en* vient.	She is coming *from there.*

Position of Personal Pronouns

All personal pronouns in French—except tonic pronouns— are normally placed BEFORE the verb. This can create a problem of order when there is more than one pronoun in the same sentence.

The sequence of personal pronouns is not determined by function. Direct objects do not always precede indirect objects, for instance. Compare the order of the pronouns in the following two sentences:

Je *le lui* donne.   I am giving *it to him.*

le = direct object

lui = indirect object

Il *me le* donne.   He is giving *it to me.*

me = indirect object

le = direct object

The direct object pronoun precedes the indirect object pronoun in the first sentence, but the order is reversed in the second.

The order of the personal pronouns is simply a matter of usage. There are many ways of learning the proper order. One helpful way to remember the order of *y* and *en* is to think of having a "yen" for something. Another device is to think of the sound of a braying donkey, *y-en!* But the easiest way to be sure of these pronouns is to memorize the following chart. Once you have learned this order, certain combinations will become automatic and you will no longer have to think consciously of the sequence.

The following sequence of pronouns is used for all kinds of sentences (declarative, negative, interrogative) with one exception: affirmative imperative sentences. (*See Table I on following page.*)

TABLE I

SUBJECT	(ne)	me te se nous vous	le la les	lui leur	y	en	VERB (or auxiliary verb)	(pas)	(past participle)

Note that pronouns of the first and second persons precede pronouns of the third person. When there are two pronouns of the third person, the direct object precedes the indirect object.

Notice that *ne* and *pas* enclose the pronoun(s) and verb, like bookends. In a compound tense, *ne* and *pas* enclose the pronoun(s) and the AUXILIARY verb; the past participle goes after *pas*.*

Some examples with more than one object pronoun in a sentence will illustrate this sequence.

Elle a rendu *sa bague à son financé.*	She returned *her ring to her fiancé.*
Elle *la lui* a rendue.	She returned *it to him.*
Nous ne donnons pas *de chocolats aux enfants.*	We don't give *the children chocolates.*
Nous ne *leur en* donnons pas.	We don't give *them any.*
As-tu parlé *à Georges de son projet?*	Did you speak *to George about his project?*
Lui en as-tu parlé?	Did you speak *to him about it?*
N'avez-vous pas pris *les billets?*	Didn't you get *the tickets?*
Ne *les* avez-vous pas pris?	Didn't you get *them?*

Affirmative imperative sentences alter this order somewhat.

**ne pas is usually placed as a unit BEFORE an infinitive. For example:

Elle préférerait *ne pas* aller *au concert.*	She would rather *not* go *to the concert.*
Elle préférerait *ne pas* y aller.	She would rather *not* go (*there*).

A brief review of this verb form might be useful. The imperative is used for exclamations and commands. It exists in the *tu, nous* and *vous* forms. To form the imperative, drop the subject pronoun.*

Tu parles.	You are talking.
Parle!	Talk!

Nous commençons.	We are beginning.
Commençons!	Let's begin!

Vous sortez.	You are going out.
Sortez!	Get out!

Three changes occur when personal (or reflexive) pronouns are used with the affirmative imperative, one of form and two of position:

1. First, all pronouns are placed AFTER the verb, and the verb and pronoun(s) are joined by hyphens.

2. Secondly,

le		me
la	PRECEDE	te
les		nous
		vous

The rest of the sequence of pronouns is unchanged.

---

*The final *s* in the *tu* form of *-er* verbs is dropped in imperative sentences, except before *y* and *en*, where it facilitates pronunciation, *e.g.*, *Vas-y! Manges-en!*

3. Finally, for added emphasis, the pronouns *me* and *te* take the tonic forms *moi* and *toi*. (*Nous* and *vous* are already tonic forms.) This change DOES NOT occur if *me* and *te* precede *y* or *en*.

Thus, the order of the personal pronouns in **affirmative imperative** sentences is:

VERB	le	moi	lui	y	en
	la	toi	leur		
	les	nous			
		vous			

For example:

Tu mets *les fleurs sur la table.*	You are putting *the flowers on the table.*
Mets-*les*-*y*!	Put *them there*!
Tu *te* tais.	You are quiet.
Tais-*toi*!	Be quiet!
Vous *me* donnez *de l'eau.*	You are giving *me some water.*
Donnez-*m'en*!	Give *me some*!
Tu rends *le livre à Suzanne.*	You are giving *the book* back *to Susan.*
Rends-*le*-*lui*!	Give *it* back *to her*!

Vous *me* passez *le pain*.   You are passing *me the bread*.

Passez-*le-moi*!   Pass *it to me*!

There is NO CHANGE from the normal form and order of personal pronouns in a NEGATIVE imperative sentence, nor are hyphens used between the elements.

NE	me	le	lui	y	en	VERB	PAS
	te	la	leur				
	nous	les					
	vous						

For example:

Tu ne mets pas *les fleurs sur la table*.   You are not putting *the flowers on the table*.

Ne *les y* mets pas!   Don't put *them there*!

Vous ne *me* donnez pas *d'eau*.   You are not giving *me any water*.

Ne *m'en* donnez pas!   Don't give *me any*!

Tu ne *te* tais pas.   You don't stop talking.

Ne *te* tais pas!   Don't stop talking!

Vous ne *me* passez pas *le pain*.   You aren't passing *me the bread*.

Ne *me le* passez pas!   Don't pass *it to me*!

Tu ne rends pas *le livre* à *Suzanne*.	You aren't giving *the book* back *to Susan*.
Ne *le lui* rends pas!	Don't give *it* back *to her*!

C. Verbs and Infinitives

The Present Infinitive

An infinitive is the "pure" form of the verb that expresses the idea of a verb without regard to person, number, or tense.

In English, infinitives are prefaced by "to": *to swim, to rain, to leave*. We frequently use infinitives after another verb.

> I like *to swim*.
>
> It's beginning *to rain*.
>
> He decided *to leave*.

The preposition "to" in English is actually part of the infinitive, a kind of "marker." The main verb in English never takes another preposition before an infinitive.

In French, however, infinitives need no external marker, since the endings **-er**, **-ir**, and **-re** clearly identify them. Moreover, the main verb can take the prepositions *à*, *de*, *par*, or no preposition at all before the infinitive:

J'aime nager.	I like to swim.
Il commence *à* pleuvoir.	It's beginning to rain.
Il a décidé *de* partir.	He decided to leave.

The use of prepositions in French is completely arbitrary. You must simply try to learn what preposition, if any, a verb uses before an infinitive when you learn the verb; or check in the VERB LIST.

The use of the infinitive in French is more extensive than in English. French uses an infinitive where English might use an infinitive or another construction, such as a gerund* or a subordinate clause:

J'aime *nager*.	I like *to swim*. OR I like *swimming*.
Il continue de *travailler*.	He continues *to work*. OR He continues *working*.
Elle m'a demandé de *rester*.	She asked me *to stay*. OR She asked *that I stay*.

FRENCH	ENGLISH
VERB + (preposition) + Infinitive	VERB + { Infinitive / Gerund / Subordinate Clause

---

*In English, when the present participle (the *-ing* form of the verb) is used as a noun, it is called a *gerund*. The present participle form in French (the *-ant* form) is NEVER used as a verbal noun; an infinitive is used instead. For example, the saying, "Seeing is believing" is translated, "*Voir, c'est croire.*"

Of course, in some cases in English one form is clearly correct. We would never say "He finished to eat" but rather, "He finished eating."

Two prepositions, *sans* and *avant de*, which take an infinitive in French, never take an infinitive in English:

Il est parti sans *payer*.	He left without *paying*.
Pensez-y avant de *répondre*.	Think about it before *answering* (*before you answer*).

The Past Infinitive

A past infinitive is simply the infinitive of the appropriate auxiliary verb (*être* or *avoir*) plus the past participle:

avoir parlé	to have spoken
être parti	to have left

French uses a past infinitive where English usually uses a gerund or a subordinate clause:

On l'accuse d'*avoir volé* la banque.	He is accused of *robbing* the bank.
Je m'excuse d'*être venu* en retard.	I'm sorry *that I'm late*.

Verbs that usually take a past infinitive in French are indicated in the VERB LIST.

Note that the preposition *après* takes a past infinitive.

Je suis sorti après *avoir dîné.*	I went out after *I ate* (*after eating*) dinner.
Ils ont regardé la télévision après *avoir fini* leurs devoirs.	They watched television after *they finished* (*after finishing*) their homework.

It is considered bad style in French to use a subordinate clause when the subject of the subordinate clause is the same person as the subject of the main clause. French uses an infinitive (past or present) to avoid this repetition.

Je regrette d'*avoir gaspillé* mon temps.	I'm sorry *that I wasted* (*to have wasted*) my time.
Je pense *pouvoir faire* le travail.	I think *that I can do* the work.

PART TWO

Verb Categories

Verbs and Nouns

I. *Direct object verbs: These verbs take* NO *preposition before a noun.*

Examples:

Je connais le chef.	I know the chef.
Je connais le restaurant.	I know the restaurant.

Substitutions:

1. Use direct object pronouns to replace most DIRECT OBJECT NOUNS, people or things.

Je connais *le chef.*	I know *the chef.*
Je *le* connais.	I know *him.*

Je connais *le restaurant.*	I know *the restaurant.*
Je *le* connais.	I know *it.*

2. Use *en* to replace a **DIRECT OBJECT NOUN** introduced by a partitive article (*du, de la, de l', des, de, d'*) or an expression of quantity (*beaucoup de, trop de, etc.*).

La reine a *des ennemis*.	The queen has *enemies*.
La reine *en* a.	The queen has *some* (enemies).
La reine a *des bijoux*.	The queen has *jewels*.
La reine *en* a.	The queen has *some* (jewels).
Elle a *beaucoup d'ennemis*.	She has *many enemies*.
Elle *en* a beaucoup.	She has many (*of them*).
Elle a *beaucoup de bijoux*.	She has *many jewels*.
Elle *en* a beaucoup.	She has many (*of them*).

Most verbs in French, as in English, are **DIRECT OBJECT VERBS**. They present no problems and, therefore, are not listed in the **VERB LIST**.

Reflexive verbs fall in this Category when the reflexive pronoun is the direct object of the verb. For example, **se coucher**, to go to bed (to put *oneself* to bed). See REFLEXIVE VERBS, p. 5.

Note: The following common verbs take a DIRECT OBJECT in French, whereas their English equivalents take a preposition before a noun.

Example:

Il demande l'addition.   He asks *for* the check.

approuver	to approve of	**mettre**	to put on
attendre	to wait for	**opérer**	to operate on
chercher	to look for	**payer**	to pay for
demander	to ask for	**pleurer**	to cry over, about
écouter	to listen to		
envoyer chercher	to send for	**prier**	to pray to
essayer	to try on, out	**puer**	to stink of
habiter	to live in, on	**regarder**	to look at
ignorer	to be unaware of	**sentir**	to smell of
marchander	to haggle with, over	**soigner**	to take care of

II. *Verbs which take À before a noun*

Examples:

Les soldats obéissent *au* capitaine.

The soldiers obey the captain.

Les soldats obéissent *à* l'ordre.

The soldiers obey the order.

Substitutions:

1. For people, use indirect object pronouns to replace *à* and the noun.

Les soldats obéissent *au capitaine.*

The soldiers obey *the captain.*

Les soldats *lui* obéissent.

The soldiers obey *him.*

2. For things, use *y* to replace *à* and the noun.

Les soldats obéissent *à l'ordre.*

The soldiers obey *the order.*

Les soldats *y* obéissent.

The soldiers obey *it.*

Note: The following common verbs take the preposition *à* before a noun, whereas their English equivalents take a direct object.

Example:

Ils assistent *à* la conférence.   They attend the lecture.

assister à	to attend	**obéir à**	to obey
s'attendre à	to expect	**s'opposer à**	to oppose
déplaire à	to displease	**plaire à**	to please
désobéir à	to disobey	**résister à**	to resist
se fier à	to trust	**ressembler à**	to resemble
goûter à	to taste	**survivre à**	to survive
jouer à	to play (a game)	**téléphoner à**	to telephone
nuire à	to harm		

III. *Verbs which take* À *before a noun but which cannot use an indirect object pronoun to substitute for that noun.*

Examples:

Je m'habitue *à* mon nouveau patron.	I'm getting used to my new boss.
Je m'habitue *à* mon nouveau poste.	I'm getting used to my new job.

Substitutions:

1. For people, keep the preposition *à* and replace the noun with a tonic pronoun.

Je m'habitue *à mon nouveau patron.*	I'm getting used to *my new boss.*
Je m'habitue *à lui.*	I'm getting used to *him.*

2. For things, use *y* to replace *à* and the noun, as in II, 2 above.

Je m'habitue *à mon nouveau poste.*	I'm getting used to *my new job.*
Je m'*y* habitue.	I'm getting used to *it.*

This category includes the following verbs and expressions:

être à	to belong to
faire attention à	to pay attention to
penser à	to think about
tenir à	to be fond of

And all reflexive verbs which take *à* before a noun, *e.g.*, **s'habituer à**, to get used to.

IV. *Verbs which take DE before a noun*

Examples:

Je me souviens *de* la chanteuse.	I remember the singer.
Je me souviens *de* la chanson.	I remember the song.

Substitutions:

1. For people, keep the preposition *de* and replace the noun with a tonic pronoun.

Je me souviens *de la chanteuse*.	I remember *the singer*.
Je me souviens *d'elle*.	I remember *her*.

2. For things, use **en** to replace *de* and the noun.

Je me souviens *de la chanson*.	I remember *the song*.
Je m'*en* souviens.	I remember *it*.

Note: The following common verbs take the preposition *de* before a noun, whereas their English equivalents take a direct object.

Example:

Le millionnaire ne manque pas *d*'argent.	The millionaire does not lack money.

s'apercevoir de	to notice	**hériter de**	to inherit
approcher de	to approach	**jouer de**	to play (an instrument)
changer de	to change		
douter de	to doubt	**jouir de**	to enjoy
se douter de	to suspect	**manquer de**	to lack
goûter de	to taste, try	**partir de**	to leave

V. *Verbs which commonly take a preposition other than À or DE before a noun*

Examples:

L'ambassadeur s'incline *devant* le roi.	The ambassador bows *to* the king.

J'entre *dans* le café.   I go *into* the café.

Substitutions:

1. For people, keep the preposition and replace the noun with a tonic pronoun.

> L'ambassadeur s'incline   The ambassador bows *to*
>   *devant le roi.*   the king.

> L'ambassadeur s'incline   The ambassador bows *to*
>   *devant lui.*   him.

2. For things:

> (a) When the preposition indicates position or location (*contre, dans, en, sous, sur*) **y** (meaning loosely, "there") is often used to replace the preposition and the noun:

> > J'entre *dans le café.*   I go *into the café.*
> >
> > J'*y* entre.   I go in (*there*).

> The prepositions *dans*, *sous*, and *sur* have special forms which are more precise and emphatic than *y*: *là-dedans* (in, into it), *là-dessous* (under it), and *là-dessus* (on, about it). These forms may be used to replace the preposition and the noun. They are placed AFTER the verb.

L'archéologue a pénétré *dans la tombe égyptienne.*	The archeologist broke *into the Egyptian tomb.*
L'archéologue a pénétré *là-dedans.*	The archeologist broke *into it.*

(b) When the preposition does not indicate position or location, the noun following the preposition is usually kept.

Le prisonnier languit *après sa liberté.*	The prisoner longs *for his liberty.*

In colloquial French, however, the noun is sometimes omitted after the prepositions *contre* and *avec*.

Il a lutté *contre sa peur.*	He struggled *against his fear.*
Il a lutté *contre.*	He struggled *against (it).*

Note: Some French verbs take a preposition before a noun, whereas their English equivalents take a direct object. For example:

Anne se marie *avec* Georges.   Anne is marrying George.

VI. *Verbs which take a direct object plus a noun introduced by* À, DE *or another preposition*

A.   Direct Object Plus À + NOUN

Step 1: To replace the DIRECT OBJECT, person or thing, use a direct object pronoun or **en** (See Category I, p. 40).

Step 2: To replace $\boxed{\text{À + NOUN}}$

    (a) When the noun following *à* is a person, replace $\boxed{\text{À + NOUN}}$ with an indirect object pronoun.

    (b) When the noun following *à* is a thing, replace $\boxed{\text{À + NOUN}}$ with *y*.

Step 3: To replace both the DIRECT OBJECT AND $\boxed{\text{À + NOUN}}$ combine Steps 1 and 2 above.*

Examples:

Le serpent offrit *la pomme à Eve*.	The serpent offered *the apple to Eve*.
1. Le serpent *l'*offrit à Eve.	The serpent offered *it* to Eve.
2a. Le serpent *lui* offrit la pomme.	The serpent offered *her* the apple.
3. Le serpent *la lui* offrit.	The serpent offered *it to her*.

---

*For order of personal pronouns, see REVIEW, p. 29.

Il a prêté *du sucre à son voisin*.	He loaned *his neighbor some sugar*.

1. Il *en* a prêté à son voisin.   He loaned his neighbor *some*.

2a. Il *lui* a prêté du sucre.   He loaned *him* some sugar.

3. Il *lui en* a prêté.   He loaned *him some*.

La faim a poussé *le pauvre au vol*.	Hunger drove *the poor man to theft*.

1. La faim *l'*a poussé au vol.   Hunger drove *him* to theft.

2b. La faim *y* a poussé le pauvre.   Hunger drove the poor man *to it*.

3. La faim *l'y* a poussé.   Hunger drove *him to it*.

B. Direct Object Plus | DE + NOUN |

> *Step 1:* To replace the DIRECT OBJECT, person or thing, use a direct object pronoun or **en** (See Category I, p. 40).

> *Step 2:* To replace | DE + NOUN |

> > (a) When the noun following *de* is a person, keep *de* and replace the noun with a tonic pronoun.

(b) When the noun following *de* is a thing, replace *de* and the noun with **en**.

Step 3: To replace both the DIRECT OBJECT AND
| DE + NOUN | combine Steps 1 and 2
above.*

Example:

Le cambrioleur a rempli *ses poches d'argent.*	The burglar filled *his pockets with money.*

1. Le cambrioleur *les* a remplies d'argent.   The burglar filled *them* with money.

2b. Le cambrioleur *en* a rempli ses poches.   The burglar filled his pockets *with it.*

3. Le cambrioleur *les en* a remplies.   The burglar filled *them with it.*

C. Direct Object Plus Prepositions Other Than
À or DE

Step 1: To replace the DIRECT OBJECT, person or
thing, use a direct object pronoun or **en** (See
Category I, p. 40).

Step 2: To replace | PREPOSITION + NOUN |

---

*For order of personal pronouns, see REVIEW, p. 29.

(a) When the noun following the preposition is a person, keep the preposition and replace the noun with a tonic pronoun.

(b) When the noun following the preposition is a thing, there are several possibilities:

When the preposition indicates position or location (*contre, dans, en, sous, sur*), **y** (meaning loosely "there") is often used to replace the preposition and noun.

The prepositions *dans, sous,* and *sur* have special forms which are more precise and emphatic than *y: là-dedans* (in, into it), *là-dessous* (under it), and *là-dessus* (on, about it). These forms may be used to replace the preposition and noun. They are placed AFTER the verb.

When the preposition does not indicate position or location, the noun following the preposition is usually kept.

Step 3: To replace both the DIRECT OBJECT AND PREPOSITION + NOUN combine Steps 1 and 2 above.

Examples:

Le vieillard a partagé *sa fortune entre ses trois filles.*	The old man divided *his fortune among his three daughters.*

1. Le vieillard *l'*a partagée
   entre ses trois filles.

   The old man divided *it*
   among his three
   daughters.

2a. Le vieillard a partagé sa
    fortune *entre elles*.

    The old man divided his
    fortune *among them*.

3. Le vieillard *l'*a partagée
   entre elles.

   The old man divided *it*
   among them.

L'ouvrier a planté *l'échelle
contre le mur*.

The workman set *the lad-
der against the wall*.

1. L'ouvrier *l'*a plantée
   contre le mur.

   The workman set *it*
   against the wall.

2b. L'ouvrier *y* a planté
    l'échelle.

    The workman set the lad-
    der *there*.

3. L'ouvrier *l'y* a plantée.

   The workman set *it there*.

La police a interrogé
l'accusé sur le crime.

The police questioned *the
suspect about the
crime*.

1. La police *l'*a interrogé
   sur le crime.

   The police questioned
   him about the crime.

2b. La police a interrogé
    l'accusé *là-dessus*.

    The police questioned the
    suspect *about it*.

3. La police *l'*a interrogé
   là-dessus.

   The police questioned
   him about it.

Verbs and Infinitives

VII. *Verbs which take NO preposition before an infinitive*

A. Verbs which take an Infinitive but which do not take a Direct or Indirect Object

Examples:

Nous devons partir tout de suite.	We have to leave immediately.
J'aime lire.	I like to read.

If the *infinitive* is followed by a noun, the noun can be replaced by a pronoun. If you are uncertain of what pronoun to use, refer to Categories I-VI, VERBS AND NOUNS, pp. 40–53.

All personal pronouns, except tonic pronouns, directly PRECEDE the infinitive.

Les singes adorent manger *les bananes.*	Monkeys love to eat *bananas.*
Les singes adorent *les* manger.	Monkeys love to eat *them.*
Tout le monde aime recevoir *des cadeaux.*	Everyone likes to get *presents.*

Tout le monde aime *en* recevoir.	Everyone likes to get *them.*
Je veux parler *au directeur*!	I want to speak *to the manager*!
Je veux *lui* parler!	I want to speak *to him*!
Elle espère gagner *à la loterie.*	She hopes to win *the lottery.*
Elle espère *y* gagner.	She hopes to win *(it).*
Il n'ose pas se disputer *avec sa femme.*	He doesn't dare argue *with his wife.*
Il n'ose pas se disputer *avec elle.*	He doesn't dare argue *with her.*

B.   Verbs which take a Direct Object Plus an Infinitive

The most common of these verbs are *amener*, to bring (someone); *emmener*, to take (someone); *envoyer*, to send (someone); and *mener*, to lead (someone).

Example:

Il emmène *les enfants* nager.	He is taking *the children* swimming.

Substitutions:

1. To replace the direct object of the main verb, use a direct object pronoun.

<table>
<tr><td>Il emmène *les enfants* nager.</td><td>He is taking *the children* swimming.</td></tr>
<tr><td>Il *les* emmène nager.</td><td>He is taking *them* swimming.</td></tr>
</table>

2. If the *infinitive* is followed by a noun, the noun can be replaced by a pronoun. If you are not certain what pronoun to use, refer to Categories I-VI, VERBS AND NOUNS, pp. 40–53.

All personal pronouns, except tonic pronouns, directly PRECEDE the infinitive.

<table>
<tr><td>Elle a emmené les écoliers voir *l'exposition de Picasso*.</td><td>She took the students to see *the Picasso exhibit*.</td></tr>
<tr><td>Elle les a emmenés *la* voir.</td><td>She took them to see *it*.</td></tr>
<tr><td>J'ai envoyé Marie acheter *du pain*.</td><td>I sent Marie to buy *some bread*.</td></tr>
<tr><td>Je l'ai envoyée *en* acheter.</td><td>I sent her to buy *some*.</td></tr>
</table>

Note: The following verbs take an infinitive followed by a noun:

faire	to make, to do
laisser	to let, to allow

And certain verbs of perception:

écouter	to listen to
entendre	to hear
regarder	to look at, to watch
sentir	to feel, to smell
voir	to see

The noun, however, is not the direct object of the infinitive; it acts as the direct object of the main verb. Therefore, when the noun direct object is replaced by a pronoun, the pronoun precedes the main verb.

Examples:

J'entends tomber *la pluie.*	I hear *the rain* falling.
Je *l'*entends tomber.	I hear *it* falling.
On a fait venir *le médecin.**	They had *the doctor* come.
On *l'*a fait venir.	They had *him* come.

---

*When the noun following the infinitive is a *thing*, the verb **faire** can take an indirect object as well as a direct object. For example:

VIII. *Verbs which take the preposition À before an infinitive*

A. Verbs which take NO Direct or Indirect Object before
   | À + INFINITIVE |

Example:

Il hésite à parler.	He is reluctant to speak.

Substitutions:

If the *infinitive* is followed by a noun, the noun can be replaced by a pronoun. If you are not certain what pronoun to use, refer to Categories I-VI, VERBS AND NOUNS, pp. 40–53.

All personal pronouns, except tonic pronouns, directly PRECEDE the infinitive.

J'ai fait réparer *la voiture.*	I had *the car* repaired.
Je *l'*ai fait réparer.	I had *it* repaired.
J'ai fait réparer *la voiture au garagiste.*	I had *the car* repaired *by the mechanic.*
Je *la lui* ai fait réparer.	I had *him* repair *it.*

In the above example, the subject of the verb *faire, je,* causes the repairs to be made; the indirect object of *faire, le garagiste,* actually makes the repairs. The direct object of *faire, la voiture,* is the thing being repaired. This construction is called the *faire causatif.* (Note that when the past participle—in this case *fait*—precedes an infinitive, there is no agreement between the past participle and the preceding direct object.)

Un peintre célèbre a consenti à faire *mon portrait*.	A famous painter has agreed to paint *my portrait*.
Un peintre célèbre a consenti à *le* faire.*	A famous painter has agreed to paint *it*.
Mon père persiste à fumer *des cigares*.	My father won't give up smoking *cigars*.
Mon père persiste à *en* fumer.	My father won't give up smoking *them*.
Nous tenons à assister *au concert*.	We are eager to attend *the concert*.
Nous tenons à *y* assister.	We are eager to attend (*it*).
Elle hésite à sortir *avec cet homme*.	She is hesitant to go out *with that man*.
Elle hésite à sortir *avec lui*.	She is hesitant to go out *with him*.

B. Verbs which take a Direct or Indirect Object before À + INFINITIVE

Verbs which take À + INFINITIVE usually take a DIRECT OBJECT.

---

*Note that when *le* and *les* are pronouns, there is no contraction with *à*.

Example:

J'ai décidé *mon ami* à venir.   I persuaded *my friend* to come.

A few verbs, however, take INDIRECT OBJECTS.*

Example:

Elle apprend *aux enfants* à   She is teaching *the children*
patiner.   to skate.

Substitutions:

1. To replace the DIRECT OBJECT of the main verb, person or thing, use a direct object pronoun.

    J'ai décidé *mon ami* à   I persuaded *my friend* to
    venir.   come.

    Je *l'*ai décidé à venir.   I persuaded *him* to come.

    Elle met *le linge* à   She is hanging *the laun-*
    sécher.   *dry* up to dry.

    Elle *le* met à sécher.   She is hanging *it* up to
                                  dry.

2. To replace the INDIRECT OBJECT of the main verb, use an indirect object pronoun.

___

*Other verbs which take an INDIRECT OBJECT plus
$\boxed{\text{À + INFINITIVE}}$ are: **enseigner** (*to teach*) and **montrer** (*to show*).

Elle apprend *aux en-fants* à patiner.	She is teaching *the children* to skate.
Elle *leur* apprend à patiner.	She is teaching *them* to skate.

3. If the *infinitive* is followed by a noun, the noun can be replaced by a pronoun. If you are not certain what pronoun to use, refer to Categories I-VI, VERBS AND NOUNS, pp. 40–53.

Le scout aide la vieille à traverser *la rue*.	The boy scout helps the old lady across *the street*.
Le scout l'aide à *la* traverser.	The boy scout helps her across *it*.
Le garçon encourage son client à prendre *des huîtres*.	The waiter urges his customer to have *some oysters*.
Le garçon l'encourage à *en* prendre.	The waiter urges him to have *some*.
On a autorisé le journaliste à parler *aux otages*.	They allowed the journalist to speak *to the hostages*.
On l'a autorisé à *leur* parler.	They allowed him to speak *to them*.

Il a invité ses amis à   He invited his friends to
aller *au théâtre*.   go *to the theatre*.

Il les a invités à y aller.   He invited them to go
                                     (*there*).

IX. *Verbs which take the preposition DE before an infinitive*

A. Verbs which take NO Direct or Indirect Object before
    DE + INFINITIVE

Example:

Le bébé refuse de manger.   The baby refuses to eat.

Substitutions:

If the *infinitive* is followed by a noun, the noun can be replaced by a pronoun. If you are not certain what pronoun to use, refer to Categories I-VI, VERBS AND NOUNS, pp. 40–53.

All personal pronouns, except tonic pronouns, directly PRECEDE the infinitive.

J'ai oublié de rendre *le livre*.   I forgot to return *the book*.

J'ai oublié de *le* rendre.*   I forgot to return *it*.

Il a offert d'apporter *du vin*.   He offered to bring *some wine*.

---

*Note that when *le* and *les* are pronouns, there is no contraction with *de*.

Il a offert d'*en* apporter.	He offered to bring *some*.
Elle a promis d'assister *à la réunion*.	She promised to attend *the meeting*.
Elle a promis d'*y* assister.	She promised to attend *(it)*.
Le chien essaye de plaire *à son maître*.	The dog tries to please *his master*.
Le chien essaye de *lui* plaire.	The dog tries to please *him*.

B. Verbs which take a Direct or Indirect Object before

$\boxed{\text{DE + INFINITIVE}}$

Examples:

On a persuadé *le fugitif* de se rendre.	They persuaded *the fugitive* to give himself up.
J'ai dit *à mon ami* d'attendre.	I told *my friend* to wait.

Substitutions:

1. To replace the DIRECT OBJECT of the main verb, person or thing, use a direct object pronoun.

On a persuadé *le fu-gitif* de se rendre.	They persuaded *the fugitive* to give himself up.
On *l'*a persuadé de se rendre,	They persuaded *him* to give himself up.
L'orage a empêché *le bateau* de partir.	The storm prevented *the ship* from leaving.
L'orage *l'*a empêché de partir.	The storm prevented *it* from leaving.

2. To replace the INDIRECT OBJECT of the main verb, use an indirect object pronoun.

J'ai dit *à mon ami* d'attendre.	I told *my friend* to wait.
Je *lui* ai dit d'attendre.	I told *him* to wait.

3. If the *infinitive* is followed by a noun, the noun can be replaced by a pronoun. If you are not certain what pronoun to use, refer to Categories I–VI, VERBS AND NOUNS, pp. 40–53.

Elle a grondé l'enfant d'avoir perdu *ses moufles*.	She scolded the child for having lost *his mittens*.

Elle l'a grondé de *les* avoir perdues.*	She scolded him for having lost *them*.
Le gardien a permis au touriste de prendre *des photos*.	The guard allowed the tourist to take *pictures*.
Le gardien lui a permis d'*en* prendre.	The guard allowed him to take *some*.
Le professeur interdit aux étudiants de dormir *en classe*.	The professor forbids the students to sleep *in class*.
Le professeur leur interdit d'*y* dormir.	The professor forbids them to sleep *there*.
J'ai persuadé mon frère de se raccomoder *avec sa femme*.	I persuaded my brother to make up *with his wife*.
Je l'ai persuadé de se raccomoder *avec elle*.	I persuaded him to make up *with her*.

X. *Verbs which take prepositions other than À or DE before an infinitive.*

Example:

Il a fini par réussir.	He finally succeeded.

---

*Note that when *le* and *les* are pronouns, there is no contraction with *de*.

There are very few verbs in this category. The most common are:

commencer par	to begin by
débuter par	to start (one's career) by
finir par	to end by, to finally
insister pour	to insist on
terminer par	to end (something) by

Substitutions:

If the *infinitive* is followed by a noun, the noun can be replaced by a pronoun. If you are not certain what pronoun to use, refer to Categories I-VI, VERBS AND NOUNS, pp. 40–53.

All personal pronouns, except tonic pronouns, directly PRECEDE the infinitive.

Le conférencier a commencé par exposer *sa théorie*.	The speaker began by stating *his theory*.
Le conférencier a commencé par *l'*exposer.	The speaker began by stating *it*.
J'ai fini par me résigner *à la situation*.	I finally resigned myself *to the situation*.
J'ai fini par m'*y* résigner.	I finally resigned myself *to it*.

PART THREE

Verb List

Key To Verb List

ROMAN NUMERALS indicate Verb Categories (pp. 40–66). Refer to the appropriate Category for detailed explanation of verb type and usage. No Category is indicated for idiomatic expressions when a pronoun substitution is not possible.

ARABIC NUMERALS at the left-hand margin are included for easy reference to verb entries. They do not indicate order of importance of the definitions.

ABBREVIATIONS:

Qn	*Quelqu'un*	(People or animate objects)
Qch	*Quelque chose*	(Things or inanimate objects)
Inf.	*Infinitif*	(Infinitive)
Inf. passé	*Infinitif passé*	(Past Infinitive)
Coll:	Colloquial Expression	
Lit:	Literary Expression	

The ending ---*ing* appears frequently in the English definition of a verb and corresponds to the French abbreviation *Inf*. For example, for the verb **cesser** we find:

> **cesser**
> 1. _____ Qch. (to stop . . .) I
> 2. _____ de *Inf*. (to stop ---*ing*) IX-A

The "---*ing*" in number 2 indicates that the present participle is used in English where French employs the infinitive, *e.g.*, "cesser de *fumer*"—"to stop *smoking*."

A

abaisser
1. ———— Qn ou Qch (to lower . . .) I
2. s'———— (to sink, subside; to lower oneself, humble oneself) I
3. s'———— à, jusqu'à *Inf.* (to stoop to, condescend to . . .) VIII-A

abandonner
1. ———— Qn ou Qch (to abandon . . .) I
2. s'———— (to let oneself go) I
3. s'———— à Qch (to give oneself up to . . .) III
4. ———— Qn ou Qch à Qch (to abandon, give up . . . to . . .) VI

abattre
1. ———— Qch (to knock down, bring down, slaughter . . .) I
2. s'———— (to fall down, crash down; to abate) I
3. s'———— sur Qch (to fall down on, swoop down on, pounce upon . . .) V

abîmer
1. ———— Qn ou Qch (to spoil, damage, ruin . . .) I
2. s'———— (to get spoiled, to spoil) I
3. s'———— *dans la douleur, dans le chagrin; dans ses pensées* (to be sunk in sorrow; in one's thoughts) V

abonder
1. ———— en Qch (to abound in . . .) V

abonner
1. s'———— à Qch (to subscribe to . . .) III
2. ———— Qn à Qch (to enroll, to take out a subscription for . . . to . . .) VI

aboutir
1. _____ à Qch (to lead to, end at, result in . . .) II
2. _____ dans, en* Qch (to end in . . .) V

aboyer
1. _____ après, à Qn ou Qch (to bark at . . . [*après* often indicates movement] Ex: *un chien qui aboie après le facteur, à la lune*, a dog that barks at the postman, at the moon) V, III

abreuver
1. _____ Qn ou Qch (to water, soak . . .) I
2. s'_____ (of people: to quench one's thirst; of animals: to drink) I
3. s'_____ de Qch (to quench one's thirst for, with . . .) IV
4. _____ Qn de Qch (to overwhelm, shower . . . with . . .) VI

abriter
1. _____ Qn ou Qch (to shelter . . .) I
2. s'_____ (to take cover, shelter) I
3. s'_____ contre Qch (to take cover from . . .) V
4. _____ Qn contre Qch (to shelter . . . from . . .) VI

absenter (s')
1. s'_____ de Qch (to absent oneself from . . .) IV

absorber
1. _____ Qn ou Qch (to absorb . . .) I
2. s'_____ dans Qch (to become engrossed in . . .) V
3. être absorbé dans Qch (to be engrossed in . . .) V

absoudre
1. _____ Qn (to forgive . . .) I
2. _____ Qn de Qch (to forgive . . . for . . .; to absolve . . . of . . .) VI

___
*See Appendix II: **DANS, EN, À**, p. 298.

abstenir (s')
1. s'_____ de Qch (to abstain, refrain from . . .) IV
2. s'_____ de *Inf.* (to abstain, refrain from ---*ing*) IX-A

abstraire
1. _____ Qch (to abstract . . .) I
2. s'_____ (to withdraw oneself) I
3. s'_____ dans, en* Qch (to become engrossed in . . .) V

abuser
1. _____ Qn (to deceive . . .) I
2. s'_____ (to be mistaken) I
3. _____ de Qch (to abuse, take advantage of . . .) IV

accabler
1. _____ Qn ou Qch (to overwhelm, overburden . . .) I
2. être accablé de Qch (to be overwhelmed, overburdened with
. . . *e.g.*, *de travail*, with work) IV
3. _____ Qn de Qch (to overwhelm, overburden, shower . . .
with . . .) VI

accéder
1. _____ à Qch (to have access to, to comply with . . .) II

accepter
1. _____ Qn ou Qch (to accept . . .) I
2. _____ Qch de Qn (to accept . . . from . . .) VI
3. _____ de *Inf.* (to agree to . . .) IX-A

accoler
1. _____ Qch (to join, place . . . side by side) I
2. s'_____ (of plants: to intertwine) I
3. être accolé à Qch (to be joined to, built onto . . .) II
4. s'_____ à Qch (to be joined to, built onto . . .) III

---

*See Appendix II: **DANS, EN, À**, p. 298.

accomoder
1. _____ Qn ou Qch (to accommodate . . .; to make . . . comfortable; to prepare [food]) I
2. s'_____ (to make oneself comfortable) I
3. s'_____ à Qch (to adapt to . . .) III
4. s'_____ de Qch (to put up with . . .) IV
5. s'_____ avec Qn (to come to an agreement, a compromise with . . .) V
6. _____ Qch à Qch (to fit, adapt . . . to . . .) VI

accompagner
1. _____ Qn ou Qch (to accompany . . .) I
2. s'_____ à Qch (to accompany oneself on . . . *e.g.*, *à la guitare*, on the guitar) III
3. s'_____ de Qch (to be accompanied by, followed by . . .) IV
4. _____ Qn ou Qch à Qch (to accompany . . . on . . . *e.g.*, *au piano*, on the piano) VI

accorder
1. _____ Qn ou Qch (to bring . . . into harmony, accord; to grant, concede . . .; to tune . . . *e.g.*, a musical instrument) I
2. s'_____ (to agree, be in accordance) I
3. s'_____ Qch (to allow oneself . . .) I
4. s'_____ avec Qch (to be in accordance, in keeping with . . .) V
5. s'_____ sur Qch (to agree upon . . .) V
6. _____ Qch à Qn (to grant, concede . . . to . . .) VI
7. _____ Qch avec Qch (to reconcile, bring . . . into accord with . . .) VI

accoter
1. s'_____ à, contre Qch (to lean against . . .) III, V
2. _____ Qch contre, sur Qch (to lean . . . against, on . . .) VI

accoucher
1. _____ de Qn ou Qch (to give birth to . . .) IV

accoutrer
1. s'_____ de Qch (to dress up ridiculously in . . .) IV
2. _____ Qn de Qch (to dress up . . . ridiculously in . . .) VI

accoutumer
1. s'_____ à Qch (to become accustomed to . . .) III
2. _____ Qn à Qch (to accustom . . . to . . .) VI
3. s'_____ à *Inf.* (to become accustomed to ---*ing*) VIII-A
4. _____ Qn à *Inf.* (to accustom . . . to ---*ing*) VIII-B

accréditer
1. _____ Qn ou Qch (to accredit, credit . . .) I
2. _____ Qn auprès de Qn ou Qch (to accredit . . . at, to, with . . .) VI

accrocher
1. _____ Qn ou Qch (to hook, to hang, to grab onto . . .) I
2. s'_____ à Qn ou Qch (to fasten, cling to . . .) III
3. _____ Qch à Qch (to hang, catch . . . on . . .) VI

acculer
1. s'_____ contre, à Qch (to set one's back against . . .) V, III
2. _____ Qn contre, à Qch (to drive . . . back against . . .) VI

accuser
1. _____ Qn (to accuse . . .) I
2. _____ Qch (to own up to . . .; to accentuate . . .) I
3. _____ Qn de Qch (to accuse . . . of . . .) VI
4. _____ Qn de *Inf.* ou *Inf. passé* (to accuse . . . of ---*ing*, of having . . .) IX-B

acharner
1. s'_____ à Qch (to persist in . . .) III
2. s'_____ sur Qn ou Qch (to swoop down on . . .) V
3. s'_____ contre Qn ou Qch (to pursue . . . relentlessly) V

acheminer
1. s'_____ vers, sur Qch (to proceed, make one's way to, towards . . .) V
2. _____ Qn ou Qch vers, sur Qch (to direct, dispatch, put . . . on the road to, towards . . .) VI

acheter
1. _____ Qch (to buy . . .) I
2. _____ Qch à Qn (to buy . . . from . . .) VI
3. _____ Qch à, pour Qn (to buy . . . for . . .) VI

achever
1. _____ Qn ou Qch (to finish, to finish off . . .) I
2. _____ de *Inf.* (to finish ---*ing*) IX-A

acoquiner (s')
1. s'_____ avec Qn (Coll: to take up with . . . [with someone disreputable]) V

acquérir
1. _____ Qch (to acquire . . .) I
2. _____ Qch à Qn (to acquire . . . for . . .) VI

acquiescer
1. _____ à Qch (to agree to, acquiesce to . . .) II

acquitter
1. _____ Qn ou Qch (to acquit . . .) I
2. s'_____ de Qch (to fulfill, carry out . . . Ex: *s'acquitter d'un devoir*, to carry out a duty; *s'acquitter d'une dette*, to pay off a debt) IV
3. s'_____ envers Qn (to repay, to pay off one's debts to . . .) V

adapter
  1. s'_____ à Qch (to adapt to . . .) III
  2. _____ Qch à Qch (to adapt . . . to . . .) VI

adhérer
  1. _____ à Qch (to adhere, stick to . . .) II

adjoindre
  1. s'_____ à Qn (to join in with . . .) III
  2. _____ Qn ou Qch à Qn ou Qch (to add, join . . . to . . .;
       to unite . . . with . . .) VI

adjuger
  1. _____ Qch à Qn (to adjudge, award . . . to . . .) VI

adjurer
  1. _____ Qn de *Inf.* (to beseech . . . to . . .) IX-B

admettre
  1. _____ Qch (to admit . . .) I
  2. _____ Qn à Qch (to let . . . into . . .) VI
  3. _____ Qn à *Inf.* (to allow . . . to . . .) VIII-B

administrer
  1. _____ Qch à Qn (to administer . . . to . . .) VI

admirer
  1. _____ Qn ou Qch (to admire . . .) I
  2. _____ Qn de *Inf.* ou *Inf. passé* (to admire . . . for ---*ing*,
       for having . . .) IX-B

adonner (s')
  1. s'_____ à Qch (to devote oneself to . . .) III

adorer
1. _____ Qn ou Qch (to adore . . .) I
2. _____ *Inf.* (to adore ---*ing*) VII-A

adosser
1. s'_____ à, contre Qch (to lean back against . . .) III, V
2. _____ Qch à Qch (to lean, to back . . . against . . .) VI

adresser
1. _____ Qch (to address . . .) I
2. s'_____ à Qn ou Qch (to apply to, speak to . . .) III
3. _____ Qn ou Qch à Qn ou Qch (to address direct . . . to . . .) VI

affairer (s')
1. s'_____ à *Inf.* (to busy oneself, to bustle about ---*ing*) VIII-A
2. être affairé à *Inf.* (to be very busy ---*ing*) VIII-A

affecter
1. _____ Qn (to move, touch . . .) I
2. _____ Qch (to affect, to feign, to assume . . .) I
3. s'_____ de Qch (to be distressed by . . .) IV
4. _____ Qch à Qch (to assign . . . to . . .; to allocate . . . for . . .) VI
5. _____ de *Inf.* (to make a pretense of ---*ing*) IX-A

afficher
1. _____ Qch (to post, display . . .) I
2. s'_____ avec Qn (to be seen everywhere with . . .) V

affilier
1. être affilié à Qn ou Qch (to be affiliated with . . .) II
2. s'_____ à Qch (to affiliate oneself with . . .) III
3. _____ Qn ou Qch à Qch (to affiliate . . . to, with . . .) VI

affliger

1. _____ Qn (to pain, distress . . .) I
2. s'_____ de Qch (to grieve, be distressed over . . .) IV
3. _____ Qn de Qch (to afflict . . . with . . .) VI
4. s'_____ de *Inf.* (to be distressed at ---*ing*) IX-A

affluer

1. _____ à, vers, dans Qch (to flow to, towards, into . . .) II, V
2. _____ à, dans Qch (to flock to . . .) II, V

affoler

1. _____ Qn (to distract, drive . . . crazy; to throw . . . into a panic) I
2. s'_____ de Qn (to fall madly in love with . . .) IV

affranchir

1. s'_____ de Qch (to free oneself of . . .) IV
2. _____ Qn de Qch (to free . . . from . . .) V!

affubler

1. s'_____ de Qch (to dress up in . . . [in something bizarre or ridiculous]) IV
2. _____ Qn de Qch (to dress up . . . in . . .) VI

agir

1. Il s'agit de Qn ou Qch (It concerns, it is a question, a matter of . . .) IV
2. _____ sur Qn ou Qch (to have an influence on . . .) V
3. Il s'agit de *Inf.* (It is a question, a matter of ---*ing*) IX-A

agrafer

1. _____ Qch (to clasp, hook . . .) I
2. s'_____ à Qn ou Qch (to cling to, hang onto . . .) III

agrémenter
1. _____ Qn ou Qch de Qch (to embellish, ornament . . . with . . .) VI

agripper
1. _____ Qch (to clutch, seize, snatch . . .) I
2. s'_____ à Qch (to cling to, clutch at . . .) III

aguerrir
1. s'_____ contre Qch (to become hardened, accustomed to . . .) III, V
2. _____ Qn à Qch (to harden, accustom . . . to . . .) VI

aider
1. _____ Qn (to help . . .) I
2. _____ à Qch (to contribute to, towards . . .) II
3. s'_____ de Qch (to make use of . . .) IV
4. _____ Qn à *Inf.* (to help . . . to . . .) VIII-B

aimer
1. _____ Qn ou Qch (to like, love . . .) I
2. _____ *mieux* Qn ou Qch (to prefer . . .) I
3. _____ *Inf.* (to like to . . .; to like, enjoy ---*ing*) VII-A
4. _____ *mieux Inf.* (to prefer ---*ing*) VII-A
5. _____ à *Inf.* (Lit: to enjoy, take pleasure in ---*ing*) VIII-A

ajouter
1. _____ Qch (to add . . .) I
2. _____ Qch à Qch (to add . . . to . . .) VI

ajuster
1. _____ Qch (to adjust, to aim at . . .) I
2. _____ Qn ou Qch avec Qch (to aim at . . . with . . .) VI
3. _____ Qch à Qch (to fit, adjust . . . to . . .) VI

alarmer
1. ——— Qn (to alarm, frighten . . .) I
2. s'——— de Qch (to be alarmed at, by . . .) IV

aller
1. ——— à Qn (of clothing: to suit, become . . . Used only in third person, Ex: *Cette robe vous va bien,* that dress becomes you) II
2. ——— à, dans, en* Qch (to go to, into . . .) II, V
3. Il y va de Qch (to be at stake, Ex: *Il y va de sa vie,* his life is at stake) IV
4. ——— chez Qn (to go to someone's home, office, establishment, Ex: *aller chez le dentiste, chez le coiffeur, chez un ami,* to go to the dentist, to the hairdresser, to a friend's house) V
5. ——— *Inf.* (to be going to . . . Ex: *Nous allons faire une promenade cet après-midi,* we're going to take a walk this afternoon; to go to . . . Ex: *Je suis allé voir la nouvelle pièce de Ionesco,* I went to see Ionesco's new play) VII-A

allier
1. ——— Qn ou Qch (to ally, unite . . .) I
2. s'——— à, avec Qn ou Qch (to form an alliance with . . .) III, V
3. ——— Qn ou Qch à, avec Qn ou Qch (to ally, unite, combine . . . with . . .) VI

alterner
1. ——— avec Qn ou Qch (to alternate with . . .) V
2. ——— pour *Inf.* (to alternate ---*ing*) X

ambitionner
1. ——— Qch (to be ambitious of, to covet . . .) I
2. ——— de *Inf.* (to aspire to . . .) IX-A

---

*See Appendix I: **PREPOSITIONS OF GEOGRAPHICAL LOCATION** and Appendix II: **DANS, EN, À**, p. 289.

amener

1. ———— Qn (to bring . . .) I
2. ———— à Qch (to lead up to, to bring about . . .) II
3. ———— Qn à Qn ou Qch (to bring . . . to . . . Ex: *amener un enfant à sa mère*, to bring a child to his mother; to bring . . . around to . . . Ex: *amener quelqu'un à une idée*, to bring someone around to an idea) VI
4. ———— Qn *Inf.* (to bring . . . to . . .) VII-B
5. ———— Qn à *Inf.* (to induce, cause . . . to . . . Ex: *Il m'a amené à voir les choses d'une façon plus réaliste*, he made me see things more realistically) VIII-B

amouracher (s')

1. s'———— de Qn (to be infatuated with . . . [often pejorative]) IV

amuser

1. ———— Qn (to amuse . . .) I
2. s'———— à Qch (to amuse oneself at, to enjoy . . .) III
3. s'———— de, aux dépens de Qn (to make fun of . . .) IV, V
4. s'———— à *Inf.* (to have a good time ---*ing*) VIII-A

annexer

1. ———— Qch (to annex . . .) I
2. ———— Qch à Qch (to attach, annex . . . to . . .) VI

annoncer

1. ———— Qch (to announce, indicate . . . Ex: *Ces nuages annoncent l'orage*, these clouds indicate a storm [is coming]) I
2. ———— Qch à Qn (to announce . . . to . . .) VI

anticiper

1. ——— Qch (to anticipate . . .) I
2. ——— sur Qch (to anticipate . . .; to encroach upon . . .; to pay or spend . . . in advance, Ex: *anticiper sur ses revenues*, to spend one's income in advance) V

apercevoir

1. ——— Qn ou Qch (to catch sight of, catch a glimpse of . . .) I
2. s'——— de Qch (to notice, realize . . .) IV

apitoyer

1. ——— Qn (to move . . . to pity) I
2. s'——— sur Qn ou Qch (to be moved to pity over . . .) V

apparaître

1. ——— à Qn (to appear to, before . . .; to become evident, apparent to . . .) II

apparenter

1. être apparenté à Qn (to be related to . . .) II
2. s'——— à Qn ou Qch (to become related by marriage to . . .; to bear a resemblance to, be of the same nature as . . .) III

appartenir

1. s'——— (to be one's own boss, to be in control of oneself) I
2. ——— à Qn ou Qch (to belong to . . .) II
3. Il appartient à Qn de *Inf.* (to be one's job, part of one's functions to . . . Ex: *Il appartient au tribunal d'administrer la justice*, it is the job of the court to administer justice) IX-B

appeler
1. _____ Qn ou Qch (to call, call for . . .) I
2. s'_____ Qch (to be named . . .) I
3. en _____ à Qn ou Qch (to appeal to . . .) II
4. _____ Qn à *Inf.* (to call on . . . to . . .) VIII-B

appesantir
1. _____ Qn ou Qch (to weigh down, dull, slow down . . .) I
2. s'_____ sur Qn (to weigh on, become oppressive to . . .) V
3. s'_____ sur Qch (to dwell on . . . *e.g., sur un sujet,* on a subject) V
4. _____ Qch sur Qch (to lean, press down . . . on . . .) VI

applaudir
1. _____ Qn ou Qch (to applaud . . .) I
2. _____ à Qch (to approve of . . . wholeheartedly) II
3. s'_____ de Qch (to pat oneself on the back for . . .) IV
4. s'_____ de *Inf.* ou *Inf. passé* (to pat oneself on the back for ---*ing*, for having . . .) IX-A
5. _____ Qn de *Inf.* ou *Inf. passé* (to commend . . . for ---*ing*, for having . . .) IX-B

appliquer
1. _____ Qch (to affix . . .) I
2. s'_____ à Qch (to work hard at . . .) III
3. s'_____ à Qn ou Qch (to apply to . . . Used only in third person, Ex: *Cette règle s'applique à vous, à votre cas,* this rule applies to you, to your case) III
4. _____ Qch sur Qch (to apply . . . to, on . . .) VI

apporter
1. _____ Qch (to bring . . .) I
2. _____ Qch à Qn (to bring . . . to . . .) VI
3. _____ *du soin à Inf.* (to take care in ---*ing*) VIII-B

apposer
1. _____ Qch (to affix . . .) I
2. _____ Qch à, sur Qch (to affix . . . to, on . . .) VI

appréhender
1. _____ Qn (to seize . . .) I
2. _____ Qn *au corps* (to arrest . . .) I
3. _____ Qch (to fear, be apprehensive about . . .) I
4. _____ de *Inf.* (to dread, fear ---*ing*) IX-A

apprendre
1. _____ Qch (to learn . . .) I
2. _____ Qch à Qn (to teach someone something) VI
3. _____ à *Inf.* (to learn [how] to . . .) VIII-A
4. _____ à Qn à *Inf.* (to teach . . . [how] to . . .) VIII-B

apprêter
1. _____ Qch (to make ready, prepare . . .) I
2. s'_____ à Qch (to prepare for . . .) III
3. s'_____ à *Inf.* (to prepare to . . .) VIII-A

approcher
1. _____ Qn (to get near, close to . . .) I
2. _____ Qch (to bring . . . near) I
3. _____ de Qn (to approach, come near, close to . . .) IV
4. _____ de Qch (to approach, come near, close to . . . Ex:
Nous approchons de Marseille, we are getting
near Marseille; *approcher du but,* to come near
the mark, the goal; *approcher de la quarantaine,*
to be nearing forty; to resemble, be close to, approximate . . . Ex: *approcher de la vérité,* to be
close to the truth) IV
5. s'_____ de Qn ou Qch (to go up to, come near, close to
. . .) IV
6. _____ Qn ou Qch de Qn ou Qch (to bring . . . near to
. . .) VI

approprier
1. s'_____ Qch (to appropriate . . . for oneself) I
2. s'_____ à Qch (to adapt oneself, itself to . . .) III
3. _____ Qch à Qch (to adapt . . . to . . .) VI

approuver
1. _____ Qn ou Qch (to approve, approve of . . .) I
2. _____ Qn de *Inf.* ou *Inf. passé* (to approve of . . . for
---*ing*, for having . . .) IX-B

approvisionner
1. _____ Qn ou Qch (to furnish . . . with supplies) I
2. s'_____ [chez un marchand] (to lay in supplies, to get one's
supplies, one's provisions [at . . .]) I
3. s'_____ en, de Qch (to supply, furnish oneself with . . .)
V, IV
4. _____ Qn ou Qch de Qch (to supply, furnish . . . with
. . .) VI

appuyer
1. _____ Qn ou Qch (to support . . .) I
2. _____ sur Qch (to press, press on . . .; to stress, emphasize . . .) V
3. s'_____ sur, contre, à Qch (to lean on, against . . .) V, III
4. s'_____ sur Qn (to lean on, rely on . . .) V
5. _____ Qch contre Qch (to lean . . . against . . .) VI
6. _____ Qch sur Qch (to press, rest . . . on . . .) VI

arguer
1. _____ de Qch (to use . . . as an argument, reason, or pre-
text) IV
2. _____ Qch de Qch (Lit: to conclude, infer, deduce . . .
from . . .) VI

armer

1. _____ Qn ou Qch (to arm, to strengthen . . .; to load, cock [a gun]) I
2. s'_____ de Qch (to arm, equip oneself with . . .) IV
3. s'_____ contre Qn ou Qch (to arm oneself against . . .) V
4. _____ Qn ou Qch de Qch (to arm . . . with . . .) VI

arracher

1. _____ Qch (to tear out, up, away . . .) I
2. s'_____ de Qch (to tear oneself away from . . . *e.g., d'un livre*, from a book) IV
3. _____ Qch à Qn (to extract, snatch . . . from . . . Ex: *arracher une dent, une promesse à quelqu'un*, to extract a tooth, a promise from someone; *s'arracher les cheveux*, to tear one's hair out) VI
4. _____ Qn à Qch (to save . . . from . . . *e.g., à un danger*, from danger; to pull, draw . . . out of . . . *e.g., au sommeil*, out of sleep) VI
5. _____ Qn ou Qch de Qch (to pull out, drive out . . . from . . .; to snatch . . . from, out of . . . *e.g., des mains de quelqu'un*, out of someone's hands) VI

arranger

1. _____ Qch (to arrange . . .) I
2. _____ Qn (to accommodate . . .) I
3. s'_____ (to manage) I
4. s'_____ de Qch (to make do with . . .) IV
5. s'_____ avec Qn (to come to terms with . . .) V
6. s'_____ pour *Inf.* (to make arrangements to . . .) X

arrêter

1. _____ Qn ou Qch (to stop, arrest . . .) I
2. s'_____ (to stop, come to a halt) I
3. s'_____ sur, à Qch (to dwell on, pay attention to, decide on . . .) V, III
4. _____ *ses regards* sur Qn (to fix one's glance on . . .) VI
5. _____ de *Inf.* (to stop ---*ing*) IX-A
6. s'_____ de *Inf.* (to leave off, give up ---*ing*) IX-A

arriver
1. _____ à Qch (to arrive at . . .) II
2. Il arrive à Qn Qch (to happen to, befall . . . Ex: *Il m'est arrivé une chose terrible*, a terrible thing [has] happened to me) VI
3. _____ à *Inf.* (to manage to . . .; to succeed in ---*ing*) VIII-A
4. en _____ à *Inf.* (to get to the point of, be at the point of ---*ing*) VIII-A
5. Il arrive à Qn de *Inf.* (to happen to . . . to . . . Ex: *Il arrive à tout le monde de se tromper*, everyone makes mistakes) IX-B

arroser
1. _____ Qch (to water, sprinkle . . .) I
2. _____ Qn ou Qch de Qch (to bathe, sprinkle . . . with . . .) VI

asperger
1. _____ Qn ou Qch (to sprinkle . . .) I
2. _____ Qn ou Qch de Qch (to sprinkle . . . with . . .) VI

aspirer
1. _____ à Qch (to aspire to, after . . .) II
2. _____ à *Inf.* (to aspire to . . .) VIII-A

assaillir
1. _____ Qn ou Qch (to assail, assault . . .) I
2. _____ Qn de Qch (to assail, assault . . . with . . .) VI

assaisonner
1. _____ Qch (to season . . .) I
2. _____ Qch de Qch (to season . . . with . . .) VI

assener
1. _____ Qch à Qn (to deal . . . to . . . Ex: *assener un coup à quelqu'un*, to deal someone a blow) VI

asseoir
1. ———— Qn ou Qch (to seat, set . . .) I
2. s'———— (to sit down) I
3. ———— Qn ou Qch sur Qch (to seat . . . on . . .; to base
. . . [*e.g.*, an opinion] on . . .) VI

asservir
1. ———— Qn ou Qch (to enslave . . .) I
2. s'———— à Qch (to submit to . . .) III
3. ———— Qn à Qch (to subject, tie . . . down to . . .) VI

assiéger
1. ———— Qn ou Qch (to besiege . . .) I
2. ———— Qn de Qch (to besiege . . . with . . .) VI

assigner
1. ———— Qn ou Qch (to assign, to allot, to subpoena . . .) I
2. ———— Qch à Qn ou Qch (to assign . . . to . . .) VI

assimiler
1. ———— Qch (to assimilate . . .) I
2. s'———— (to become assimilated) I
3. s'———— à Qn ou Qch (to become assimilated into . . . *e.g.*,
à un groupe, into a group; to compare oneself
with . . .) III

assister
1. ———— Qn (to assist . . .) I
2. ———— à Qch (to attend . . .) II

associer
1. ———— Qn ou Qch (to associate, bring together . . .) I
2. s'———— à, avec Qn (to associate with, go into partnership
with . . .) III ,V
3. s'———— à Qch (to share in, participate in . . .) III
4. ———— Qn ou Qch à Qn ou Qch (to associate . . . with
. . .; to include . . . in . . .) VI

assommer

1. _____ Qn (to stun, kill . . . with a blow; to beat up . . .;
Coll: to bore . . .) I
2. _____ Qn de Qch (to strike . . . with . . .; Coll: to tire,
bore, pester . . . with . . .) VI

assortir

1. _____ Qn ou Qch (to put together, match . . .) I
2. s'_____ (to match, harmonize) I
3. _____ Qch à Qch (to match . . . with . . .; to suit . . . to
. . .) VI

assouvir

1. _____ Qn ou Qch (to sate, assuage . . .) I
2. s'_____ de Qch (to become sated with . . .) IV

assujettir

1. _____ Qn ou Qch (to subjugate . . .; to fasten, secure
. . .) I
2. s'_____ à Qch (to subject oneself to, submit to . . .) III
3. _____ Qn ou Qch à Qch (to subject . . . to . . .) VI

assurer

1. _____ Qn ou Qch (to assure, to insure, to secure . . .) I
2. s'_____ de Qch (to make certain of . . .; to secure . . .) IV
3. s'_____ contre Qch (to protect, insure oneself against . . .)
V
4. _____ Qn de Qch (to assure . . . of . . .) VI
5. _____ Qch à Qn (to vouch for . . . to . . .) VI

astreindre

1. _____ Qn (to compel . . .) I
2. s'_____ à Qch (to tie oneself down to, subject oneself to
. . .) III
3. _____ Qn à Qch (to subject . . . to . . .) VI
4. s'_____ à *Inf.* (to force oneself to . . .) VIII-A
5. _____ Qn à *Inf.* (to compel . . . to . . .) VIII-B

attacher
1. _____ Qch (to attach . . .) I
2. s'_____ à Qn (to be attached to, fond of . . .) III
3. s'_____ à Qch (to be attached to, fasten onto, stick to . . .) III
4. _____ Qn ou Qch à Qn ou Qch (to attach, make . . . attached to . . .) VI
5. s'_____ à *Inf.* (to strive to . . .) VIII-A

attaquer
1. _____ Qn ou Qch (to attack . . .) I
2. s'_____ à Qn ou Qch (to attack, criticize . . .) III
3. s'_____ à Qch (to tackle . . . *e.g.*, a problem) III

attarder
1. _____ Qn (to delay, keep . . . late) I
2. s'_____ (to be late, stay late, lag behind, dally) I
3. s'_____ à *Inf.* (to linger, stay late ---*ing*) VIII-A

atteindre
1. _____ Qn ou Qch (to reach, attain . . .) I
2. _____ à Qch (to reach . . . with difficulty, effort) II
3. _____ Qn de Qch (to hit . . . with . . .) VI

atteler
1. _____ Qch (to harness, yoke . . .) I
2. s'_____ à Qch (to buckle down, settle down to . . . *e.g.*, *à une tâche*, to a task) III
3. _____ Qn ou Qch à Qch (to harness, put . . . to . . .) VI

attendre
1. _____ Qn ou Qch (to wait for . . .) I
2. s'_____ à Qch (to expect . . .) III
3. _____ Qch de Qn (to expect . . . from . . .) VI
4. s'_____ à *Inf.* (to expect to . . .) VIII-A
5. _____ de *Inf.* (to wait to . . .) IX-A

attendrir
1. _____ Qn (to move . . . to pity) I
2. _____ Qch (to tenderize [meat]; to soften . . .) I
3. s'_____ sur Qch (to be moved to pity by . . .) V

attenter
1. _____ à Qch (to make an attempt on, against . . . Ex: *attenter à la vie de quelqu'un*, to make an attempt on someone's life) II

attester
1. _____ Qch (to attest . . .; to testify to . . .) I

attirer
1. _____ Qn ou Qch (to attract, entice . . .) I
2. s'_____ Qch (to bring . . . upon oneself) I
3. _____ Qn à Qn ou Qch (to attract . . . to . . .) VI
4. _____ Qn dans Qch (to lure . . . into . .)VI
5. _____ Qch à, sur Qn (to bring . . . to, on, upon . . .) VI
6. _____ Qch sur Qch (to draw . . . [*e.g.*, one's attention] to . . .) VI

attraper
1. _____ Qn ou Qch (to catch, trap, trick . . .) I
2. _____ Qn à Qch (to catch . . . at . . .) VI
3. _____ Qn à *Inf.* (to catch . . . ---*ing*) VIII-B

attribuer
1. s'_____ Qch (to claim, assume . . .) I
2. _____ Qch à Qn ou Qch (to attribute . . . to . . .; to assign, allot . . . to . . .) VI

augurer
1. _____ Qch de Qch (to augur . . . of . . .; to predict . . . from, for . . .) VI

autoriser
1. _____ Qn ou Qch (to authorize . . .) I
2. s'_____ de Qn ou Qch (to cite . . . as an authority; to act on the authority of . . .) IV
3. _____ Qn à *Inf.* (to authorize . . . to . . .) VIII-B

avancer
1. _____ Qn ou Qch (to advance . . .) I
2. s'_____ (to move forward, advance) I
3. _____ de [un certain temps] (to be . . . fast, Ex: *La pendule avance de dix minutes,* the clock is ten minutes fast) IV
4. _____ Qch à Qn (to advance [money] to . . .) VI

aventurer
1. _____ Qch (to venture, risk . . .) I
2. s'_____ (to take a chance) I
3. s'_____ à *Inf.* (to venture to . . .) VIII-A

avertir
1. _____ Qn (to warn, notify . . .) I
2. _____ Qn de Qch (to warn, notify . . . of . . .) VI
3. _____ Qn de *Inf.* (to warn . . . to . . .) IX-B

aveugler
·1. _____ Qn ou Qch (to blind, to plug up, wall up . . .) I
2. s'_____ sur Qch (to shut one's eyes to . . .) V

avilir
1. _____ Qn ou Qch (to debase . . .) I
2. s'_____ (to debase, demean oneself) I
3. s'_____ à *Inf.* (to stoop to . . .; to demean oneself to the point of ---*ing*) VIII-A

aviser

1. _____ Qn (to inform . . .) I
2. _____ à Qch (to see to, to deal with . . .) II
3. s'_____ de Qch (to realize . . .) IV
4. _____ Qn de Qch (to inform . . . of . . .) VI
5. _____ à *Inf.* (to see about, think about ---*ing*) VIII-A
6. s'_____ de *Inf.* (to take it into one's head to . . .) IX-A

avoir

1. _____ Qn ou Qch (to have . . .) I
2. _____ *affaire* à Qn (to have to deal with . . .) III
3. _____ *affaire* avec Qn (to have dealings with . . .) V
4. en _____ à, contre, après Qn (to be angry with . . .) II, V
5. en _____ pour Qch (to take, require . . . Ex: *Elle en a pour trois jours*, it will take her three days) V
6. _____ à *Inf.* (to have to . . .; to have [something] to . . . Ex: *J'ai à travailler*, I have to work, I have work to do) VIII-A
7. _____ Qch à *Inf.* (to have . . . to . . . Ex: *avoir une lettre à écrire*, to have a letter to write) VIII-B

avouer

1. _____ Qch (to acknowledge, confess . . .) I
2. _____ Qn pour Qn ou Qch (to acknowledge, recognize . . . as . . . *e.g.*, *pour fils*, as one's son) VI
3. _____ Qch à Qn (to confess, admit . . . to . . .) VI
4. _____ *Inf. passé* (to admit having . . .) VII-A

B

badiner

1. _____ avec Qch (to trifle, play with . . .) V

baigner
1. _____ Qn ou Qch (to bathe, wash . . .) I
2. être baigné de Qch (to be bathed in . . . *e.g., les yeux baignés de larmes,* eyes bathed in tears) IV
3. _____ dans Qch (to soak in . . .) V
4. _____ Qn ou Qch dans Qch (to immerse, dip . . . in . . .) VI

balancer
1. _____ Qn ou Qch (to balance, to swing, rock . . .) I
2. _____ Qch par Qch (to [counter] balance . . . with . . .) VI

bannir
1. _____ Qn (to banish, exile . . .) I
2. _____ Qn ou Qch de Qch (to banish . . . from . . .) VI

barbouiller
1. _____ Qch (to smear, to daub . . .) I
2. _____ Qn ou Qch de Qch (to smear . . . with . . .) VI

barrer
1. _____ Qch (to bar, block . . . *e.g.,* a door, a road; to cross out . . .) I
2. _____ Qch à, contre Qn (to bar, close off . . . to, against . . .) VI

baser
1. se _____ sur Qch (to be based on, founded on . . .) V
2. _____ Qch sur Qch (to base . . . on . . .) VI

battre
1. _____ Qn ou Qch (to beat . . .) I
2. _____ *des mains* (to clap one's hands)
3. _____ *des pieds* (to stamp one's feet)
4. se _____ avec, contre Qn (to fight with, against . . .) V
5. _____ contre Qch (to beat against . . .) V
6. _____ Qn à Qch (to beat . . . at . . . *e.g.*, *au tennis*, at tennis) VI
7. _____ Qn par Qch (to beat, be ahead of . . . by . . . *e.g.*, *par trois points*, by three points) VI

bénéficier
1. _____ de Qch (to profit by . . .) IV

bercer
1. _____ Qn (to rock . . .) I
2. se _____ de Qch (to delude oneself with . . .) IV
3. _____ Qn de Qch (to beguile . . . with . . .) VI

blâmer
1. _____ Qn ou Qch (to blame . . .) I
2. _____ Qn de Qch (to blame . . . for . . .) VI
3. _____ Qn de *Inf.* ou *Inf. passé* (to blame . . . for ---*ing*, for having . . .) IX-B

blaser
1. _____ Qn ou Qch (to cloy, to blunt . . .) I
2. se _____ de Qch (to become tired of, indifferent to . . .) IV
3. être blasé de, sur Qch (to be tired of, indifferent to . . .) IV, V

blesser
1. _____ Qn ou Qch (to wound, injure, offend . . .) I
2. être blessé à Qch (to be wounded, injured, hurt in . . . *e.g.*, *au bras*, in the arm) II
3. se _____ de Qch (to take offense at . . .) IV
4. se _____ avec Qch (to injure oneself with . . .) V
5. _____ Qn à Qch (to wound, injure . . . in . . . *e.g.*, *au genou*, in the knee, *à la tête*, in the head [exception: *dans le dos*, in the back]) VI
6. _____ Qn de Qch (to wound, injure . . . with . . .) VI

bombarder
1. _____ Qn ou Qch (to bombard . . .) I
2. _____ Qn ou Qch de Qch (to bombard . . . with . . .) VI

bondir
1. _____ de Qch (to leap with . . . *e.g., de joie*, with joy) IV
2. _____ sur Qn ou Qch (to pounce on, leap at . . .) V

border
1. _____ Qn ou Qch (to border . . .; to tuck in . . . Ex: *border quelqu'un dans son lit*, to tuck someone in bed) I
2. _____ Qch de, avec Qch (to border . . . with . . .) VI

borner
1. _____ Qch (to mark out, form the boundary of . . .; to limit . . .) I
2. se _____ à Qch (of people: to restrict oneself to . . .; of things: to be limited to . . . Ex: *Son répertoire se borne à des morceaux classiques*, his repertory is limited to classical pieces) III

bouder
1. _____ Qn ou Qch (to be sulky with, distant toward . . .) I
2. _____ contre Qn (to be sulky with . . .) V

bourrer
1. _____ Qn ou Qch (to stuff, cram . . .) I
2. _____ Qn *de coups* (to pummel, thrash . . .) I
3. se _____ de Qch (to stuff oneself with . . .) IV
4. _____ Qn ou Qch de Qch (to stuff, cram . . . with . . .) VI

braquer
1. _____ Qch (to aim, level, point . . .) I
2. se _____ contre Qn ou Qch (to be stubbornly opposed to, dead set against . . .) V
3. _____ Qn contre Qn ou Qch (to set . . . against . . .) VI
4. _____ *les yeux* sur Qn ou Qch (to fix one's gaze on, to stare at . . . Ex: *Tout le monde avait les yeux*

braqués sur la vedette, everyone was staring at the movie star) VI

briser
1. _____ Qn ou Qch (to break, shatter . . .) I
2. _____ avec Qn (to break with . . .) V

brouiller
1. _____ Qn ou Qch (to mix up, confuse . . .) I
2. se _____ avec Qn (to have a falling out with . . .) V

brûler
1. _____ Qn ou Qch (to burn . . .) I
2. _____ de Qch (to be burning with . . . *e.g., de fièvre,* with fever; *d'amour,* with love) IV
3. _____ de *Inf.* (to be eager to, anxious to . . .) IX-A

buter
1. se _____ à Qn ou Qch (to come up against . . . *e.g.,* a difficulty) III
2. _____ contre Qch (of people: to knock against, stumble over . . .; of things: to butt, strike against . . .) V
3. se _____ contre Qch (to prop oneself up against . . .) V
4. se _____ à *Inf.* (to be dead set on ---*ing*) VIII-A

C

cabrer
1. se _____ (of horses: to rear) I
2. se _____ contre Qch (to balk at, to revolt against . . .) V

cacher
1. _____ Qn ou Qch (to hide . . .) I
2. se _____ à Qn (to hide from . . .) III
3. se _____ de Qn (to keep out of the way of, to hide one's feelings from . . .) IV

4. se ―― de Qch (to make a secret of . . . Usually in the negative, Ex: *Il ne s'en cache pas*, he makes no secret of it) IV

5. ―― Qch à Qn (to hide . . . from . . .) VI

cadrer

1. ―― avec Qch (to agree, tally with . . .) V

calquer

1. ―― Qn ou Qch (to trace, to imitate . . .) I

2. ―― Qch sur Qch (to trace . . . from . . .; to model . . . on . . .) VI

causer

1. ―― Qch (to cause . . .; to talk . . . Ex: *causer politique*, to talk politics) I

2. ―― à Qn (Coll: to talk to . . .) II

3. ―― de Qch (to talk of, about . . .) IV

4. ―― avec Qn (to have a talk with, a chat with . . .) V

céder

1. ―― Qch (to give up . . .) I

2. ―― à Qn ou Qch (to yield to . . .) II

3. ne ―― *en rien* à Qn (to be someone's equal, Ex: *Elle ne lui cède en rien*, she is his equal in every respect) II

4. ―― Qch à Qn (to give up . . . to . . .; to give in to someone's . . . Ex: *céder à quelqu'un tous ses caprices*, to give in to someone's every whim) VI

ceindre

1. ―― Qn ou Qch (to gird, encircle . . .) I

2. ―― Qch à Qn (to gird . . . on . . .) VI

3. ―― Qn ou Qch de Qch (to gird, encircle . . . with . . .) VI

celer

1. _____ Qch (to hide, conceal . . .) I
2. _____ Qch à Qn (to hide, conceal . . . from . . .) VI

centrer

1. _____ Qch (to center . . .) I
2. _____ Qch sur Qn ou Qch (to center . . . on . . .) VI

certifier

1. _____ Qch (to certify, vouch for . . .) I
2. _____ Qch à Qn (to assure someone of something) VI

cesser

1. _____ Qch (to stop . . .) I
2. _____ de *Inf.* (to stop ---*ing*) IX-A

changer

1. _____ Qn ou Qch (to change, alter . . .) I
2. _____ de Qn ou Qch (to change . . . Ex: *changer d'avis*, to change one's mind; *changer de place*, to change places) IV
3. se ____ en Qn ou Qch (to change into . . .) V
4. _____ Qch contre Qch (to exchange . . . for . . .) VI

charger

1. _____ Qn ou Qch (to load, to transport, to charge . . .) I
2. se ____ de Qch (to take . . . upon oneself) IV
3. _____ Qn de Qch (to charge . . . with . . . *e.g., d'un crime*, with a crime; to entrust . . . with . . . *e.g., d'une mission*, with a mission) VI
4. _____ Qn ou Qch de Qch (to load, overburden . . . with . . .) VI
5. _____ Qn de *Inf.* (to charge, entrust . . . with ---*ing*) IX-B

charmer

1. ———— Qn ou Qch (to charm, bewitch . . .) I
2. être charmé de Qch (to be delighted with . . .) IV
3. être charmé de *Inf.* (to be delighted to . . .) IX-A

chasser

1. ———— Qn ou Qch (to chase, hunt, drive out . . .) I
2. ———— Qn ou Qch de Qch (to drive out . . . from . . .) VI

chausser

1. ———— Qch (to put on . . . on one's feet) I
2. ———— du 38, 40, etc. (to wear size 38, 40, etc. shoe [French sizes]) IV

chercher

1. ———— Qn ou Qch (to look for . . .) I
2. ———— à *Inf.* (to attempt to . . .) VIII-A

chicaner

1. ———— Qn (to quibble with, start a quarrel with . . .) I
2. ———— sur Qch (to quibble over . . .) V
3. ———— Qn sur Qch (to quibble with . . . over . . .) VI
4. ———— Qch à Qn (to quibble over . . . with . . .) VI

chiper

1. ———— Qch (Coll: to swipe . . .) I
2. ———— Qch à Qn (Coll: to swipe . . . from . . .) VI

choisir

1. ———— Qn ou Qch (to choose . . .) I
2. ———— de *Inf.* (to choose to . . .) IX-A

choquer

1. ———— Qn ou Qch (to shock, offend . . .; to clink [glasses]) I
2. se ——— de Qch (to be shocked by, at . . .; to take offense at . . .) IV
3. être choqué de Qch (to be shocked by, at . . .) IV
4. se ——— contre Qch (to collide with . . .) V

circonscrire

1. _____ Qch (to circumscribe . . .) I
2. _____ Qch à Qch (to draw [a circle] around . . . Ex: *circonscrire un cercle à un polygone*, to circumscribe a polygon) VI
3. _____ Qch par Qch (to surround, encircle . . . with . . .) VI

clabauder

1. _____ sur, contre Qn (to speak ill of . . .) V

coiffer

1. _____ Qn (to do someone's hair) I
2. _____ Qch (to cover, cap . . .; to be at the head of, to encompass . . .) I
3. se _____ (to fix, do one's hair) I
4. se _____ de Qch (to put on, wear . . . [on one's head]) IV
5. être coiffé de Qch (to be wearing . . . [on one's head]) IV

coincer

1. _____ Qn (Coll: to corner, catch . . .) I
2. _____ Qch (to wedge, jam . . .) I
2. être coincé dans Qch (Coll: to be caught, stuck in . . .) V

coïncider

1. _____ avec Qch (to coincide with . . .) V

collaborer

1. _____ à Qch (to contribute to . . . *e.g.*, *à une revue*, to a magazine) II
2. _____ avec Qn (to collaborate with . . .) V

coller

1. _____ Qn (Coll: to fail, flunk [a student]) I
2. _____ Qch (to paste, stick, glue . . .) I
3. _____ à Qn ou Qch (to cling, stick, adhere to . . .) II
4. se _____ à, contre Qn ou Qch (to stand close to, cling to . . .) III, V
5. _____ Qch à Qch (to stick, paste, glue . . . to . . .) VI
6. _____ *une gifle* à Qn (Coll: to give . . . a slap, a smack in the face) VI

colleter

1. _____ Qn (to collar . . .) I
2. se _____ avec Qn (to fight, scuffle with . . .) V

colorer

1. _____ Qch (to color . . .) I
2. _____ Qch en Qch (to color something . . . Ex: *colorer une toile en bleu*, to color a canvas blue) VI
3. _____ Qch avec Qch (to color . . . with . . . *e.g., avec un vernis rouge*, with a red glaze) VI
4. _____ Qch de Qch (to embellish, gloss over . . . with . . .) VI

combiner

1. _____ Qch (to combine, to concoct, devise . . .) I
2. se _____ à, avec Qch (in chemistry: to combine with . . .) III, V
3. _____ Qch avec Qch (to combine . . . with . . .) VI

combler

1. _____ Qch (to fill in, fill . . . to the brim) I
2. être comblé de Qn ou Qch (to be filled with . . .; to be showered with . . . *e.g., d'honneurs*, with honors) IV
3. _____ Qn de Qch (to shower, overwhelm . . . with . . .) VI

commander

1. _____ Qch (to command . . .; to order . . . *e.g.*, a book, a dinner) I
2. _____ à Qn (to give orders to, have authority over . . .) II
3. _____ *à ses passions* (to curb one's passions) II
4. _____ Qch à Qn ou Qch (to order . . . from . . .) VI
5. _____ à Qn de *Inf.* (to order . . . to . . .) IX-B

commencer

1. _____ Qch (to begin . . .) I
2. _____ Qn dans Qch (to start, initiate . . . in . . .) VI
3. _____ à ou de *Inf.* (to begin to . . . *À* is more common; *de* is more literary) VIII-A, IX-A
4. _____ par *Inf.* (to begin by ---*ing*) X

commercer

1. _____ avec Qn ou Qch (to trade, deal with . . .) V

commettre

1. _____ Qch (to commit . . . *e.g.*, a crime, an error; to risk . . . *e.g.*, one's reputation) I
2. se _____ (to commit oneself) I
3. se _____ avec Qn (to throw in one's lot with . . . [and thereby compromise oneself]) V

commuer

1. _____ Qch (to commute [a sentence]) I
2. _____ Qch en Qch (to commute . . . to . . .) VI

communiquer

1. _____ Qch (to communicate, convey, impart . . .) I
2. se _____ à Qch (to spread to . . .) III
3. _____ avec Qn (to be in communication with, in touch with . . .) V
4. _____ avec Qch (to lead into . . . Ex: *une porte qui communique avec le salon*, a door which leads into the living room) V
5. _____ Qch à Qn ou Qch (to communicate, convey, transmit . . . to . . .) VI

comparer

1. _____ Qn ou Qch à Qn ou Qch (to compare . . . [in a general way] to, with . . .) VI
2. _____ Qn ou Qch avec Qn ou Qch (to compare . . . [methodically] with . . .) VI

compatir
1. _____ à Qch (to sympathize with, feel for . . . Ex: *Nous compatissons à leur douleur*, we feel for them in their sorrow) II

complaire
1. _____ à Qn (Lit: to please . . .) II
2. se _____ dans, en* Qch (to take pleasure in . . .) V
3. se _____ à *Inf.* (to take pleasure in ---*ing*) VIII-A

complimenter
1. _____ Qn (to compliment, congratulate . . .) I
2. _____ Qn pour Qch (to compliment, congratulate . . . for . . .) VI
3. _____ Qn sur, de Qch (to compliment, congratulate . . . on . . .) VI

comploter
1. _____ Qch (to plot, scheme . . .) I
2. _____ de *Inf.* (to plot to . . .) IX-A

composer
1. _____ Qch (to compose, make up . . .) I
2. se _____ de Qn ou Qch (to be composed of, consist of . . .) IV
3. _____ avec Qn ou Qch (to come to terms with . . .) V

comprendre
1. _____ Qn ou Qch (to understand . . . .) I
2. ne _____ *rien* à Qch (to know nothing about, to not understand anything in . . . Ex: *Je ne comprends rien à la géométrie*, I don't know the first thing about geometry) II

*See Appendix II: **DANS, EN, À**, p. 298.

compromettre
1. _____ Qn ou Qch (to compromise . . .) I
2. se _____ (to compromise oneself) I
3. se _____ avec Qn (to compromise oneself with . . .) V
4. être compromis dans Qch (to be implicated in . . .) V

compter
1. _____ Qn ou Qch (to count . . .) I
2. _____ avec Qn ou Qch (to reckon with . . .) V
3. _____ sur Qn ou Qch (to count on, rely on . . .) V
4. _____ Qch à Qn [pour Qch] (to pay someone . . . [for
. . .] Ex: *compter mille francs à quelqu'un,* to
pay someone a thousand francs) VI

concéder
1. _____ Qch (to concede, grant . . .) I
2. _____ Qch à Qn (to grant . . . to . . .) VI

concentrer
1. _____ Qch (to concentrate, focus . . .) I
2. se _____ [sur Qch] (to concentrate [on . . .] Ex: *Laissez-moi
tranquille, j'essaye de me concentrer,* leave me
alone, I'm trying to concentrate) V

concerter
1. _____ Qch (to concert, arrange . . .) I
2. se _____ avec Qn (to act in concert with, to connive with
. . .) V

concilier
1. _____ Qn ou Qch (to conciliate, reconcile . . .) I
2. se _____ Qch (to win over, gain . . . Ex: *se concilier l'es-
time de tout le monde,* to gain the esteem of
everyone) I
3. se _____ avec Qn ou Qch (to agree with, jibe with . . .) V
4. _____ Qn ou Qch avec Qn ou Qch (to reconcile, harmonize . . . with . . .) VI

concorder

1. _____ avec Qch (to agree, tally with . . .) V

concourir

1. _____ à Qch (to contribute toward, be directed toward
. . .) II
2. _____ avec Qn (to cooperate with . . .) V
3. _____ pour Qch (to compete for . . .) V
4. _____ à *Inf.* (to combine, unite, conspire to . . . Ex:
Tout concourt à prouver son innocence, everything tends to prove his innocence) VIII-A

condamner

1. _____ Qn (to condemn, sentence . . .) I
2. _____ Qn à Qch (to condemn, sentence . . . to . . .) VI
3. _____ Qn à *Inf.* (to condemn . . . to . . .) VIII-B

condenser

1. _____ Qch (to condense . . .) I
2. _____ Qch en Qch (to condense . . . into . . .) VI

condescendre

1. _____ à Qch (to condescend to, agree [with disdain] to
. . .) II
2. _____ à *Inf.* (to condescend to, deign to . . .) VIII-A

conduire

1. _____ Qn ou Qch (to conduct, lead, drive . . .) I
2. _____ Qn ou Qch à Qch (to lead, take . . . to . . .) VI
3. _____ Qn à *Inf.* (to lead, induce . . . to . . .) VIII-B

confédérer

1. _____ avec Qn ou Qch (to unite with . . .) V

conférer

1. _____ de Qch (to talk over, confer about . . .) IV
2. _____ avec Qn (to confer with . . .) V
3. _____ Qch à Qn (to confer . . . on . . .) VI
4. _____ de Qch avec Qn (to confer about . . . with . . .) IV

confesser

1. _____ Qch (to confess . . .) I
2. _____ Qn (to receive the confession of . . . Ex: *Le prêtre confessa le pénitent*, the priest confessed the penitent) I
3. se _____ (to confess one's sins) I
4. se _____ à Qn (to confess one's sins to . . .) III
5. se _____ de Qch (to confess having done . . .) IV
6. _____ Qch à Qn (to confess . . . to . . .) VI

confier

1. se _____ à, en Qn ou Qch (to put one's trust in, to confide in . . .) III, V
2. _____ Qch à Qn (to entrust someone with something; to tell someone something in confidence) VI

confiner

1. _____ Qn ou Qch (to confine, imprison, shut up . . .) I
2. _____ à Qch (to border on . . . *e.g.*, a country; to verge on . . . *e.g.*, madness) II
3. se _____ dans Qch (to limit oneself to, specialize in . . .) V
4. _____ Qn dans Qch (to shut up . . . in . . .) VI

confisquer

1. _____ Qch (to confiscate . . .) I
2. _____ Qch à Qn (to confiscate . . . from . . .) VI

confondre
1. _____ Qn ou Qch (to confuse, mix up, confound . . .) I
2. se _____ (to become bewildered, confused; to intermingle, be indistinguishable) I
3. être confondu de Qch (to be dumbfounded at . . .) IV
4. se _____ en Qch (to blend into . . .; to be profuse in . . . Ex: *se confondre en excuses*, to apologize profusely) V
5. se _____ avec Qch (to be confused with, indistinguishable from . . .) V
6. _____ Qn ou Qch avec Qn ou Qch (to mistake . . . for . . .) VI

conformer
1. _____ Qch (to form, shape . . .) I
2. se _____ à Qch (to conform to, comply with . . .) III
3. _____ Qch à Qch (to make . . . conform to . . .) VI

confronter
1. _____ Qn ou Qch (to confront, compare . . .) I
2. _____ Qn ou Qch avec Qn ou Qch (to confront, compare . . . with . . .) VI

conjurer
1. _____ Qch (to conjure up or away, to ward off . . .) I
2. se _____ contre Qn (to plot together, conspire against . . .) V
3. se _____ à *Inf.* (to unite, conspire to . . .) VIII-A
4. _____ Qn de *Inf.* (to beseech . . . to . . .) IX-B

connaître
1. _____ Qn ou Qch (to know, be acquainted with . . .) I
2. se _____ en Qch (to know a lot about, to be a good judge of . . .) V

consacrer
1. ———— Qn ou Qch (to consecrate . . .) I
2. se ———— à Qch (to devote oneself to . . .) III
3. ———— Qch à Qn ou Qch (to dedicate, devote . . . to . . .)
   VI

conseiller
1. ———— Qn ou Qch (to advise, counsel . . .) I
2. ———— Qch à Qn (to recommend . . . to . . .) VI
3. ———— à Qn de *Inf.* (to advise . . . to . . .) IX-B

consentir
1. ———— à Qch (to consent to . . .) II
2. ———— à *Inf.* (to consent to, be willing to . . .) VIII-A

consister
1. ———— dans* Qch (to consist of, to lie in . . . Ex: *La valeur de l'or consiste dans sa rareté*, the value of gold lies in its scarcity) V
2. ———— en* Qch (to consist of, be composed of . . . Ex: *Ce travail consiste en recherches minutieuses*, this job consists of very detailed research; *le problème consiste en ceci*, the problem is this) V
3. ———— à *Inf.* (to consist of, to lie in ---*ing*) VIII-A

consoler
1. ———— Qn (to console, comfort . . .) I
2. se ———— de Qch (to get over . . .) IV
3. ———— Qn de Qch (to console . . . for . . .) VI

conspirer
1. ———— contre Qn ou Qch (to plot against . . .) V
2. ———— à *Inf.* (to conspire to . . .) VIII-A

———
*See Appendix II: **DANS, EN, À**, p. 298.

constituer

1. _____ Qn ou Qch (to constitute, form, make up . . .) I
2. se _____ en Qch (to form, set oneself up as . . . Ex: *Ils se constituèrent en gouvernement révolutionnaire,* they formed a revolutionary government; *ils se constituèrent en arbitre du bon goût,* they set themselves up as the arbiter of good taste) V
3. _____ Qch à Qn (to settle . . . on . . . Ex: *constituer une annuité à quelqu'un,* to settle an annuity on someone) VI

consulter

1. _____ Qn ou Qch (to consult . . .) I
2. _____ avec Qn (to consult with, confer with . . .) V
3. _____ Qn sur Qch (to consult . . . on, about . . .) VI

contenter

1. _____ Qn ou Qch (to satisfy, gratify . . .) I
2. se _____ de Qch (to be content, satisfied with . . .) IV
3. se _____ de *Inf.* (to be content, satisfied with ---*ing*) IX-A

contester

1. _____ Qch (to contest, dispute . . .) I
2. _____ sur Qch (to wrangle, argue over . . .) V

continuer

1. _____ Qch (to continue . . .) I
2. _____ à ou de *Inf.* (to continue to . . .; to keep on ---*ing*) VIII-A, IX-A

contraindre

1. _____ Qn ou Qch (to constrain, restrain . . .) I
2. se _____ à ou de *Inf.* (to stop oneself from ---*ing*) VIII-A, IX-A
3. _____ Qn à *Inf.* (to compel, force . . . to . . .) VIII-B
4. être contraint de *Inf.* (to be obliged to . . .) IX-A

contrarier
1. _____ Qn ou Qch (to thwart, oppose, vex . . .) I
2. être contrarié de Qch (to be annoyed, vexed by, at . . .) IV

contraster
1. _____ Qch (to contrast, set . . . in contrast) I
2. _____ avec Qch (to stand in contrast to, form a contrast with . . .) V

contrevenir
1. _____ à Qch (to contravene, violate . . .) II

contribuer
1. _____ Qch (to contribute . . .) I
2. _____ à Qch (to contribute to, play a part in . . .) II
3. _____ Qch à Qch (to contribute . . . to . . .) VI

convaincre
1. _____ Qn (to convince . . .) I
2. se _____ de Qch (to convince oneself of . . .) IV
3. _____ Qn de Qch (to convince . . . of . . .; to prove . . . guilty of . . .) VI

convenir
1. _____ à Qn ou Qch (to suit, be suited to, for . . .; to be agreeable to . . .) II
2. _____ de Qch (to agree on . . .; to acknowledge, admit . . .) IV
3. _____ de *Inf.* (to agree to . . .) IX-A
4. Il convient de *Inf.* (It is fitting, advisable to . . .) IX-A

converger
1. _____ sur, vers Qn ou Qch (to coverge on, towards . . .) V

converser
1. _____ avec Qn (to converse with . . .) V

convertir
1. _____ Qn ou Qch (to convert . . .) I
2. se _____ à Qch (to convert to . . . Ex: *se convertir au christianisme,* to convert to Christianity) III
3. _____ Qn à Qch (to convert . . . to . . .) VI
4. _____ Qch en Qch (to convert . . . to, into . . .) VI

convier
1. _____ Qn (to invite . . .) I
2. _____ Qn à Qch (to invite . . . to . . .) VI
3. _____ Qn à *Inf.* (to invite, urge . . . to . . .) VIII-B

coopérer
1. _____ à Qch (to cooperate on, in . . .) II
2. _____ avec Qn (to cooperate with . . .) V

coordonner
1. _____ Qch (to coordinate . . .) I
2. _____ Qch à, avec Qch (to coordinate . . . with . . .) VI

copier
1. _____ Qn ou Qch (to copy, imitate . . .) I
2. _____ sur Qn ou Qch (to copy from . . .) V
3. _____ Qch sur Qn ou Qch (to copy . . . from . . .) VI

correspondre
1. _____ à Qch (to tally, agree with, correspond to . . .) II
2. _____ avec Qn (to correspond with . . .) V

corriger
1. _____ Qn ou Qch (to correct . . .) I
2. se _____ de Qch (to break oneself of . . . *e.g., d'une mauvaise habitude,* of a bad habit) IV
3. _____ Qn de Qch (to cure, break . . . of . . .) VI

costumer
1. ———— Qn (to dress . . . up) I
2. se —— en Qch (to dress up as . . .) V
3. ———— Qn en Qch (to dress . . . up as . . .) VI

coucher
1. ———— Qn ou Qch (to put . . . to bed; to put down, lay down, flatten . . .) I
2. se —— (to go to bed) I
3. ———— Qch dans Qch (to write down, enter . . . in . . .) VI
4. ———— Qn *sur son testament*, to mention someone in one's will) VI

coudre
1. ———— Qch (to sew . . .) I
2. ———— Qch à Qch (to sew . . . on, to . . .) VI

courir
1. ———— Qch (to run . . . *e.g.*, a risk; to pursue, to roam, to frequent . . .) I
2. ———— à Qch (to race to, flock to . . .) II
3. ———— après Qn ou Qch (to run after, pursue . . .) V
4. ———— *Inf.* (to run to . . . Ex: *J'ai couru lui dire les nouvelles*, I ran to tell him the news) VII-A

couronner
1. ———— Qn (to crown . . .) I
2. ———— Qn de Qch (to crown . . . with . . .) VI

coûter
1. ———— Qch (to cost . . .) I
2. ———— Qch à Qn (to cost, cause someone something, Ex: *Cela lui a coûté la vie*, that cost him his life; *cela lui a coûté une fortune*, that cost him a fortune) VI
3. Il en coûte à Qn de *Inf.* (It is painful, difficult for . . . to . . .) IX-B

couvrir
1. _____ (to cover . . .) I
2. se _____ de Qch (to become covered with . . .) IV
3. être couvert de Qch (to be covered with . . .) IV
4. _____ Qn ou Qch de Qch (to cover . . . with . . .) VI

craindre
1. _____ Qn ou Qch (to fear . . .) I
2. _____ pour Qn ou Qch (to fear for . . .) V
3. _____ de *Inf.* (to fear, be afraid of ---*ing*) IX-A

cramponner
1. _____ Qn (Coll: to pester . . .) I
2. _____ Qch (to clamp . . . together) I
3. se _____ à Qn (Coll: to cling to, hang on to . . .) III
4. se _____ à Qch (to cling to, hold fast to, hang on to . . .) III

créditer
1. _____ Qch de Qch (to credit . . . with . . . Ex: *créditer un compte de vingt dollars*, to credit an account with twenty dollars) VI

crever
1. _____ Qn (to exhaust, work . . . to death) I
2. _____ Qch (to burst, split . . .; to puncture [a tire]) I
3. _____ de Qch (Coll: to be bursting with . . . Ex: *crever de rire*, to split one's sides laughing; Coll: to be dying of . . . e.g., *de faim*, of hunger; *d'ennui*, of boredom) IV

cribler
1. _____ Qch (to sift, riddle . . .) I
2. _____ Qn ou Qch de Qch (to riddle . . . with . . .) VI

crier
1. _____ Qch (to cry, cry out, shout . . .) I
2. _____ *au feu* (to cry out "fire") II
3. _____ *au secours* (to cry out for help) II
4. _____ de Qch (to cry out with . . . *e.g., de douleur,*
with pain) IV
5. _____ contre Qn (to cry out against, rail against . . .) V
6. _____ après Qn (to carp at, bawl out . . .) V
7. _____ Qch à Qn (to shout, cry out . . . at, to . . .) VI
8. _____ à Qn de *Inf.* (to shout to . . . to . . .) IX-B

croire
1. _____ Qn ou Qch (to believe . . .) I
2. se ____ Qch (to think oneself . . . Ex: *Il se croit un
génie,* he thinks he's a genius) I
3. _____ à Qch (to believe in: to have faith in the reality,
veracity, truth, or likelihood of . . . Ex: *Le médecin croit à une tuberculose,* the doctor thinks that
it's tuberculosis; *croire aux promesses de quelqu'un,* to believe someone's promises; *croire aux
revenants,* to believe in ghosts; *croire à la pos-
sibilité d'une guerre,* to believe that war is possible) II
4. _____ en Qn (to believe in, have confidence in . . . Ex:
croire en ses amis, to trust one's friends; *croire
en Dieu,* to believe in God) V
5. _____ *Inf.* (to think, believe that . . . Ex: *Il croit entendre des voix,* he thinks he hears voices) VII-
A

croiser
1. _____ Qn ou Qch (to cross, thwart, meet, pass . . .) I
2. se ____ (to cross, Ex: *Nos lettres se sont croisées,* our letters crossed [in the mail]) I
3. se ____ avec Qn ou Qch (to meet, pass . . .; of letters: to
cross with . . .) V

croître
1. _____ en Qch (to grow, increase in . . . *e.g., en nombre,*
in number) V

croupir
1. _____ dans Qch (to wallow in . . .) V

cuirasser
1. _____ Qn (to armor . . .) I
2. se _____ (to put on armor) I
3. se _____ contre Qn ou Qch (to steel oneself, protect one-self against . . .) V

cuire
1. _____ Qch (to cook . . .) I
2. _____ [Qch] à Qch (to cook [. . .] in, on . . . Ex: *cuire au four*, to bake, roast; *cuire à l'eau*, to boil; *cuire à la broche*, to cook on a spit) VI

D

daigner
1. _____ *Inf.* (to deign to, condescend to . . .) VII-A

danser
1. _____ Qch (to dance . . . *e.g.*, the polka) I
2. _____ avec Qn (to dance with . . .) V

dater
1. _____ Qch (to date . . .) I
2. _____ de Qch (to date from . . .; to be dated . . .) IV

débarrasser
1. _____ Qch (to disencumber . . .; to clear . . . *e.g.*, the table) I
2. se _____ de Qn ou Qch (to get rid of . . .; to extricate one-self from . . .) IV
3. _____ Qn de Qn ou Qch (to rid, relieve . . . of . . .) VI

débattre

1. ⸺ Qch (to debate, discuss . . .) I
2. se ⸺ avec Qch (to struggle with . . . *e.g.*, *avec un problème*, with a problem) V
3. se ⸺ contre Qch (to struggle against . . .) V

débiter

1. ⸺ Qn ou Qch de Qch (to debit . . . with . . . *e.g.*, *d'une somme*, with an amount) VI
2. ⸺ Qch à Qn ou Qch (to debit . . . to . . .) VI

déblatérer

1. ⸺ Qch (to bluster, hurl . . . *e.g.*, insults, threats) I
2. ⸺ contre Qn (to shout abuse, rail at . . .) V
3. ⸺ Qch contre Qn (to hurl . . . [*e.g.*, abuse] at . . .) VI

déborder

1. ⸺ de Qch (to overflow with . . . *e.g.*, *d'enthousiasme*, with enthusiasm) IV
2. être débordé de Qch (to be overwhelmed, snowed under with . . . *e.g.*, *de travail*, with work) IV

déboucher

1. ⸺ Qch (to clear, unstop, uncork . . .) I
2. ⸺ dans Qch (to empty into . . .) V
3. ⸺ sur Qch (to open onto . . .) V

débrouiller

1. ⸺ Qch (to unravel, disentangle, make out . . .) I
2. se ⸺ (to extricate oneself [from a difficult situation]; Coll: to get along, manage) I
3. se ⸺ avec Qch (Coll: to get by on, manage with . . . Ex: *se débrouiller avec $90 par semaine*, to get by on $90 a week) V

débuter

1. ———— dans Qch (to start in, make one's debut in . . .) V
2. ———— par *Inf.* (to begin by ---*ing*) X

décerner

1. ———— Qch à Qn (to bestow . . . on . . .; to award . . . to . . .) VI
2. ———— *un mandat d'arrêt* contre Qn (to issue a warrant for someone's arrest) VI

décevoir

1. ———— Qn (to disappoint . . .) I
2. être déçu par Qn ou Qch (to be disappointed by, in . . .) V

déchaîner

1. ———— Qn ou Qch (to unleash, let loose . . .) I
2. se ———— (to be unleashed; of a storm: to break out) I
3. se ———— contre Qn ou Qch (to fly into a rage against . . .) V
4. ———— Qn ou Qch contre Qn ou Qch (to let loose, trigger . . . against . . .) VI

décharger

1. ———— Qn ou Qch (to unburden, unload . . .) I
2. se ———— de Qn ou Qch (to get rid of, free oneself of . . .) IV
3. se ———— de Qch sur Qn (to shift the responsibility for . . . onto . . .) IV
4. se ———— dans Qch (to flow, empty into . . .) V
5. ———— Qn de Qch (to relieve, discharge, acquit . . . of . . .) VI
6. ———— Qch sur Qn (to vent . . . [*e.g.*, one's anger] on . . .) VI
7. ———— Qch sur, contre Qn ou Qch (to fire [a gun] at . . .) VI

décider
1. _____ Qch (to decide, settle . . .) I
2. _____ de Qch (to determine, to determine the outcome of . . .) IV
3. se _____ pour, contre Qch (to decide in favor of, against . . .; to decide on, against . . . Ex: *Je me suis décidé pour une Renault*, I've decided on [decided to buy] a Renault) V
4. se _____ à *Inf.* (to make up one's mind, resolve to . . .) VIII-A
5. être décidé à *Inf.* (to be determined, resolved to . . .) VIII-A
6. _____ Qn à *Inf.* (to persuade . . . to . . .) VIII-B
7. _____ de *Inf.* (to decide to . . .) IX-A

déclamer
1. _____ Qch (to declaim . . .) I
2. _____ contre Qn ou Qch (to inveigh against . . .) V

déclarer
1. _____ Qn ou Qch (to declare . . .) I
2. se _____ pour, contre Qn ou Qch (to come out in favor of, against . . .) V
3. _____ Qch à Qn (to make . . . known to . . .; to declare [war] on . . .) VI

déconseiller
1. _____ Qch à Qn (to advise someone against something) VI
2. _____ à Qn de *Inf.* (to advise . . . not to . . .) IX-B

décorer
1. _____ Qn ou Qch (to decorate . . .) I
2. _____ Qn ou Qch de Qch (to decorate . . . with . . .) VI

découler
1. _____ de Qch (to derive, follow, issue from . . .) IV

découper
1. _____ Qch (to cut out, carve . . .) I
2. se ____ sur Qch (to stand out against . . .) V

décourager
1. _____ Qn ou Qch (to discourage, dishearten . . .) I
2. se ____ (to become discouraged) I
3. _____ Qn de Qch (to discourage . . . from . . .) VI
4. _____ Qn de *Inf.* (to discourage . . . from ---*ing*) IX-B

découvrir
1. _____ Qn ou Qch (to uncover, discover . . .; to discern
          . . . [in the distance]) I
2. se ____ (to take off one's hat; to lower one's guard; to
          come into sight, come to light; of the sky: to
          clear up) I
3. se ____ à Qn (to confide in . . .) III
4. _____ Qch à Qn (to divulge, expose . . . to . . .) VI

dédaigner
1. _____ Qn ou Qch (to scorn, disdain . . .) I
2. _____ de *Inf.* (to not deign to . . .) IX-A

dédier
1. _____ Qch à Qn (to dedicate . . . to . . .) VI

dédire (se)
1. se ____ de Qch (to take back, retract, go back on . . .) IV

dédommager
1. _____ Qn (to compensate, indemnify . . .) I
2. se ____ de Qch (to recoup oneself for . . .) IV
3. _____ Qn de Qch (to compensate, indemnify . . . for
          . . .) VI

déduire
1. _____ Qch (to deduce, infer, deduct . . .) I
2. _____ Qch de Qch (to deduce, infer, deduct . . . from
          . . .) VI

défaire

1. _____ Qn ou Qch (to undo, destroy . . .) I
2. se _____ de Qn (to get rid of . . .) IV
3. se _____ de Qch (to rid oneself of . . .; to break oneself of . . . e.g., *d'une mauvaise habitude*, of a bad habit) IV

défendre

1. _____ Qn ou Qch (to defend, protect . . .) I
2. se _____ (to defend oneself; Coll: to get along, to hold one's own) I
3. se _____ de, contre Qch (to protect, shield oneself from, against . . .) IV, V
4. _____ Qch à Qn (to forbid someone something) VI
5. _____ Qn ou Qch contre Qn ou Qch (to defend, protect . . . from, against . . .) VI
6. se _____ de *Inf.* ou *Inf. passé* (to deny ---*ing*, having . . .) IX-A
7. se _____ de *Inf.* (Lit: to refrain from, keep from --- *ing*; often in the negative, Ex: *Je ne pus me défendre de rire*, I couldn't keep from laughing) IX-A
8. Il est défendu de *Inf.* (It is forbidden to . . . Ex: *Il est défendu de fumer*, "smoking is prohibited") IX-A
9. _____ à Qn de *Inf.* (to forbid . . . to . . .) IX-B

déférer

1. _____ à Qn (to defer to . . .) II
2. _____ à Qch (to comply with, accede to . . .) II

défier

1. _____ Qch (to defy, brave . . .) I
2. se _____ de Qn ou Qch (to mistrust . . .) IV
3. _____ Qn à Qch (to challenge . . . to . . .) VI
4. _____ Qn de *Inf.* (to defy, dare . . . to . . .) IX-B

dégager
1. _____ Qn ou Qch (to disengage, to redeem . . .) I
2. se _____ (to emerge, to become apparent) I
3. se _____ de Qch (to free oneself of, extricate oneself from
. . .; of vapors, odors: to be given off by, to
emanate, escape from . . .) IV
4. _____ Qn ou Qch de Qch (to extricate, release, separate
. . . from . . .) VI

dégarnir
1. _____ Qch (to clear, empty, strip . . .) I
2. se _____ (to thin out, empty out) I
3. _____ Qch de Qch (to clear, empty, strip . . . of . . .) VI

dégénérer
1. _____ de Qch (to degenerate from . . .) IV
2. _____ en Qch (to degenerate into . . .) V

dégorger
1. _____ Qch (to disgorge, unstop . . .) I
2. _____ dans Qch (to overflow, discharge into . . .) V

dégoûter
1. _____ Qn (to disgust . . .) I
2. se _____ de Qn ou Qch (to take a dislike to, become fed
up with . . .) IV
3. être dégoûté de Qch (to be tired of, sick of . . .) IV
4. _____ Qn de Qch (to make someone dislike . . .; to disgust . . . with . . .) VI

dégoutter
1. _____ de Qch (to drip, trickle from . . .; to be dripping
with . . .) IV

déguiser
1. _____ Qn ou Qch (to disguise . . .) I
2. se _____ en Qch (to disguise oneself as . . .) V
3. _____ Qn en Qch (to disguise . . . as . . .) VI

déjeuner
1. _____ de Qch (to breakfast, lunch on . . .; to have a breakfast, lunch of . . .) IV

délayer
1. _____ Qch (to thin, add water to . . .) I
2. _____ Qch dans Qch (to thin . . . with . . .; to mix . . . with . . . [something liquid]) VI

délecter
1. se _____ à, de Qch (to delight in, take pleasure in . . .) III, IV
2. se _____ à *Inf.* (to delight in, take pleasure in ---*ing*) VIII-A

déléguer
1. _____ Qn ou Qch (to delegate . . .) I
2. _____ Qn à Qch (to delegate, appoint . . . to . . .) VI
3. _____ Qch à Qn (to delegate, hand over . . . to . . .) VI
4. _____ Qn pour *Inf.* (to delegate . . . to . . .) X

délibérer
1. _____ Qch (to deliberate over, discuss . . .) I
2. _____ de Qch (to deliberate . . .; to decide . . . [by debate or deliberation]) IV
3. _____ avec Qn (to deliberate with . . .) V
4. _____ sur Qch (to deliberate on . . .) V

délier
1. _____ Qch (to untie, undo . . .) I
2. _____ Qn de Qch (to release . . . from . . . *e.g.*, *d'une promesse*, from a promise) VI

délivrer
1. _____ Qn (to rescue, free . . .) I
2. se _____ de Qn ou Qch (to free oneself, rid oneself of . . .) IV
3. _____ Qn de Qch (to free . . . of . . .; to rescue, deliver . . . from . . .) VI

déloger
1. _____ de Qch (to move out of . . . *e.g., d'une maison,* out of a house) IV
2. _____ Qn ou Qch de Qch (to oust, evict . . . from . . .; to drive . . . out of . . .) VI

demander
1. _____ Qn ou Qch (to ask, ask for . . .) I
2. se _____ Qch (to wonder . . .) I
3. _____ Qch à Qn (to ask someone [for] something) VI
4. _____ à *Inf.* (to ask to . . .) VIII-A
5. _____ à Qn de *Inf.* (to ask . . . to . . .) IX-B

démarrer
1. _____ de Qch (to cast off from, get out of . . .) IV

démettre
1. _____ Qch (to dislocate . . . *e.g.,* a shoulder) I
2. _____ Qn (to dismiss . . . [from a job]) I
3. se _____ de Qch (to resign from . . . *e.g., de ses fonctions,* from office) IV
4. _____ Qn de Qch (to dismiss . . . from . . .) VI

démontrer
1. _____ Qch (to demonstrate, prove . . .) I
2. _____ Qch à Qn (to demonstrate, prove . . . to . . .) VI

démordre
1. _____ de Qch (to let go of, abandon . . . Usually in the negative, Ex: *Il ne démordra pas de sa résolution,* he won't give up his resolution) IV

démunir
1. _____ Qch (to strip, deplete . . .) I
2. se _____ de Qch (to allow oneself to run short of, to part with . . .) IV
3. être démuni de Qch (to be out of, short of . . .) IV
4. _____ Qch de Qch (to strip, empty . . . of . . .) VI

dénier
1. _____ Qch (to deny, disclaim . . .) I
2. _____ Qch à Qn (to deny someone something) VI

dénoncer
1. _____ Qch (to denounce, expose, reveal . . .) I
2. _____ Qn (to denounce, inform against . . .) I
3. se _____ à Qn (to give oneself up to . . . *e.g., à la police*, to the police) III
4. _____ Qn à Qn (to denounce . . . to . . .) VI

dénuer
1. se _____ de Qch (Lit: to part with, deprive oneself of . . .) IV
2. être dénué de Qch (to be devoid of, without . . . Ex: *être dénué de tout intérêt*, to be totally lacking in interest) IV

départir
1. _____ Qch (Lit: to divide, dispense, distribute . . .) I
2. se _____ de Qch (to give up, abandon, depart from . . . Ex: *Il ne se départait pas de son calme*, he kept his composure) IV

dépêcher
1. _____ Qn ou Qch (to dispatch . . .) I
2. se _____ (to hurry) I
3. se _____ de *Inf.* (to hurry to . . .) IX-A

dépendre
1. _____ de Qn ou Qch (to depend on . . . Ex: *Le succès de ce projet dépend de vous*, the success of this project depends on you) IV
2. Il dépend de Qn de *Inf.* (It is up to, it rests with . . . to . . .) IX-B

dépenser
1. _____ Qch (to spend, consume . . . *e.g.*, money, energy)
I
2. se _____ pour Qn (to exert oneself, to go to a lot of trouble for . . .) V

dépêtrer
1. se _____ de Qch (to extricate oneself from . . .) IV
2. _____ Qn de Qch (to extricate . . . from . . .; to get . . . out of . . .) VI

dépiter
1. _____ Qn (to vex . . .) I
2. se _____ (to take offense) I
3. se _____ de *Inf.* (to be vexed, annoyed to . . .; at ---*ing*)
IX-A

déplaire
1. _____ à Qn (to displease, offend . . .) II
2. N'en déplaise à Qn (Ex: *Ne vous en déplaise*, [ironic] with your permission, if you have no objection) II
3. Il déplaît à Qn de *Inf.* (It displeases . . . to . . . Ex: *Il me déplaît de les voir souffrir*, I don't like to see them suffer) IX-B

déplorer
1. _____ Qch (to deplore, grieve over . . .) I
2. _____ de *Inf.* ou *Inf. passé* (to regret very much ---*ing*, having . . .) IX-A

déposséder
1. _____ Qn (to dispossess . . .) I
2. _____ Qn de Qch (to dispossess, deprive . . . of . . .; to oust . . . from . . .) VI

dépouiller
1. _____ Qn ou Qch (to skim, strip, despoil . . .) I
2. se _____ de Qch (to strip oneself, divest oneself of . . .) IV
3. _____ Qn de Qch (to deprive, strip . . . of . . .) VI

dépourvoir
1. être dépourvu de Qch (to be devoid of, lacking in . . .) IV

députer
1. ———— Qn (to deputize . . .) I
2. ———— Qn à Qch (to appoint . . . to . . .) VI

déranger
1. ———— Qn ou Qch (to disturb, trouble . . .; to put . . . out of order) I
2. se ———— pour Qn ou Qch (to go out of one's way for . . .) V
3. se ———— pour *Inf.* (to go out of one's way to . . .) X

dériver
1. ———— Qch (to divert . . . *e.g.,* a stream) I
2. ———— de Qch (to arise from, be derived from . . .; of streams, rivers: to be diverted from . . . *e.g.,* from a course) IV
3. ———— Qch de Qch (to divert . . . from . . .) VI

dérober
1. ———— Qn ou Qch (Lit: to steal . . .; to hide . . .) I
2. se ———— (to give way, Ex: *Le sol se déroba sous leurs pas,* the ground gave way under their feet) I
3. se ———— à Qch (to escape, evade . . . *e.g., à ses obligations,* one's obligations) III
4. ———— Qch à Qn (Lit: to steal . . . from . . . Ex: *On m'a dérobé mes bijoux,* someone has taken my jewels) VI

déroger
1. ———— à Qch (to depart from . . . *e.g., à l'usage,* from custom; to derogate from . . .) II

désabonner
1. se ———— à Qch (to cancel one's subscription to . . .) III
2. ———— Qn à Qch (to cancel someone's subscription to . . .) VI

désabuser
1. _____ Qn (to disabuse, enlighten . . .) I
2. se _____ de Qch (to have one's eyes opened, lose one's illusions about . . .) IV
3. _____ Qn de Qch (to disabuse . . . of . . .) VI

désaccoutumer
1. se _____ de Qch (to get out of the habit of . . .) IV
2. se _____ de *Inf.* (to get out of the habit of, become unused to ---*ing*) IX-A
3. _____ Qn de *Inf.* (to break . . . of the habit of, to get . . . out of the habit of ---*ing*) IX-B

descendre
1. _____ Qn ou Qch (Coll: to knock . . . down) I
2. _____ Qch (to go down . . . *e.g.*, a street, the stairs; to bring down, lower . . .) I
3. _____ à Qch (to get off [*e.g.*, the train, bus] at . . .) II
4. _____ de Qn ou Qch (to be descended from . . .) IV
5. _____ de Qch (to get off, to come down from . . .) IV
6. _____ *Inf.* (to go down[stairs] to . . .; to stop off to . . .) VII-A

désenchanter
1. _____ Qn (to disenchant, disillusion . . .) I
2. être désenchanté de Qch (to be disenchanted, disillusioned with . . .) IV
3. _____ Qn de Qch (to disenchant, disillusion . . . with . . .) VI

désencombrer
1. _____ Qch (to disencumber, clear . . . *e.g.*, a road) I
2. _____ Qch de Qch (to clear, free . . . of . . .) VI

désennuyer
1. _____ Qn (to divert, cheer up [someone who is bored]) I
2. se _____ à *Inf.* (to relieve one's boredom [by] ---*ing*) VIII-A

désespérer

1. _____ Qn (to discourage, dishearten . . .) I
2. _____ de Qn ou Qch (to despair of . . .; to lose hope in . . .) IV
3. _____ de *Inf.* (to despair of ---*ing*) IX-A

déshabituer

1. se _____ de Qch (to break oneself of the habit of . . .; to become unaccustomed to . . .) IV
2. _____ Qn de Qch (to break . . . of the habit, to make . . . lose the habit of . . .) VI
3. se _____ de *Inf.* (to break oneself of the habit of, to lose the habit of ---*ing*) IX-A
4. _____ Qn de *Inf.* (to break . . . of the habit of ---*ing*; to disaccustom . . . to ---*ing*) IX-B

désigner

1. _____ Qn ou Qch (to designate, point out, appoint . . .) I
2. _____ Qn à, pour Qch (to appoint . . . to . . .; to nominate . . . for . . .; to recommend . . . for . . .) VI
3. _____ Qch à Qn (to point out . . . to . . .) VI
4. _____ Qn pour *Inf.* (to appoint, designate, qualify . . . to . . .) X

désintéresser

1. _____ Qn (to buy out . . .; to pay off [a creditor]) I
2. se _____ de Qn ou Qch (to lose interest, to take no further interest in . . .) IV

désirer

1. _____ Qn ou Qch (to desire, want . . .) I
2. _____ *Inf.* (to want to, wish to . . .) VII-A

désister (se)

1. se _____ de Qch (to desist from . . .; to waive . . . *e.g.*, a claim) IV

désobéir
1. _____ à Qn ou Qch (to disobey . . .; to break . . . *e.g.*, a rule, a law) II

désoler
1. _____ Qn (to distress, grieve . . .) I
2. se ____ de *Inf.* (to be distressed to . . .; at ---*ing*) IX-A
3. être désolé de *Inf.* ou *Inf. passé* (to be sorry to . . ., to have . . .) IX-A

désolidariser (se)
1. se ____ de, d'avec Qn ou Qch (to break one's ties with, separate oneself from . . .) IV, V

dessaisir
1. se ____ de Qch (to relinquish, give up . . .) IV
2. _____ Qn de Qch (to dispossess . . . of . . .) VI

destiner
1. se ____ à Qch (to intend to take up . . . *e.g.*, a profession) III
2. _____ Qn ou Qch à Qch (to intend, mean . . . for . . .; to destine . . . to . . .; to plan a career for . . . in . . .) VI
3. être destiné à *Inf.* (to be destined, doomed to . . .) VIII-A

destituer
1. _____ Qn (to dismiss, remove . . . from office) I
2. être destitué de Qch (to be deprived of, lacking in, without . . .) IV
3. _____ Qn de Qch (to dismiss . . . from . . .; to deprive . . . of . . .) VI

détacher
1. se ____ de Qn ou Qch (to separate, break away from . . .) IV
2. se ____ sur Qch (to stand out against . . .) V
3. _____ Qn ou Qch de Qn ou Qch (to separate, detach . . . from . . .) VI

déteindre
1. _____ Qch (to take the color out of . . .) I
2. _____ sur Qn (to influence, make its mark on . . .) V
3. _____ sur Qch (of colors: to fade, bleed, run on . . .) V

déterminer
1. _____ Qch (to determine, settle, cause . . .) I
2. se _____ à *Inf.* (to make up one's mind to . . .) VIII-A
3. _____ Qn à *Inf.* (to induce, decide . . . to . . .) VIII-B
4. _____ de *Inf.* (to resolve, decide to . . .) IX-A

détester
1. _____ Qn ou Qch (to detest, hate . . .) I
2. _____ *Inf.* (to hate to . . .; to detest ---*ing*) VII-A

détourner
1. _____ Qch (to divert, turn aside . . .) I
2. se _____ de Qn ou Qch (to turn away, turn aside from . . .) IV
3. _____ Qn ou Qch de Qn ou Qch (to divert, turn . . . aside from . . .; to entice . . . away from . . .) VI

déverser
1. _____ Qch (to pour, pour out, dump . . .) I
2. se _____ dans Qch (to flow, pour into . . .) V
3. _____ Qch sur Qch (to pour, dump . . . on . . .) VI

dévêtir
1. _____ Qn (to undress . . .) I
2. se _____ (to disrobe) I
3. se _____ de Qch (to divest oneself of . . .) IV

devoir
1. _____ Qch (to owe . . . *e.g.*, money) I
2. se _____ à Qn ou Qch (to have a duty, an obligation to . . . *e.g.*, *à sa patrie*, to one's country; *à ses enfants*, to one's children) III

3. _____ Qch à Qn (to owe someone something) VI
4. _____ *Inf.* (to have to, be supposed to, must . . . Ex: *Je dois partir tout de suite,* I have to leave immediately; *Elle doit être malade,* she must be sick) VII-A
5. se _____ de *Inf.* (to be one's duty to . . .) IX-A
6. _____ à Qn de *Inf.* (to owe it to . . . to . . .) IX-B

dévouer
1. être dévoué à Qn (to be devoted to . . .) II
2. se _____ pour Qn (to sacrifice oneself for . . .) V
3. se _____ pour *Inf.* (to sacrifice oneself [in order] to . . .) X

dicter
1. _____ Qch (to dictate, impose . . .) I
2. _____ Qch à Qn (to dictate, prescribe . . . to . . .) VI

différencier
1. se _____ de Qn ou Qch (to distinguish oneself from, be different from . . .) IV
2. _____ entre Qch et Qch (to distinguish between . . . and . . .) V
3. _____ Qn ou Qch de Qn ou Qch (to differentiate . . . from . . .) VI

différer
1. _____ Qch (to defer, put off, postpone . . .) I
2. _____ de Qch (to differ in . . . *e.g., d'opinion,* in opinion; to be different in . . .) IV
3. _____ de Qn ou Qch (to differ from . . .) IV
4. _____ sur Qch (to differ on . . .) V
5. _____ de, à *Inf.* (Lit: to put off, postpone ---*ing*) IX-A, VIII-A

diminuer
1. _____ Qch (to reduce . . .) I
2. _____ de Qch (to diminish in . . .) IV

dîner
  1. _____ de Qch (to dine on . . .) IV

dire
  1. _____ Qch (to say, tell . . .) I
  2. _____ Qch à Qn (to tell, say . . . to . . .) VI
  3. _____ Qch de Qn ou Qch (to say . . . about . . .) VI
  4. _____ à Qn de *Inf.* (to tell, order . . . to . . .) IX-B

diriger
  1. _____ Qch (to direct, manage, guide . . .) I
  2. se _____ vers Qn ou Qch (to head for, go up to . . .) V
  3. _____ Qch contre Qn (to aim, level . . . [*e.g.*, an accusation] at . . .) VI
  4. _____ Qch sur, vers Qn ou Qch (to direct, aim, point . . . at, towards . . .) VI

disconvenir
  1. _____ de Qch (to disagree with . . .; usually in negative: to admit, not deny . . . Ex: *Je n'en disconviens pas*, I don't deny it) IV

discourir
  1. _____ sur Qch (to discourse, hold forth on . . .) V

discréditer
  1. _____ Qn ou Qch (to discredit, disparage . . .) I
  2. se _____ auprès de Qn (to fall into discredit with, lose the esteem of . . .) V

disculper
  1. se _____ de Qch (to exculpate oneself from, clear oneself of . . .) IV
  2. _____ Qn de Qch (to clear . . . of . . .; to exonerate . . . from . . .) VI

discuter
1. ———— Qch (to discuss, debate, question . . .) I
2. ———— de Qch [avec Qn] (to discuss, talk over . . . [with . . .]) IV
3. ———— sur Qch [avec Qn] (to discuss, to quibble about . . . [with . . .]) V

disparaître
1. ———— de Qch (to disappear from . . .) IV

dispenser
1. se ——— de Qch (to excuse oneself from, to get out of . . .) IV
2. ———— Qch à Qn (to dispense, distribute . . . to . .) VI
3. ———— Qn de Qch (to exempt, excuse . . . from . . .) VI
4. se ——— de *Inf.* (to excuse oneself from, to get out of ---*ing*) IX-A
5. ———— Qn de *Inf.* (to excuse, exempt . . . from ---*ing*) IX-B

disposer
1. ———— Qch (to arrange, set out . . .) I
2. ———— de Qn ou Qch (to dispose of . . .; to have . . . at one's disposal) IV
3. ———— Qn à Qch (to dispose . . . to . . .; to prepare . . . [psychologically] for . . .) VI
4. se ——— à *Inf.* (to get ready to . . .) VIII-A
5. ———— Qn à *Inf.* (to dispose, incline, prepare . . . to . . .) VIII-B

disputer
1. ———— Qch (to dispute, contest . . .) I
2. se ——— avec Qn (to quarrel with . . .) V
3. se ——— pour Qch (to quarrel, wrangle over, about . . .) V
4. ———— Qch à Qn (to contend with someone for something) VI

disserter
1. ———   sur Qch (to hold forth on [a subject]) V

dissimuler
1. ———   Qch (to hide, cover up . . .) I
2. ———   Qch à Qn (to hide, keep . . . from . . .) VI

dissuader
1. ———   Qn de Qch (to dissuade . . . from . . .) VI
2. ———   Qn de *Inf.* (to dissuade . . . from ---*ing*) IX-B

distinguer
1. ———   Qn ou Qch (to distinguish . . .) I
2. se ——   de Qn ou Qch (to distinguish oneself from, stand out from . . .) IV
3. se ——   [de Qn ou Qch] par Qch (of people: to distinguish oneself by . . .; of things: to be remarkable for . . .) V
4. ———   entre deux choses (to distinguish between . . .) V
5. ———   Qn ou Qch de, d'avec Qn ou Qch (to distinguish . . . from . . .) VI

distraire
1. ———   Qn ou Qch (to divert, distract, entertain . . .) I
2. ———   Qn de Qch (to divert, distract . . . from . . .; to take someone's mind off . . .) VI

distribuer
1. ———   Qch (to distribute, give out, arrange . . .) I
2. ———   Qch à Qn (to distribute, give out . . . to . . .) VI

diverger
1. ———   de Qch (to diverge from . . .) IV

divertir
1. _____ Qn ou Qch (to divert, amuse . . .) I
2. se _____ (to amuse oneself) I
3. se _____ de Qn ou Qch (to be amused by . . .) IV
4. se _____ à *Inf.* (to amuse oneself [by] ---*ing*) VIII-A

diviser
1. _____ Qch (to divide . . .) I
2. se _____ en Qch (to divide, be divided into . . .) V
3. _____ Qch entre Qn (to divide . . . among . . .) VI
4. _____ Qch en Qch (to divide . . . into . . .) VI

divorcer
1. _____ d'avec, avec Qn (to divorce . . .) V

documenter
1. _____ Qch (to document . . .) I
2. se _____ sur Qch (to collect material, gather documentary evidence on . . .) V
3. _____ Qn sur Qch (to furnish someone with information, documents on, about . . .) VI

dominer
1. _____ Qn ou Qch (to dominate, to tower above . . .) I
2. se _____ (to be in control of oneself) I
3. _____ sur Qn ou Qch (to prevail, have dominion over . . .) V

donner
1. _____ Qch (to give . . .) I
2. se _____ à Qn ou Qch (to give oneself up to, to devote oneself to . . .) III
3. _____ dans Qch (to fall into . . . *e.g.*, *dans un piège*, into a trap; to fall into, go in for . . . Ex: *Il donne dans le fanatisme*, he is becoming a fanatic) V
4. se _____ pour Qn ou Qch (to claim to be, to present oneself as . . .) V
5. _____ sur Qch (to look out on, to face . . . *e.g.*, the garden, the street) V

6. _____ Qn ou Qch à Qn (to give . . . to . . .) VI
7. _____ Qch pour, contre Qch (to exchange . . . for . . .) VI
8. _____ à *Inf.* à Qn (to give someone something to . . . Ex: *donner à boire à quelqu'un,* to give someone something to drink) VIII-B
9. _____ à Qn de *Inf.* (to permit, enable . . . to . . .) IX-B
10. Il est donné à Qn de *Inf.* (It is possible for . . . to . . .) IX-B

doter

1. _____ Qn (to give a dowry to . . .) I
2. _____ Qch (to endow, equip . . .) I
3. _____ Qn ou Qch de Qch (to endow, equip . . . with . . .; Lit: [figurative sense] to endow . . . with . . .) VI

doubler

1. _____ Qn (to pass . . . *e.g.,* on a road; to replace [an actor]) I
2. _____ Qch (to double . . .; to fold . . . in half; to line . . . *e.g.,* a coat; to dub . . . *e.g.,* a film; to pass . . . *e.g.,* on a highway) I
3. _____ Qch de Qch (to line, dub . . . with . . .) VI

douer

1. être doué pour Qch (to have a gift for . . .) V
2. _____ Qn de Qch (to endow . . . with . . .) VI

douter

1. _____ de Qn (to doubt, mistrust . . .) IV
2. _____ de Qch (to doubt . . .) IV
3. se _____ de Qch (to suspect, surmise . . .) IV
4. _____ de *Inf.* ou *Inf. passé* (to doubt that one will, has . . . Ex: *Je doute d'arriver à l'heure,* I doubt that I will arrive on time; *je doute de lui avoir dit cela,* I doubt that I told him that) IX-A

draper
1. _____ Qch (to drape, cover . . .) I
2. se _____ dans, de Qch (to drape oneself in . . .; to make a show of . . . Ex: *se draper dans sa vertu*, to make a show of one's virtue) V, IV

dresser
1. _____ Qn (to train . . .) I
2. _____ Qch (to raise, erect, prepare, draw up . . .) I
3. se _____ contre Qn ou Qch (to rise up against . . .) V
4. _____ Qn à *Inf.* (to train . . . to . . .) VIII-B

E

ébahir
1. _____ Qn (to astound, flabbergast . . .) I
2. s'_____ de Qch (to be amazed, dumbfounded at, by . . .) IV
3. s'_____ de *Inf.* (to be amazed, dumbfounded at ---*ing*) IX-A

éblouir
1. _____ Qn (to dazzle . . .) I
2. être ébloui de Qch (to be dazzled by . . .) IV

écarter
1. _____ Qn ou Qch (to separate . . .; to divert, move . . . aside) I
2. s'_____ de Qch (to deviate, stray from . . .) IV
3. _____ Qn ou Qch de Qch (to separate . . . from . . .; to move, lead . . . away from . . .) VI

échanger
1. _____ Qch (to exchange . . .) I
2. _____ Qch contre, pour Qch (to exchange, barter . . . for . . .) VI

échapper
1. _____ à Qn ou Qch (to escape, escape from . . . Ex: *Son nom m'échappe*, his name escapes me; *Il alla au Mexique pour échapper à la police*, he went to Mexico to escape from the police; to slip out of, away from . . . Ex: *La tasse m'a échappé des mains*, the cup slipped out of my hands; *Une remarque indiscrète m'a échappé*, I let slip an indiscreet remark) II

échoir
1. _____ à Qn (to fall to, befall . . .) II

éclaircir
1. _____ Qch (to clear up, lighten, explain, clarify . . .) I
2. _____ Qn sur Qch (to enlighten . . . on . . .) VI

éclater
1. _____ en Qch (to burst into . . . e.g., *en applaudissements*, into applause; *en sanglots*, into sobs) V
2. _____ *de rire* (to burst out laughing)

écouter
1. _____ Qn ou Qch (to listen to . . .) I
2. _____ *Inf.* Qn ou Qch (to listen to someone or something . . .) VII-B

écraser
1. _____ Qn ou Qch (to crush, run over . . .) I
2. être écrasé de Qch (to be overburdened, overwhelmed with . . .) IV
3. être écrasé par Qch (to be crushed, run over by . . .) V
4. _____ Qn de Qch (to overwhelm, overburden . . . with . . .) VI

écrire
1. _____ Qch (to write . . .) I
2. _____ à Qn (to write to . . .) II
3. _____ Qch à Qn (to write . . . to . . .) VI

effacer

1. _____   Qch (to erase, obliterate . . .) I
2. s'_____   devant Qn ou Qch (to yield, accede to . . .) V
3. _____   Qch de Qch (to erase . . . from . . .) VI

effarer

1. _____   Qn (to scare, bewilder . . .) I
2. s'_____   de Qn ou Qch (to be scared, frightened by, at . . .) IV

effaroucher

1. _____   Qn (to scare away, startle . . .) I
2. s'_____   de Qn ou Qch (to be scared, startled by . . .) IV

efforcer (s')

1. s'_____   de *Inf.* (to strive, try hard to . . .) IX-A

effrayer

1. _____   Qn (to frighten . . .) I
2. s'_____   de Qch (to be frightened at, by . . .) IV

élancer

1. _____   à Qn (to cause pain to . . . by a throbbing, twinging sensation, Ex: *Le doigt m'élance,* my finger is throbbing) II
2. s'_____   *sur un cheval, sur une moto, sur une bicyclette,* to leap onto, astride a horse, a motorcycle, a bicycle) V

élever

1. _____   Qn ou Qch (to bring up . . . *e.g.,* a child; to raise, erect . . .) I
2. s'_____   à Qch (to rise to . . .; to amount to . . . Ex: *L'addition s'élève à 20 francs,* the bill comes to 20 francs) III
3. s'_____   au-dessus de Qch (to rise above . . .) V
4. s'_____   contre Qn ou Qch (to protest against . . .) V

éliminer
1. _____ Qn ou Qch (to eliminate . . .) I
2. _____ Qn ou Qch de Qch (to eliminate . . . from . . .) VI

éloigner
1. _____ Qn ou Qch (to remove, distance, send away . . .) I
2. s'_____ de Qn ou Qch (to stray, digress, move away from, become estranged from . . .) IV
3. _____ Qn ou Qch de Qch (to move, remove, send . . . away from . . .) VI
4. _____ Qn de Qn (to alienate, separate . . . from . . .) VI

émailler
1. _____ Qch (to enamel, glaze . . .) I
2. _____ Qch de Qch (to sprinkle . . . with . . . Ex: *émailler un texte de citations*, to sprinkle a text with quotations) VI

émanciper
1. _____ Qn ou Qch (to emancipate . . .) I
2. s'_____ de Qch (to free oneself from . . .) IV
3. _____ Qn de Qch (to free . . . from . . .) VI

émaner
1. _____ de Qn ou Qch (to emanate from . . .) IV

emballer
1. _____ Qn (Coll: to excite, thrill . . .) I
2. _____ Qch (to wrap up, pack . . .; to race [a motor]) I
3. s'_____ (of horses: to run away; of people [Coll.]: to get carried away) I
4. s'_____ de Qn ou Qch (Coll: to be crazy about, to have a sudden passion for . . .) IV
5. être emballé par Qch (to be crazy about, to have a sudden passion for . . .) V

embarquer
1. _____ Qn ou Qch (to embark, to ship, to load . . .) I
2. s'_____ dans Qch (to embark in, get into . . . [especially a risky affair]) V
3. _____ Qn dans Qch (to draw . . . into . . . [especially something risky]) VI
4. _____ Qch dans Qch (to load . . . in . . .) VI

embarrasser
1. _____ Qn ou Qch (to encumber, hamper, obstruct . . .) I
2. s'_____ de Qch (to burden, trouble oneself with . . .) IV
3. _____ Qn de Qch (to encumber . . . with . . .) VI

embrancher
1. _____ Qch (to join up . . . *e.g.*, roads, pipes) I
2. s'_____ sur Qch (to branch off from . . .) V

émerger
1. _____ de Qch (to emerge from . . .) IV

émerveiller
1. _____ Qn (to amaze, astonish . . .) I
2. s'_____ de Qch (to marvel at, be astonished at, by . . .) IV

emmitoufler
1. _____ Qn (to bundle up . . .) I
2. s'_____ dans, de Qch (to bundle up in . . .) V, IV
3. _____ Qn dans, de Qch (to bundle up . . . in . . .) VI

émouvoir
1. _____ Qn (to stir up, affect, move . . .) I
2. s'_____ (to be moved, anxious, upset) I
3. s'_____ de Qch (to be moved, upset by . . .) IV
4. être ému par Qch (to be moved, upset by . . .) V

empaqueter
1. _____ Qch (to wrap up . . .) I
2. _____ Qch dans Qch (to wrap up . . . in . . .) VI

emparer (s')
1. s'_____ de Qn ou Qch (to seize, take hold of . . .) IV

empêcher
1. _____ Qch (to prevent, hinder . . .) I
2. s'_____ de *Inf.* (to refrain from ---*ing*; Especially in the negative: Ex: *Elle ne pouvait s'empêcher de rire*, she couldn't help laughing) IX-A
3. _____ Qn ou Qch de *Inf.* (to prevent . . . from ---*ing*) IX-B

empêtrer
1. _____ Qn ou Qch (to entangle, involve, hamper . . .) I
2. s'_____ de Qn ou Qch (to become entangled, involved with . . .; to hamper, burden oneself with . . .) IV
3. s'_____ dans Qch (to become entangled in . . .) V
4. _____ Qn dans Qch (to involve, entangle . . . in . . .) VI

empiéter
1. _____ sur Qn ou Qch (to encroach upon . . .) V

empiffrer
1. s'_____ de Qch (Coll: to stuff oneself with . . . *e.g., de bonbons*, with candy) IV
2. _____ Qn de Qch (Coll: to stuff . . . with . . .) VI

employer
1. _____ Qn ou Qch (to use, employ . . .) I
2. s'_____ (to be used, Ex: *Cette expression ne s'emploie plus*, that expression is no longer used) I
3. s'_____ à Qch (to apply oneself, devote oneself to . . .) III
4. _____ Qn à Qch (to employ . . . at, in . . .; to occupy . . . with . . .) VI
5. _____ Qn comme Qch (to employ . . . as . . . *e.g., comme secrétaire*, as a secretary) VI
6. s'_____ à *Inf.* (to spend one's time ---*ing*; to work hard at ---*ing*) VIII-A
7. _____ [son temps, son argent] à *Inf.* (to use . . . to, for . . . Ex: *J'ai employé mon après-midi de congé à faire des courses en ville*, I used my afternoon off to do errands downtown) VIII-B

emporter

1. _____ Qn ou Qch (to carry away, take away . . .) I
2. s'_____ (to lose one's temper) I
3. s'_____ contre Qn ou Qch (to flare up at, inveigh against . . .) V
4. l'_____ sur Qn ou Qch (to prevail over, get the better of, overcome . . .) V

empreindre

1. _____ Qch (to imprint, stamp . . .) I
2. _____ Qch de Qch (to imprint, stamp . . . with . . .) VI

empresser (s')

1. s'_____ auprès de Qn (to be attentive to, to make a fuss over . . .) V
2. s'_____ à *Inf.* (to be eager to . . .) VIII-A
3. s'_____ de *Inf.* (to hurry, hasten to . . .) IX-A

emprunter

1. _____ Qch (to borrow . . .) I
2. _____ Qch à Qn ou Qch (to borrow . . . from . . .) VI

enamourer (s')

1. s'_____ de Qn (Lit: to become enamored of . . .) IV
2. être enamouré de Qn (Lit: to be enamored of . . .) IV

encadrer

1. _____ Qch (to frame . . .) I
2. _____ Qch de Qch (to frame . . . with . . .) VI

enchanter

1. _____ Qn ou Qch (to bewitch, charm, delight . . .) I
2. être enchanté de Qch (to be delighted with . . .) IV
3. être enchanté de *Inf.* (to be delighted to . . .) IX-A

enchasser
1. ———— Qch (to enshrine, set [a stone], insert . . .) I
2. ———— Qch dans Qch (to enshrine, set, insert . . . in . . .)
   VI

enchérir
1. ———— sur Qn (to outbid . . . *e.g.*, in an auction; to outdo . . .) V
2. ———— sur Qch (to surpass, go beyond . . .) V

enchevêtrer
1. ———— Qch (to mix up, confuse, tangle up . . .) I
2. s'———— dans Qch (to become confused, mixed up, tangled
   up in . . .) V

enclaver
1. ———— Qch (to enclose, wedge in, dovetail . . .) I
2. ———— Qch dans Qch (to enclose, wedge . . . in . . .) VI

encombrer
1. ———— Qn ou Qch (to encumber, congest, load down . . .)
   I
2. s'———— de Qch (to burden oneself, saddle oneself with
   . . .) IV

encourager
1. ———— Qn ou Qch (to encourage . . .) I
2. ———— Qn à *Inf.* (to encourage . . . to . . .) VIII-B

enduire
1. ———— Qch (to coat, smear, plaster . . .) I
2. ———— Qch de Qch (to coat, smear, plaster . . . with
   . . .) VI

endurcir
1. ———— Qn ou Qch (to harden, toughen . . .) I
2. s'———— à Qch (to become inured, hardened to . . .) III
3. ———— Qn à Qch (to inure . . . to . . .) VI

enfermer
1. ———— Qn ou Qch (to shut, lock . . . up; to enclose . . .) I
2. ———— Qn ou Qch dans Qch (to enclose, shut . . . up in . . .) VI

enfuir (s')
1. s'———— (to run away, escape, flee) I
2. s'———— de Qch (to run away, escape, flee from . . .) IV

engager
1. ———— Qn ou Qch (to pledge, engage, begin, involve, enlist . . .) I
2. s'———— chez Qn (to enter the service of . . .) V
3. s'———— dans Qch (to enter, venture into . . .) V
4. s'———— à *Inf.* (to undertake to . . .; to pledge one's word to . . .) VIII-A
5. ———— Qn à *Inf.* (to advise, urge . . . to . . .) VIII-B

englober
1. ———— Qch (to include, embrace . . .) I
2. ———— Qch dans Qch (to include . . . in . . .; to join, annex . . . to . . .) VI

engouer (s')
1. s'———— de Qn (to become infatuated with . . .) IV

engraisser
1. ———— Qn (to fatten [animals]) I
2. ———— Qch (to fertilize [land]) I
3. s'———— de Qch (to thrive on, grow fat, rich on . . .) IV

enhardir
1. ———— Qn (to embolden . . .) I
2. s'———— à, jusqu'à *Inf.* (to venture to, to be so bold as to . . .) VIII-A
3. ———— Qn à *Inf.* (to encourage . . . to . . .) VIII-B

enivrer
1. _____ Qn (to intoxicate, inebriate . . .) I
2. s'_____ de Qch (to become intoxicated, inebriated with . . .) IV

enjamber
1. _____ Qch (to step over, stride over, span . . .) I
2. _____ sur Qch (to project over . . .; to encroach on . . .) V

enjoindre
1. _____ Qch (to enjoin . . .) I
2. _____ à Qn de *Inf.* (to enjoin, direct . . . to . . .) IX-B

enlever
1. _____ Qn ou Qch (to remove, take away, take up, lift up, carry away . . .) I
2. _____ Qn ou Qch à Qn (to take . . . from, away from . . .) VI
3. _____ Qch de Qch (to remove . . . from . . .) VI

ennuyer
1. _____ Qn (to bore, annoy, bother . . .) I
2. s'_____ (to be bored) I
3. s'_____ de Qn (to miss . . .) IV
4. s'_____ à *Inf.* (to be bored [with] ---*ing*) VIII-A
5. s'_____ à *mourir* à *Inf.* (to be bored to death ---*ing*) VIII-A

enorgueillir
1. _____ Qn (to make . . . proud, puffed up) I
2. s'_____ de Qch (to pride oneself on, to boast of . . .) IV
3. s'_____ de *Inf. passé* (to pride oneself on, to boast of having . . .) IX-A

enquérir (s')
1. s'_____ de Qn ou Qch (to ask, inquire about . . .) IV

enrager
1. faire *enrager* Qn (to drive . . . crazy) I
2. _____ de Qch (to be furious about . . .) IV
3. être enragé contre Qn (to be furious at . . .) V
4. _____ de *Inf.* ou *Inf. passé* (to be furious at ---*ing*, at having . . . Ex: *Il enrageait d'avoir agi si bête-ment*, he was furious at having acted so stupid-ly) IX-A

enrichir
1. _____ Qn ou Qch (to enrich, make . . . wealthy) I
2. s'_____ de Qch (to grow rich on, grow richer in . . .) IV
3. s'_____ en Qch (to grow rich, richer in . . .) V
4. _____ Qch de Qch (to enrich . . . with . . .) VI

enrober
1. _____ Qch (to coat, cover, wrap . . .) I
2. _____ Qch de Qch (to coat, cover . . . with . . .) VI
3. _____ Qch dans Qch (to wrap . . . in . . .) VI

enrôler
1. _____ Qn (to enroll, recruit, enlist . . .) I
2. s'_____ dans Qch (to enroll, enlist in . . .) V
3. _____ Qn dans Qch (to enroll, enlist . . . in . . .) VI

enrouler
1. _____ Qch (to roll up, wind, wrap up . . .) I
2. s'_____ autour de Qch (to wind, coil around . . .) V
3. _____ Qch dans Qch (to wrap up . . . in . . .) VI

enseigner
1. _____ Qch (to teach . . .) I
2. _____ Qch à Qn (to teach . . . to . . .) VI
3. _____ à Qn à *Inf.* (to teach . . . to, how to . . .) VIII-B

entendre

1. _____ Qn ou Qch (to hear, understand, intend, mean . . .) I
2. s'_____ (to understand one another, to get along) I
3. ne _____ *rien* à Qch (to know nothing about . . . Ex: *Je n'entends rien aux mathématiques,* I don't know the first thing about mathematics) II
4. _____ *parler* de Qn ou Qch (to hear of, about . . .) IV
5. s'_____ avec Qn (to get along with . . .) V
6. _____ *Inf.* (to intend, mean to . . .) VII-A
7. _____ *Inf.* Qn ou Qch (to hear someone or something . . . Ex: *J'entends chanter les oiseaux,* I hear the birds singing) VII-B
8. s'_____ à *Inf.* (to understand, know how to . . .) VIII-A

enter

1. _____ Qch (to graft . . .) I
2. _____ Qch sur Qch (to graft . . . on, onto . . .) VI

entêter

1. _____ Qn (to give . . . a headache; to make . . . giddy; to go to someone's head) I
2. s'_____ dans Qch (to persist [obstinately] in . . .) V
3. s'_____ à *Inf.* (to be bent on ---*ing*; to persist in ---*ing*) VIII-A

enthousiasmer

1. _____ Qn (to fill . . . with enthusiasm) I
2. s'_____ pour Qn ou Qch (to be enthusiastic, go into raptures over . . .) V

enticher

1. s'_____ de Qn ou Qch (to be infatuated with, crazy about . . .) IV
2. être entiché de Qn ou Qch (to be infatuated with, crazy about . . .) IV

entortiller

1. _____ Qn (to get the better of, outwit . . .) I
2. _____ Qch (to twist, complicate . . .) I
3. s'_____ autour de Qch (to twist, wind around . . .) V
4. s'_____ dans Qch (to get entangled in . . .) V
5. _____ Qch autour de Qch (to wind, twist . . . around . . .) VI
6. _____ Qch dans Qch (to wrap up . . . in . . .) VI

entourer

1. _____ Qn ou Qch (to surround . . .) I
2. s'_____ de Qn ou Qch (to surround oneself with . . .) IV
3. _____ Qn ou Qch de Qn ou Qch (to surround . . . with . . .) VI

entraîner

1. _____ Qn ou Qch (to carry along or away, to entail, to lead to . . .; to train . . . *e.g.*, an athlete) I
2. _____ Qn à Qch (to train, coach . . . in . . .) VI
3. _____ Qn dans Qch (to lead . . . into . . ., involve . . . in . . . Ex: *entraîner quelqu'un dans le vice, dans une aventure*, to lead someone into vice, into an adventure) VI
4. s'_____ à *Inf.* (to train, accustom oneself to . . .) VIII-A
5. _____ Qn à *Inf.* (to lead, cause . . . to . . .) VIII-B

entrecouper

1. _____ Qch (to interrupt, intersect . . .) I
2. _____ Qch de Qch (to interrupt, intersperse . . . with . . .) VI

entrelarder

1. _____ Qch (to lard . . .) I
2. _____ Qch de Qch (to lard, interlard . . . with . . .) VI

entremêler
1. ———— Qch (to blend, mix . . .) I
2. s'———— (to intermingle) I
3. s'———— dans Qch (to interfere in . . .) V
4. ———— Qch de, parmi Qch (to intermingle, intersperse . . . with, among . . .) VI

entremettre (s')
1. s'———— dans Qch (to intervene in . . .) V
2. s'———— pour Qn dans Qch (to intercede, act as a go-between for . . . in . . .) V
3. s'———— pour Qn auprès de Qn (to intercede for, on behalf of . . . with . . .) V

entreprendre
1. ———— Qch (to undertake . . .) I
2. ———— Qn (to start a discussion with . . .; to attempt to convince, seduce . . .) I
3. ———— de *Inf.* (to undertake to . . .) IX-A

entrer
1. ———— dans, en, à* Qch (to enter, go into, come into, be included in, play a part in . . .; *entrer dans une colère terrible*, to fly into a rage) V, II
2. ———— *en ménage* (to set up housekeeping) V
3. ———— *en religion* (to enter a religious order) V

entretenir
1. ———— Qn ou Qch (to maintain, support, keep up . . .) I
2. s'———— avec Qn (to converse, chat with . . .) V
3. s'———— de Qch (to converse, talk about . . .) IV
4. ———— Qn de Qch (to talk to . . . about . . .) VI

envier
1. ———— Qn ou Qch (to be envious of . . .) I
2. ———— Qch à Qn (to envy someone something) VI

---

*See Appendix II: **DANS, EN, À**, p. 298.

environner
1. _____ Qn ou Qch (to surround . . .) I
2. s'_____ de Qn ou Qch (to surround oneself with . . .) IV
3. être environné de Qch (to be surrounded with, by . . .) IV

envoyer
1. _____ Qn ou Qch (to send . . .) I
2. _____ *chercher* Qn ou Qch (to send for . . .) I
3. _____ Qn ou Qch à Qn ou Qch (to send . . . to . . .) VI
4. _____ Qn *Inf.* (to send . . . to . . .) VII-B

épargner
1. _____ Qn ou Qch (to save, spare, be sparing with . . .) I
2. _____ Qch à Qn (to spare someone something, Ex: *Epargnez-moi les détails*, spare me the details) VI

épiloguer
1. _____ sur Qch (to split hairs, go on endlessly about . . .) V

époumoner (s')
1. s'_____ à *Inf.* (to talk, shout oneself hoarse, out of breath ---*ing*) VIII-A

épouvanter
1. _____ Qn (to terrify . . .) I
2. être épouvanté de Qch (to be astounded, appalled by . . . Ex: *être épouvanté de la montée des prix*, to be astounded by the rise in prices) IV
3. être épouvanté par Qch (to be terrified by . . .) V

éprendre (s')
1. s'_____ de Qn (to become infatuated with, to fall in love with . . .) IV
2. s'_____ de Qch (to take a fancy to, develop a passion for . . .) IV

épuiser
1. _____ Qn ou Qch (to exhaust, use up, wear out . . .) I
2. s'_____ en Qch (to exhaust oneself in . . . Ex: *s'épuiser en efforts inutiles*, to exhaust oneself in useless endeavors) V
3. s'_____ à *Inf.* (to exhaust oneself ---*ing*) VIII-A

équivaloir
1. _____ à Qch (to be equivalent to . . .) II
2. _____ à *Inf.* (to be equivalent to, tantamount to ---*ing*) VIII-A

éreinter
1. _____ Qn ou Qch (to break the back of . . . *e.g.*, of a horse; to criticize . . . unmercifully, Ex: *Ce film a été éreinté par les critiques*, this film was panned by the critics) I
2. s'_____ à Qch (to wear oneself out at . . .) III
3. s'_____ à *Inf.* (to wear oneself out ---*ing*) VIII-A

ergoter
1. _____ sur Qch (to split hairs, quibble about . . .) V

ériger
1. _____ Qch (to erect, establish . . .) I
2. s'_____ en Qch (to set oneself up as, to pose as . . . Ex: *Il s'érige en expert*, he sets himself up as an expert) V
3. _____ Qn ou Qch en Qch (to set . . . up as . . .; to elevate . . . to . . .) VI

escrimer (s')
1. s'_____ à *Inf.* (to try hard to . . .; to peg away at ---*ing*) VIII-A

escroquer
1. _____ Qn (to swindle . . .) I
2. _____ Qch à Qn (to rob, cheat someone out of something) VI

espérer
1. _____ Qch (to hope for . . .) I
2. _____ en Qn ou Qch (to trust in, put one's trust in . . . *e.g., en Dieu*, in God) V
3. _____ Qch de Qn ou Qch (to expect . . . from . . .) VI
4. _____ *Inf.* (to hope to . . .) VII-A

esquinter
1. _____ Qn ou Qch (Coll: to exhaust, ruin, smash, criticize severely . . .) I
2. s'_____ Qch (Coll: to ruin, "wreck" one's . . . Ex: *s'esquinter les yeux*, to ruin one's eyes; *s'esquinter le tempérament*, to worry too much) I
3. s'_____ à *Inf.* (Coll: to exhaust oneself, "kill" oneself ---*ing*) VIII-A
4. s'_____ Qch à *Inf.* (Coll: to ruin one's . . . ---*ing*, Ex: *s'esquinter les yeux à lire sans lumière*, to ruin one's eyes reading without light) VIII-B

essayer
1. _____ Qch (to try, try on, try out . . .) I
2. s'_____ à Qch (to try one's hand, one's skill at . . .) III
3. _____ de Qch (to try . . . *e.g.*, wine, food, a restaurant) IV
4. s'_____ à *Inf.* (to try one's hand, one's skill at ---*ing*) VIII-A
5. _____ de *Inf.* (to try to . . .) IX-A

étayer
1. _____ Qch (to prop up, stay, support . . .) I
2. s'_____ contre Qch (to steady oneself against . . .) V
3. _____ Qch de Qch (to prop up, support . . . with . . .) VI

étendre

1. _____ Qch (to spread, stretch out, extend, dilute . . .) I
2. s'_____ sur Qch (to stretch out on . . . *e.g., sur l'herbe,* on the grass; to expatiate on . . . *e.g., sur un sujet,* on a subject) V
3. _____ Qch de Qch (to dilute, stretch . . . with . . .) VI

étonner

1. _____ Qn (to surprise, astonish . . .) I
2. s'_____ de Qch (to be surprised, astonished at, by . . .) IV

être

1. _____ à, dans, en* Qch (to be at, in . . . Ex: *Elle est à San Francisco,* she is in San Francisco) II, V
2. en _____ à Qch (to have reached, to be at . . . Ex: *J'en suis au deuxième chapitre,* I'm on the second chapter)
3. _____ *tout* à Qch (to be involved in, devoting one's time to . . . Ex: *Elle est tout à son travail,* she is involved in her work)
4. _____ à Qn (to belong to . . . Ex: *Ce livre est à moi,* this is my book; to be at someone's disposal, Ex: *Je suis à vous dans un instant,* I'll be with you in a moment) III
5. _____ de Qn (to be by, be created by . . . Ex: *Ce tableau est d'Ingres,* this painting is by Ingres) IV
6. _____ de* Qch (to be from . . . *e.g.,* from Chicago; to be a member of, to participate in . . . Ex: *Il est de la famille,* he is one of the family) IV
7. _____ en Qch (to be dressed in . . . Ex: *Ils étaient en tenue de soirée,* they were wearing evening clothes) V
8. en _____ pour Qch (to have spent, expended . . . to no avail; to have nothing for . . . Ex: *Il en est pour ses frais,* he has nothing for his trouble, for what he spent) V

*See Appendix I: **PREPOSITIONS OF GEOGRAPHICAL LOCATION,** p. 289.

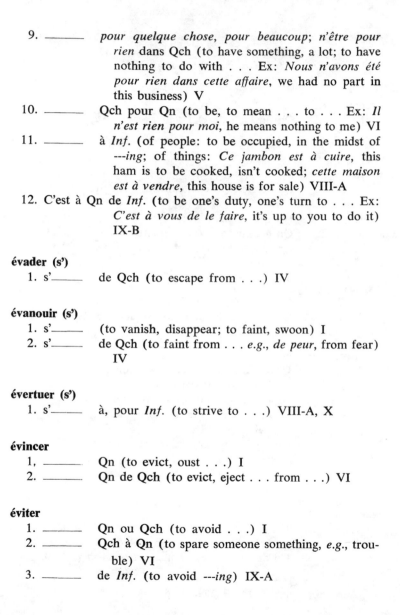

9. —————   *pour quelque chose, pour beaucoup*; *n'être pour rien* dans Qch (to have something, a lot; to have nothing to do with . . . Ex: *Nous n'avons été pour rien dans cette affaire*, we had no part in this business) V

10. —————   Qch pour Qn (to be, to mean . . . to . . . Ex: *Il n'est rien pour moi*, he means nothing to me) VI

11. —————   à *Inf.* (of people: to be occupied, in the midst of ---*ing*; of things: *Ce jambon est à cuire*, this ham is to be cooked, isn't cooked; *cette maison est à vendre*, this house is for sale) VIII-A

12. C'est à Qn de *Inf.* (to be one's duty, one's turn to . . . Ex: *C'est à vous de le faire*, it's up to you to do it) IX-B

évader (s')

1. s'————   de Qch (to escape from . . .) IV

évanouir (s')

1. s'————   (to vanish, disappear; to faint, swoon) I

2. s'————   de Qch (to faint from . . . *e.g.*, *de peur*, from fear) IV

évertuer (s')

1. s'————   à, pour *Inf.* (to strive to . . .) VIII-A, X

évincer

1, —————   Qn (to evict, oust . . .) I

2. —————   Qn de Qch (to evict, eject . . . from . . .) VI

éviter

1. —————   Qn ou Qch (to avoid . . .) I

2. —————   Qch à Qn (to spare someone something, *e.g.*, trouble) VI

3. —————   de *Inf.* (to avoid ---*ing*) IX-A

exceller
1. _____ dans, en* Qch (to excel in, at . . .) V
2. _____ à *Inf.* (to excel at ---*ing*) VIII-A

excepter
1. _____ Qn ou Qch de Qch (to except, exclude . . . from
   . . .) VI

exciter
1. _____ Qn ou Qch (to excite, arouse, stir up, provoke . . .)
   I
2. s'_____ (to get excited, worked up) I
3. _____ Qn à Qch (to exhort, incite . . . to . . .) VI
4. _____ Qn contre Qn (to set . . . against . . .) VI

exclure
1. _____ Qn ou Qch (to exclude, preclude . . .) I
2. _____ Qn ou Qch de Qch (to exclude . . . from . . .) VI

excuser
1. _____ Qn ou Qch (to excuse, pardon . . .) I
2. s'_____ de Qch (to apologize for . . .) IV
3. s'_____ auprès de Qn (to make apologies to . . .) V
4. s'_____ de *Inf.* ou *Inf. passé* (to apologize for ---*ing*, for
   having . . .) IX-A
5. _____ Qn de *Inf.* ou *Inf. passé* (to excuse . . . for ---*ing*,
   for having . . .; to excuse, exempt . . . from
   ---*ing*) IX-B

exempter
1. _____ Qn de Qch (to exempt, excuse . . . from . . .) VI
2. s'_____ de *Inf.* (to abstain from, get out of ---*ing*) IX-A
3. _____ Qn de *Inf.* (to exempt . . . from ---*ing*) IX-B

---

*See Appendix II: **DANS, EN, À**, p. 298.

exercer

1. _____ Qn ou Qch (to train, exert, exercise, practice . . .) I
2. s'_____ à Qch (to practice . . .) III
3. s'_____ à *Inf.* (to practice ---*ing*) VIII-A
4. _____ Qn à *Inf.* (to train . . . to . . .) VIII-B

exhorter

1. _____ Qn à Qch (to exhort . . . to . . .) VI
2. _____ Qn à *Inf.* (to exhort, urge . . . to . . .) VIII-B

exiger

1. _____ Qch (to demand, require . . .) I
2. _____ Qch de Qn (to demand, require, exact . . . from . . .) VI

exonérer

1. _____ Qn ou Qch (to exonerate, exempt . . .) I
2. _____ Qn ou Qch de Qch (to exonerate, exempt, free . . . from . . .) VI

expliquer

1. _____ Qch (to explain . . .) I
2. s'_____ avec Qn (to justify oneself to . . .; to have it out with . . .) V
3. s'_____ sur Qch (to explain one's views on, one's conduct in . . .) V
4. _____ Qch à Qn (to explain . . . to . . .) VI

exposer

1. _____ Qn ou Qch (to expose, exhibit, set forth . . .) I
2. s'_____ à Qch (to expose oneself to . . . *e.g., à un danger,* to danger; to lay oneself open to . . . *e.g., à des critiques,* to criticism) III
3. _____ Qn ou Qch à Qch (to expose . . . to . . .) VI

exprimer

1. _____ Qch (to express, to squeeze out . . .) I
2. _____ Qch à Qn (to express . . . to . . .) VI
3. _____ Qch de Qch (to squeeze out . . . from . . . *e.g.,* juice from an orange) VI

expulser
1. _____ Qn ou Qch (to expel, eject . . .) I
2. _____ Qn ou Qch de Qch (to expel, eject . . . from . . .)
    VI

extasier (s')
1. s'_____ sur Qch (to go into raptures over . . .) V

exténuer
1. _____ Qn (to exhaust, tire out . . .) I
2. s'_____ à *Inf.* (to exhaust oneself ---*ing*) VIII-A

extorquer
1. _____ Qch (to extort . . .) I
2. _____ Qch à Qn (to extort . . . from . . .) VI

extraire
1. _____ Qch (to extract, take out, excerpt . . .) I
2. s'_____ de Qch (to extricate oneself from . . .) IV
3. _____ Qn ou Qch de Qch (to extract, excerpt . . . from
    . . .) VI

F

fâcher
1. _____ Qn (to anger . . .) I
2. se _____ (to get angry) I
3. se _____ de Qch (to be angered by . . .) IV
4. être fâché de Qch (to be angry at, sorry for . . .) IV
5. se _____ avec Qn (to have a falling out with . . .) V
6. se _____ contre Qn (to get angry with . . .) V
7. être fâché contre Qn (to be angry with, sore at . . .) V
8. être fâché de *Inf.* ou *Inf. passé* (to be vexed, angry, sorry to
    . . ., to have . . .) IX-A

faciliter

1. _____   Qch (to facilitate, make . . . easier) I
2. _____   Qch à Qn (to facilitate, make . . . easier for . . .) VI

façonner

1. _____   Qn ou Qch (to work, shape, form . . .) I
2. se _____   à Qch (to accustom oneself to . . .) III

faillir

1. _____   *Inf.* (to almost . . . Ex: *J'ai failli manquer le train*, I almost missed the train) VII-A

faire

1. _____   Qch (to make, do . . .) I
2. se _____   à Qn ou Qch (to get accustomed to . . .) III
3. _____   *attention* à Qn ou Qch (to pay attention to . . .) III
4. être fait pour Qn ou Qch (to be made for, cut out for . . .) V
5. _____   Qch à Qn (to make, do . . . for, to . . .) VI
6. _____   Qn ou Qch de Qn ou Qch (to make . . . from, out of . . .) VI
7. ne _____   que *Inf.* (to only, to do nothing but . . . Ex: *Elle ne fait que travailler*, she does nothing but work) VII-A
8. se _____   *Inf.* (to have oneself, get oneself . . . Ex: *Il s'est fait nommer à un poste important*, he got himself appointed to an important position) VII-A
9. _____   *Inf.* Qn ou Qch (to have, make someone or something . . . Ex: *Il fait attendre ses clients*, he makes his clients wait) VII-B
10. _____   *Inf.* Qch à Qn (to have something done by someone, to someone, or for someone, Ex: *J'ai fait lire la lettre à mon frère*, I had my brother read the letter OR I had the letter read to my brother: to avoid ambiguity, use *par* for the first meaning in place of *à*. *J'ai fait faire une robe à ma mère*, I had a dress made for my mother OR I had my mother make a dress: to avoid ambiguity, use *pour* for the first meaning in place of *à*.) VII-B

11. ne —— que de *Inf.* (to have just, to have only just . . .
Ex: *Il ne fait que d'arriver*, he has [only] just
arrived) IX-A

12. être fait pour *Inf.* (to be made to . . ., for ---*ing*) X

falloir
[Impersonal verb]

1. Il faut Qch à Qn (to be lacking, necessary to . . . Must be
used with an indirect object pronoun, Ex: *Il me
faut un nouveau parapluie*, I need a new um-
brella) VI

2. Il faut *Inf.* (to be necessary to . . . Ex: *Il faut travailler pour
réussir*, one must work in order to succeed; *Il
faut partir*, [I] [you] [we] [they] must leave) VII-
A

3. Il faut à Qn *Inf.* (to need to, to have to . . . Must be used
with an indirect object pronoun, Ex: *Il lui faut
rentrer tout de suite*, he has to go home immediately) VII-B

familiariser

1. se —— avec Qch (to familiarize oneself with, to get to
know . . .) V

2. —— Qn avec Qch (to familiarize . . . with . . .; to accustom . . . to . . .) VI

farcir

1. —— Qch (to stuff . . .) I

2. —— Qch de Qch (to stuff . . . with . . .) VI

farfouiller

1. —— dans Qch (Coll: to rummage [about] in . . .) V

fatiguer

1. —— Qn ou Qch (to fatigue, tire, tire out . . .) I

2. être fatigué de Qn ou Qch (to be tired of . . .) IV

3. se —— à *Inf.* (to get tired ---*ing*) VIII-A

4. —— Qn ou Qch à *Inf.* (to tire someone or something
---*ing*) VIII-B

feindre
  1. _____ Qch (to feign . . .) I
  2. _____ de *Inf.* (to pretend to . . .) IX-A

féliciter
  1. se _____ de Qch (to be pleased with . . .; to pat oneself on the back for . . .) IV
  2. _____ Qn de, pour ou sur Qch (to congratulate, compliment . . . for, on . . .) VI
  3. _____ Qn de *Inf. passé* (to congratulate, compliment . . . for, on having . . .) IX-B

fendre
  1. _____ Qch (to cleave, split . . .; to break [one's heart]) I
  2. se _____ (to split, crack) I
  3. se _____ de Qch (Coll: to fork out, to offer to pay . . .) IV

fermer
  1. _____ Qch (to close, shut . . .) I
  2. _____ Qch à Qn (to close . . . to, on . . . Ex: *fermer la porte à quelqu'un*, to close the door on someone) VI

ferrer
  1. _____ Qn ou Qch (to fit, mount . . . with iron; to shoe a [horse]) I
  2. être ferré en Qch (Coll: to be skilled in, good in . . . Ex: *Il n'est pas très ferré en français*, he is not very good in French) V
  3. être ferré sur Qch (Coll: to know all about . . .) V

fiancer
  1. se _____ avec, à Qn (to become engaged to . . .) V, III

ficher
  1. se _____ de Qn ou Qch (Coll: to not care about, to make fun of . . .) IV

fier (se)
1. se ——— à Qn ou Qch (to trust, rely on, confide in . . .) III

figurer
1. ——— Qn ou Qch (to represent . . .) I
2. se ——— Qch (to imagine, fancy . . .) I
3. ——— dans Qch (to figure in, appear in, play a role in . . .) V
4. ——— sur Qch (to appear on . . .) V

finir
1. ——— Qch (to finish, end . . .) I
2. en ——— avec Qn ou Qch (to have done with, be done with . . .) V
3. ——— de *Inf.* (to finish ---*ing*) IX-A
4. ——— par *Inf.* (to finish, end, end up by ---*ing*) X

fixer
1. ——— Qn (to stare at . . .) I
2. ——— Qch (to fix, fasten, determine . . .) I
3. se ——— à Qch (to stick to, hold fast to . . . *e.g., à une opinion*, to an opinion; to be fastened to . . .) III
4. se ——— à, dans, en* Qch (to settle in . . . *e.g., à Paris,* in Paris) III, V
5. se ——— sur Qch (to be set on, fixed on . . .) V
6. être fixé sur Qn ou Qch (to have no further doubts about . . .) V
7. ——— Qn sur Qch (to give . . . definite information about . . .) VI
8. ——— Qch sur Qn ou Qch (to fix, fasten . . . on . . . Ex: *fixer les yeux sur quelqu'un*, to gaze at, fix one's eyes on someone) VI

———
*See Appendix I: **PREPOSITIONS OF GEOGRAPHICAL LOCATION**, p. 289.

flatter
1. ———— Qn (to flatter . . .; to stroke [an animal]) I
2. se ———— de Qch (to give oneself credit for . . .) IV
3. être flatté de Qch (to feel flattered by . . .) IV
4. ———— Qn de Qch (to delude, lead . . . on with . . .) VI
5. se ———— de *Inf.* (to flatter oneself, feel sure that one will
. . . Ex: *Il se flatte de réussir,* he is quite confi-
dent that he will succeed) IX-A
6. se ———— de *Inf. passé* (to give oneself credit for having
. . .) IX-A

flirter
1. ———— avec Qn ou Qch (to flirt with . . .) V

foisonner
1. ———— de Qch (to be swarming with . . .) IV
2. ———— en Qch (to abound in . . .) V

foncer
1. ———— Qch (to darken . . .; to dig a [well]; to fit a bot-
tom to [a cask]) I
2. ———— sur Qn (to rush, charge [at] . . .) V

fonder
1. ———— Qch (to found, start, set up . . .) I
2. se ———— sur Qch (to put one's reliance on, to be based on
. . .) V
3. ———— Qch sur Qch (to ground, base . . . on . . .) VI
4. être fondé à *Inf.* (to be entitled to . . .; to be justified in
---*ing*) VIII-A

fondre
1. ———— Qch (to melt, dissolve . . .) I
2. ———— sur Qn (to swoop down on, pounce on . . .) V
3. ———— en Qch (to melt, dissolve into . . . Ex: *fondre en
larmes,* to dissolve into tears) V

forcer
1. ———— Qn ou Qch (to force, compel, break open, break through . . .) I
2. se ———— à *Inf.* (to force oneself to . . .) VIII-A
3. ———— Qn à ou de *Inf.* (to force, compel . . . to . . . *À* is more common; *de* is more literary) VIII-B, IX-B
4. être forcé de *Inf.* (to be forced to . . .) IX-A

forfaire
1. ———— à Qch (Lit: to forfeit . . . *e.g., à l'honneur,* one's honor; to fail in . . . Ex: *forfaire à ses engagements,* to fail to uphold one's commitments) II

formaliser (se)
1. se ———— de Qch (to take offense at . . .) IV

former
1. ———— Qn ou Qch (to form, shape, train . . .) I
2. ———— Qn à Qch (to train, school . . . in . . .) VI

fortifier
1. ———— Qn ou Qch (to strengthen, fortify, confirm . . .) I
2. se ———— dans Qch (to strengthen one's . . . Ex: *se fortifier dans sa résolution,* to strengthen one's resolve) V
3. ———— Qn dans Qch (to encourage, strengthen . . . in . . .) VI

fouiller
1. ———— dans Qch (to search, rummage in . . .) V

fourmiller
1. ———— de Qn ou Qch (to be swarming with, full of . . .) IV

fournir

1. _____ à Qch (to provide for, supply, defray . . . Ex: *fournir à l'entretien de quelqu'un*, to provide for someone's needs) II

2. _____ Qn en Qch (to supply, provide . . . with . . . Ex: *Je peux vous fournir en livres*, I can provide you with books) VI

3. _____ Qch à Qn (to supply, provide . . . to, for . . . Ex: *Cette pâtisserie me fournit mes gâteaux*, I buy cakes at this pastry shop) VI

fourrer

1. se _____ dans Qch (Coll: to get entangled in . . . *e.g.*, *dans une mauvaise affaire*, in a bad affair) V

2. _____ Qch dans Qch (Coll: to stuff, cram, bury, poke . . . in, into . . .) VI

frapper

1. _____ Qn ou Qch (to strike, hit . . .) I

2. être frappé de Qch (to be stricken with . . . *e.g.*, *d'une maladie*, with a disease; to be struck, surprised by . . .) IV

3. _____ à la porte (to knock at, on the door) II

4. être frappé de *Inf.* (to be surprised to . . .) IX-A

fraterniser

1. _____ avec Qn (to fraternize with . . .) V

frayer

1. _____ Qch (to clear, open up . . . *e.g.*, a road) I

2. _____ avec Qn (to associate, consort with . . .) V

3. _____ Qch à Qn (to clear, open up . . . for . . . Ex: *frayer un passage à quelqu'un*, to clear a path for someone) VI

frémir

1. _____ de Qch (to shudder, quiver with . . . *e.g.*, *de peur*, with fear) IV

froisser

1. _____ Qn (to offend . . .; to hurt someone's feelings) I
2. _____ Qch (to rumple, crumple, bruise . . .) I
3. se ___ (to take offense) I
4. se ___ de Qch (to take offense at . . .) IV

frotter

1. _____ Qn ou Qch (to rub, polish . . .) I
2. se ___ à Qn ou Qch (to provoke, to meddle with . . .; to rub shoulders with . . .) III
3. se ___ contre Qn ou Qch (person or animal as subject: to rub against . . .) V
4. _____ contre Qch (thing as subject [*e.g.*, a piece of a mechanism]: to rub, grind against . . .) V

frustrer

1. _____ Qn (to frustrate, disappoint, defraud . . .) I
2. _____ Qn de Qch (to defraud . . . of . . .) VI

fulminer

1. _____ contre Qn ou Qch (to inveigh against . . .) V

G

gagner

1. _____ Qn ou Qch (to earn, win, reach . . .) I
2. se ___ (of diseases: to be catching) I
3. _____ à Qch (to win at, in . . . Ex: *gagner aux échecs*, to win at chess; *gagner à la loterie*, to win [in] the lottery; to profit, gain by . . .) II
4. _____ en Qch (to gain, increase in . . . *e.g.*, *en prestige*, in prestige) V

5. être gagné par Qch (to be overcome by, with . . . *e.g., par l'émòtion*, by, with emotion) V
6. ———— Qn à Qch (to win . . . over to . . . *e.g., à une cause*, to a cause) VI
7. ———— Qch à Qch (to win . . . at, in . . . Ex: *gagner de l'argent au jeu*, to win money gambling) VI
8. ———— à *Inf.* (to gain, profit by ---*ing*, Ex: *Elle gagne à être connue*, the better you know her, the more you like her) VIII-A
9. ———— de *Inf.* (to obtain the result, the advantage of ---*ing*) IX-A

garantir
1. ———— Qch (to guarantee, vouch for . . .) I
2. ———— Qch à Qn (to guarantee someone something) VI
3. ———— Qn ou Qch de Qch (to protect, shelter . . . from . . .) VI
4. ———— Qn ou Qch contre Qch (to protect, insure . . . against . . .) VI

garder
1. ———— Qn ou Qch (to keep, guard, protect . . .; to stay in . . . Ex: *garder le lit*, to stay in bed) I
2. se —— de Qn ou Qch (to beware of . . .) IV
3. ———— Qn ou Qch de Qch (to protect . . . from . . .) VI
4. se —— de *Inf.* (to take care not to . . .) IX-A

garer
1. ———— Qch (to park, garage . . .) I
2. se —— (to get out of the way; to park one's car) I
3. se —— de Qch (to get out of the way of . . .) IV

garnir
1. ———— Qch (to furnish, trim, garnish, decorate . . .) I
2. ———— Qch de Qch (to furnish, trim, garnish, decorate . . . with . . . Ex: *garnir un balcon de fleurs*, to decorate a balcony with flowers) VI

gausser (se)
1. se ———— de Qn ou Qch (Lit: to poke fun at . . .) IV

gaver
1. ———— Qn (to cram [poultry]; to feed . . . forcibly) I
2. se ———— (to eat excessively) I
3. se ———— de Qch (to gorge oneself on . . .) IV
4. être gavé de Qch (Coll: to be showered with . . . *e.g.*, *d'hon-neurs*, with honors) IV

gémir
1. ———— de Qch (to groan, moan with . . . *e.g.*, *de douleur*, with pain) IV
2. ———— sur Qch (to bemoan . . . Ex: *gémir sur son sort*, to bemoan one's fate) V

gendarmer (se)
1. se ———— contre Qn ou Qch (to fly off the handle at . . .; to be up in arms against . . .) V

glisser
1. ———— de Qch (to slip out of . . . Ex: *Le verre m'a glissé des mains*, the glass slipped out of my hands) IV
2. se ———— dans Qch (to slip, steal into . . .) V
3. ———— sur Qch (to slip, slide, glide over, on . . .) V
4. ———— sur Qn (to make little or no impression on . . .) V
5. ———— Qch à Qn (to slip . . . to . . .) VI
6. ———— Qch dans Qch (to slip . . . into . . .) VI
7. ———— Qch sous Qch (to slip . . . under . . .) VI

glorifier
1. ———— Qn ou Qch (to glorify, praise, celebrate . . .) I
2. se ———— de Qch (to boast of . . .) IV
3. se ———— de *Inf.* ou *Inf. passé* (to boast of ---*ing*, of having . . .) IX-A

gloser

1. _____ Qch (to gloss [a text]) I
2. _____ sur Qch (to discuss . . . exhaustively and often futilely) V

gonfler

1. _____ Qn ou Qch (to inflate, swell . . .) I
2. se _____ (to become inflated, distended) I
3. se _____ de Qch (to swell up with . . . *e.g., d'orgueil,* with pride) IV
4. _____ Qn ou Qch de Qch (to fill, inflate . . . with . . .) VI

gorger

1. _____ Qn (to cram [poultry]) I
2. _____ Qch (to glut, saturate . . .) I
3. se _____ (to stuff, gorge oneself) I
4. être gorgé de Qch (to be stuffed, filled, glutted, saturated with . . . Ex: *La terre était gorgée d'eau,* the ground was saturated with water) IV

goûter

1. _____ (to taste, enjoy . . .) I
2. _____ à Qch (to sample, take a little of . . .; to taste . . . critically) II
3. _____ de Qch (to try out, try . . . for the first time, *e.g.,* a food, a trade) IV

grandir

1. _____ Qch (to enlarge, increase . . .) I
2. _____ en Qch (to grow, increase in . . . *e.g., en sagesse,* in wisdom) V

gratifier

1. _____ Qn de Qch (to bestow, confer something on someone) VI

gratter

1. _____ Qn ou Qch (to scratch . . .) I
2. _____ *de la guitare, du violon* (to play the guitar, the violin mediocrely) IV

graver
1. _____ Qch (to engrave, carve . . .; to cut [a record]) I
2. _____ Qch dans Qch (to engrave, carve, imprint . . . in . . .) VI
3. _____ Qch sur Qch (to engrave, carve . . . on . . .) VI

greffer
1. se _____ sur Qch (to be added to . . .) V
2. _____ Qch sur Qch (to graft . . . on, onto . . .; to add . . . to . . .) VI

grever
1. _____ Qch (to burden . . . financially; to encumber, entail [an estate]; to mortgage, assess [property]) I
2. être grevé de Qch (to be burdened with, saddled with . . . Ex: *un homme grevé de dettes*, a man burdened with debts) IV
3. _____ Qn ou Qch de Qch (to burden, saddle . . . with . . .) VI

griller
1. _____ Qch (to grill, broil, toast . . .) I
2. _____ de *Inf.* (to be anxious, itching to . . .) IX-A

grimper
1. _____ Qch (to climb . . .) I
2. _____ à Qch (to climb, climb up, climb to . . .) II
3. _____ sur Qch (to climb up on . . .) V

griser
1. _____ Qn (to intoxicate . . .; to go to someone's head, Ex: *Les succès l'ont grisé*, success has gone to his head) I
2. se _____ (to get tipsy) I
3. se _____ de Qch (to become intoxicated with, to revel in . . .) IV
4. _____ Qn de Qch (to intoxicate, turn someone's head with . . .) VI

gronder
1. _____ Qn (to scold . . .) I
2. _____ Qn de *Inf. passé* (to scold . . . for having . . .) IX-B

grouiller
1. _____ de Qch (to swarm, teem with, be crawling with . . .) IV

guérir
1. _____ Qn ou Qch (to cure, heal . . .) I
2. se _____ (to recover, to cure oneself) I
3. _____ de Qch (to recover from, get over . . .) IV
4. se _____ de Qch (to cure, rid oneself of . . .) IV
5. _____ Qn de Qch (to cure . . . of . . .) VI

guerroyer
1. _____ contre Qn ou Qch (to wage war against . . .) V

guider
1. _____ Qn ou Qch (to guide . . .) I
2. se _____ sur Qch (to follow, to use . . . as a point of reference) V

H

habiliter
1. _____ Qn à *Inf.* (to enable, entitle . . . to . . .) VIII-B

habiller
1. _____ Qn ou Qch (to dress . . .) I
2. s'_____ de Qch (to dress in . . . *e.g., d'une vieille robe de chambre*, in an old bathrobe) IV
3. s'_____ en Qn (to dress as . . . *e.g., en Pierrot*, as a clown) V
4. s'_____ en [une couleur] (to dress in . . . *e.g., en bleu*, in blue) V
5. _____ Qn ou Qch de Qch (to dress . . . in . . .) VI
6. _____ Qn ou Qch en Qn (to dress . . . as . . .) VI
7. _____ Qn ou Qch en [une couleur] (to dress . . . in . . .) VI

habiter

1. ———— [un endroit] (to reside, live in . . . Ex: *habiter un palais, la campagne, Paris,* to live in a palace, in the country, in Paris) I

2. ———— à [un endroit] (to have one's home in, at . . . Ex: *habiter à la campagne, à Paris,* to live in the country, in Paris) II

3. ———— chez Qn (to live at the home of . . .) V

4. ———— dans* *une rue, une avenue* (to live on a street, an avenue) V

5. ———— sur* *une route, un boulevard* (to live on a highway, a boulevard) V

habituer

1. s'———— à Qn ou Qch (to get used to . . .) III

2. ———— Qn à Qn ou Qch (to accustom . . . to . . .) VI

3. s'———— à *Inf.* (to get used to ---*ing*) VIII-A

4. ———— Qn à *Inf.* (to accustom . . . to ---*ing*) VIII-B

haler

1. ———— Qch (to haul, tow . . .) I

2. ———— sur Qch (to haul, pull on . . .) V

harceler

1. ———— Qn (to harass, pester . . .) I

2. ———— Qn de Qch (to pester . . . with . . .) VI

harmoniser

1. ———— Qch (to harmonize, match, blend . . .) I

2. s'———— avec Qn ou Qch (to harmonize, to be in keeping with . . .) V

hasarder

1. ———— Qch (to risk . . .) I

2. se ———— à *Inf.* (to venture to, dare to . . .) VIII-A

hâter

1. ———— Qn ou Qch (to hasten, hurry . . .) I

2. se ———— de *Inf.* (to hasten, hurry to . . .) IX-A

————
*See Appendix I: **PREPOSITIONS OF GEOGRAPHICAL LOCATION**, p. 289.

hérisser
1. _____ Qch (to bristle, stiffen, ruffle . . .) I
2. se _____ *de peur* (to bristle, stiffen with fear)
3. être hérissé de Qch (to be spiked, studded with . . .) IV
4. _____ Qch de Qch (to spike, stud . . . with . . .) VI

hériter
1. _____ de Qn (to be the heir of . . .) IV
2. _____ de Qch (to inherit . . .) IV
3. _____ Qch de Qn (to inherit . . . from . . .) VI

hésiter
1. _____ à *Inf.* (to hesitate to . . .) VIII-A

heurter
1. _____ Qn ou Qch (to run into, collide with . . .) I
2. se _____ à Qch (to come up against, run into . . . Ex: *se heurter à un obstacle,* to run into a problem) III
3. _____ contre Qch (to beat against . . .) V
4. se _____ contre Qn (to encounter, bump into . . .) V
5. _____ sur Qch (to beat on . . .) V
6. _____ Qch contre Qch (to knock . . . against . . . Ex: *heurter son pied contre la porte,* to stub one's foot against the door) VI

hocher
1. _____ (de) *la tête* (to nod, shake one's head)

honorer
1. _____ Qn ou Qch (to honor . . .) I
2. s'_____ de Qch (to feel honored by . . .; to pride oneself on . . .) IV
3. _____ Qn ou Qch de Qch (to honor . . . by, with . . .) VI
4. s'_____ de *Inf.* ou *Inf. passé* (to be honored, proud to . . ., to have . . .) IX-A

humilier
1. _____ Qn (to humiliate . . .) I
2. s'_____ de *Inf.* ou *Inf. passé* (to be humiliated by, at
        ---*ing*, by, at having . . .) IX-A

hypnotiser
1. _____ Qn (to hypnotize . . .) I
2. s'_____ sur Qch (to be fascinated by . . .) V
3. être hypnotisé par Qn ou Qch (to be hypnotized, enthralled
        by . . .) V

I

identifier
1. _____ Qn ou Qch (to identify . . .) I
2. s'_____ avec, à Qn ou Qch (to identify with . . .) V, III
3. _____ Qn ou Qch avec Qn ou Qch (to identify . . . with
        . . .) VI

ignorer
1. _____ Qn ou Qch (to be unaware of . . .) I

illuminer
1. _____ Qn ou Qch (to illuminate . . .) I
2. s'_____ de Qch (to light up with . . . *e.g., de joie,* with
        joy) IV

illustrer
1. _____ Qch (to illustrate . . .) I
2. s'_____ dans Qch (to become famous in . . .) V
3. s'_____ par Qch (to become famous for, through . . .) V

imaginer
1. _____ Qch (to imagine, suppose . . .) I
2. s'_____ être Qn ou Qch (to fancy oneself . . . Ex: *Il s'imagine être un homme galant,* he thinks he's a ladies' man) VII-A
3. s'_____ *Inf.* (to imagine, believe that . . . Ex: *Il s'imagine chanter comme Caruso,* he thinks he sings like Caruso) VII-A
4. _____ de *Inf.* (to have the idea to . . .) IX-A

imbiber
1. _____ Qch (to absorb . . .) I
2. s'_____ de Qch (to become saturated with . . .) IV
3. _____ Qn ou Qch de Qch (to saturate, imbue . . . with . . .) VI

imiter
1. _____ Qn ou Qch (to imitate . . .) I
2. être imité de Qn (to be imitated by . . .) IV

immiscer
1. s'_____ dans Qch (to interfere in, with . . .) V
2. _____ Qn dans Qch (to involve . . . in . . .) VI

immoler
1. _____ Qn ou Qch (to immolate, sacrifice . . .) I
2. _____ Qn ou Qch à Qn ou Qch (to sacrifice . . . to . . .) VI

immuniser
1. _____ Qn (to immunize . . .) I
2. _____ Qn contre Qch (to immunize . . . against . . .) VI

impatienter
1. _____ Qn (to make . . . impatient) I
2. s'_____ (to lose patience) I
3. s'_____ de Qch (to get tired of . . .) IV
4. s'_____ contre Qn (to lose patience with . . .) V
5. s'_____ de *Inf.* (to grow annoyed with, tired of ---*ing*) IX-A

implanter
1. _____ Qch (to implant . . .) I
2. s'_____ dans Qch (to take root in . . .) V
3. _____ Qch dans Qch (to implant . . . in . . .) VI

impliquer
1. _____ Qn (to implicate, involve . . .) I
2. _____ Qch (to imply, indicate . . .) I
3. _____ Qn dans Qch (to implicate, involve . . . in . . .) VI

importer
[Only in third person]
1. _____ à Qn ou Qch (to be important, to matter to . . . Ex: *Les notes importent aux étudiants*, grades are important to students) II
2. *Il importe de Inf.* (it is important, essential to . . .) IX-A
3. *Il importe à Qn de Inf.* (it is important, essential to . . . to . . . Ex: *Il importe à Pierre de terminer son projet*, Pierre is very anxious to finish his project) IX-B

importuner
1. _____ Qn (to importune, bother . . .) I
2. _____ Qn de Qch (to bother, annoy . . . with . . .) VI

imposer
1. _____ Qch (to impose . . . Ex: *imposer un impôt*, to impose a tax) I
2. en _____ (to inspire respect, admiration)
3. en _____ à Qn (to impose on, deceive . . .) II
4. s'_____ à, chez Qn (to force oneself on . . .) III, V
5. _____ Qch à Qn (to impose, force . . . on . . .) VI

imprégner
1. _____ Qn ou Qch (to impregnate . . .) I
2. s'_____ de Qch (to imbue oneself with . . .) IV
3. _____ Qn ou Qch de Qch (to impregnate . . . with . . .) VI

impressionner
1. _____ Qn (to impress . . .) I
2. s'_____ de Qch (to be impressed with . . .) IV
3. être impressionné par Qn ou Qch (to be impressed by . . .) V

imputer
1. _____ Qch à Qn ou Qch (to attribute [something nega-tive] to . . .; to accuse someone of something) VI
2. _____ Qch à, sur Qch (to deduct . . . from . . .; to charge . . . to . . . Ex: *imputer une somme à un compte*, to deduct a sum from an account) VI
3. _____ à Qn de *Inf.* (to accuse . . . of ---*ing*) IX-B

inciter
1. _____ Qch (to urge, incite to . . .) I
2. _____ Qn à Qch (to incite . . . to . . .) VI
3. _____ Qn à *Inf.* (to incite . . . to . . .) VIII-B

incliner
1. _____ Qch (to slant, lower . . .) I
2. s'_____ (to bow) I
3. _____ à Qch (to favor, lean towards . . .) II
4. s'_____ devant Qch (to yield to . . .) V
5. s'_____ devant Qn ou Qch (to bow to . . .) V
6. s'_____ sur Qn ou Qch (to bend over . . .) V
7. _____ à *Inf.* (to be disposed to . . .) VIII-A
8. _____ Qn à *Inf.* (to predispose . . . to . . .) VIII-B

incomber
[Only in third person]
1. _____ à Qn (to be incumbent on, Ex: *Les affaires d'état incombent au souverain*, duties of state are in-cumbent on the ruler) II
2. *Il incombe à Qn de Inf.* (it behoves one to . . .) IX-B

incorporer
1. ——— Qn ou Qch (to incorporate, draft . . .) I
2. s'——— avec Qn ou Qch (to become one with . . .) V
3. s'——— dans, à Qch (to incorporate oneself in . . .) V, III
4. ——— Qn ou Qch dans, à Qch (to incorporate, blend . . . into . . .; to draft . . . into . . .) VI

incriminer
1. ——— Qn ou Qch (to incriminate, indict . . .) I
2. ——— Qn dans Qch (to incriminate . . . in . . .) VI

incruster
1. ——— Qch (to encrust, inlay . . .) I
2. s'——— dans Qch (to get stuck in . . .) V
3. ——— Qch de Qch (to inlay . . . with . . .) VI
4. ——— Qn ou Qch dans Qch (to embed . . . in . . .) VI

inculper
1. ——— Qn de Qch (to charge . . . with . . . *e.g.*, *de meurtre*, with murder) VI

inculquer
1. ——— Qch (to instill, inculcate . . .) I
2. ——— Qch à Qn (to instill . . . in . . .) VI

indemniser
1. ——— Qn (to compensate . . .) I
2. ——— Qn de Qch (to compensate . . . for . . .) VI

indigner
1. ——— Qn (to make someone indignant) I
2. s'——— (to become indignant) I
3. s'——— de Qch (to become indignant at, about . . .) IV
4. s'——— contre Qn (to become indignant at, with . . .) V

indiquer
1. _____ Qn ou Qch (to indicate, point out . . .) I
2. _____ Qn ou Qch à Qn (to indicate, point out . . . to . . .) VI

indisposer
1. _____ Qn (to make someone ill; to disagree with . . .) I
2. _____ Qn contre Qn ou Qch (to set . . . against . . .) VI

induire
1. _____ Qn *en erreur, en tentation* (to lead . . . into error, into temptation) I

infecter
1. _____ Qn ou Qch (to infect, contaminate . . .) I
2. _____ Qn ou Qch de Qch (to infect, contaminate . . . with . . .) VI

inféoder
1. s'_____ à Qn ou Qch (to swear allegiance to . . .) III

inférer
1. _____ Qch (to infer . . .) I
2. _____ Qch de Qch (to infer . . . from . . .) VI

infester
1. _____ Qch (to infest . . .) I
2. être infesté de Qch (to be infested with . . .) IV
3. _____ Qch de Qch (to infest . . . with . . .) VI

infiltrer (s')
1. s'_____ dans Qch (to seep into . . .) V
2. s'_____ à travers Qch (to seep through . . .) V

infliger
1. _____ Qch (to inflict, impose . . .) I
2. _____ Qch à Qn ou Qch (to inflict, impose . . . on . . .) VI

influer
1. ———— sur Qn ou Qch (to have an effect on . . .; to influence . . .) V

informer
1. ———— Qn (to inform . . .) I
2. s'———— de Qn ou Qch (to find out about . . .) IV
3. ———— contre Qn (to inform, testify against . . .) V
4. ———— sur Qn ou Qch (to investigate . . .) V
5. ———— Qn de Qch (to inform . . . of . . .) VI

infuser
1. ———— Qch (to infuse, steep . . .) I
2. ———— Qch à Qn (to instill . . . in . . .; to inspire someone with something) VI
3. ———— Qch dans Qch (to steep, infuse . . . in . . .) VI

ingénier
1. s'———— à *Inf.* (to figure out how to . . .; to be clever enough to . . .) VIII-A

ingérer
1. ———— Qch (to ingest . . .) I
2. s'———— dans Qch (to meddle in . . .) V

initier
1. ———— Qn ou Qch (to initiate . . .) I
2. s'———— à Qch (to become familiar with . . .) III
3. ———— Qn à Qch (to familiarize . . . with . . .; to reveal something to someone) VI

innocenter
1. ———— Qn (to clear, justify . . .) I
2. s'———— de Qch (to clear oneself of . . .) IV
3. ———— Qn de Qch (to clear . . . of . . .; to declare . . . not guilty of . . .) VI

inoculer
1. _____ Qch à Qn (to infect someone with something) VI
2. _____ Qn contre Qch (to vaccinate . . . against . . .) VI

inonder
1. _____ Qn ou Qch (to inundate, flood . . .) I
2. être inondé de Qch (to be deluged with, *e.g., de travail*, with work) IV
3. _____ Qn ou Qch de Qch (to deluge, inundate . . . with . . .) VI

inquiéter
1. _____ Qn (to trouble . . .; to make . . . uneasy) I
2. s'_____ de Qn ou Qch (to worry about . . .) IV

inscrire
1. _____ Qn (to enroll, register . . .) I
2. _____ Qch (to inscribe . . .) I
3. s'_____ à Qch (to enroll oneself at . . . *e.g., à l'université*, at college) III
4. s'_____ dans, sur Qch (to put one's name down in, on . . . *e.g., dans le registre*, in the register; *sur la liste*, on the list) V
5. s'_____ pour Qch (to sign up for . . .) V
6. _____ Qn à Qch (to enroll, register . . . in . . . *e.g., inscrire un enfant à l'école*, to régister a child in school) VI
7. _____ Qch dans, sur Qch (to inscribe . . . in, on . . . *e.g., inscrire son nom sur la liste*, to inscribe one's name on the list) VI

insérer
1. _____ Qch (to insert . . .) I
2. _____ Qch dans, sous Qch (to insert . . . in, under . . .) VI

insinuer
1. ———— Qch (to insinuate . . .) I
2. s'———— dans Qch (to insinuate oneself into . . .; to worm one's way into . . .) V
3. s'———— entre Qch (to work one's way between . . .) V
4. ———— Qch à Qn (to insinuate . . . to . . .) VI

insister
1. ———— sur Qch (to insist on, emphasize . . .) V
2. ———— pour, à *Inf.* (to insist on ---*ing*) X, VIII-A

inspirer
1. ———— Qn ou Qch (to inspire . . .) I
2. s'———— de Qn ou Qch (to take one's inspiration from . . .; to base one's work on . . .) IV
3. être inspiré par Qn ou Qch (to be inspired by . . .) V
4. ———— Qch à Qn (to inspire, fill someone with something, Ex: *Il a inspiré son enthousiasme aux autres*, he filled the others with his enthusiasm) VI

instruire
1. ———— Qn (to instruct . . .) I
2. s'———— de Qch (to inform oneself, to find out about . . .) IV
3. s'———— dans, en* Qch (to learn, learn how to do . . .) V
4. être instruit par Qch (to learn by . . . *e.g.*, *par l'expérience*, by experience) V
5. ———— Qn de Qch (to inform . . . of . . .) VI
6. ———— Qn dans, en* Qch (to teach someone . . .; to teach someone how to do . . .) VI
7. ———— Qn à *Inf.* (to instruct . . . to . . .) VIII-B

instrumenter
1. ———— Qch (to score, orchestrate . . .) I
2. ———— contre Qn (to order legal proceedings against . . .) V

———
*See Appendix II: **DANS, EN, À**, p. 298.

insulter
1. _____ Qn (to insult . . .) I
2. _____ à Qch (to lack respect for . . . Ex: *insulter aux dieux*, to lack respect for the gods) II

insurger
1. _____ contre Qn ou Qch (to revolt against . . .) V

intégrer
1. _____ Qch (to integrate . . .) I
2. s'_____ dans Qch (to combine with . . .; to become assimilated into . . .) V

intenter
1. _____ Qch à, contre Qn (to bring . . . against . . . Ex: *intenter un procès contre quelqu'un*, to bring a suit against someone, to sue someone) VI

intercaler
1. _____ Qch (to intercalate . . .) I
2. _____ Qch dans Qch (to intercalate, insert . . . in . . .) VI

intercéder
1. _____ pour Qn ou Qch auprès de Qn (to intercede for . . . with . . .) V

interdire
1. _____ Qch (to forbid, prohibit . . .) I
2. s'_____ Qch (to refuse oneself something) I
3. _____ Qch à Qn (to forbid someone something; to not allow someone something) VI
4. _____ Qn de Qch (to suspend . . . from . . . e.g., *de ses fonctions*, from his or her duties) VI
5. _____ à Qn de *Inf.* (to forbid . . . to . . .) IX-B

intéresser
1. ———— Qn ou Qch (to interest, concern . . .) I
2. s'———— à Qn ou Qch (to be interested in . . .) III
3. s'———— dans Qch (to have a financial, vested interest in . . .) V
4. ———— Qn à Qch (to interest . . . in . . .) VI
5. ———— Qn dans Qch (to involve, give . . . a financial interest in . . .) VI

interner
1. ———— Qn (to intern, imprison . . .) I
2. ———— Qn dans Qch (to intern, imprison . . . in . . .) VI

interpeller
1. ———— Qn (to question, call out to, heckle . . .) I
2. ———— Qn sur Qch (to question . . . about . . .) VI

interposer
1. s'———— (to intervene) I
2. s'———— dans Qch (to intervene in . . .) V
3. s'———— entre Qn ou Qch (to come between . . .) V
4. ———— Qn ou Qch entre Qn ou Qch (to place . . . between . . .) VI

interroger
1. ———— Qn (to interrogate, question . . .) I
2. ———— Qn sur Qn ou Qch (to interrogate . . . about . . .) VI

intervenir
1. ———— dans Qch (to intervene in . . .) V

intimer
1. ———— Qch (to indicate, signify . . .; to intimate . . .) I
2. ———— Qch à Qn (to indicate, signify, intimate . . . to . . .) VI

introduire
1. _____ Qn ou Qch (to insert, bring in, present . . .) I
2. s'_____ dans Qch (to penetrate, to slip into . . .) V
3. _____ Qn ou Qch dans Qch (to insert . . . in . . .; to usher . . . into . . .) VI

invectiver
1. _____ Qn ou Qch (to abuse . . .; to call . . . names) I
2. _____ contre Qn ou Qch (to inveigh against . . .) V

inventer
1. _____ Qch (to invent, make up . . .) I
2. _____ de *Inf.* (to have the idea to . . .) IX-A

investir
1. _____ Qch (to invest . . .; to besiege . . .) I
2. _____ Qn de Qch (to invest, entrust . . . with . . . Ex: *investir quelqu'un de pleins pouvoirs*, to grant full powers to someone) VI

inviter
1. _____ Qn (to invite . . .) I
2. _____ Qn à Qch (to invite, ask . . . to . . .) VI
3. _____ Qn à *Inf.* (to invite, ask . . . to . . .) VIII-B

irriter
1. _____ Qn ou Qch (to irritate . . .) I
2. s'_____ de Qch (to grow angry about . . .) IV
3. s'_____ contre Qn (to grow angry with . . .) V
4. s'_____ à *Inf.* (to get irritated at ---*ing*) VIII-A

isoler
1. _____ Qn ou Qch (to isolate . . .) I
2. s'_____ de Qn ou Qch (to isolate oneself from . . .) IV
3. _____ Qn de, d'avec Qn ou Qch (to isolate . . . from . . .) VI

J

jaillir
1. _____ de Qch (to spurt from . . .) IV

jalonner
1. _____ Qch (to stake, mark out . . .) I
2. _____ Qch à Qn (to stake out, mark . . . for . . .) VI

jalouser
1. _____ Qn ou Qch (to envy, be jealous of . . .) I

jaser
1. _____ de Qn ou Qch (to chatter about . . .) IV

jeter
1. _____ Qn ou Qch (to throw . . .) I
2. se _____ à Qch (to throw oneself at, in . . . *e.g., aux pieds de quelqu'un,* at someone's feet; *à l'eau,* in the water) III
3. se _____ dans, en* Qch (to throw oneself into, in . . .; to flow, empty into . . . Ex: *La Seine se jette dans l'Atlantique,* the Seine empties into the Atlantic Ocean) V
4. se _____ contre, par, sur Qn ou Qch (to throw oneself against, through, on . . .) V
5. _____ Qch à Qn (to throw . . . to . . .) VI
6. _____ Qn ou Qch contre, dans, en*, par, sur Qn ou Qch (to throw . . . against, in, through, on . . .) VI

joindre
1. _____ Qn ou Qch (to join, clasp . . .) I
2. se _____ à Qn ou Qch [pour *Inf.*] (to join with . . . [in order to . . .]) III
3. _____ Qn ou Qch à Qn ou Qch (to join . . . to . . .; to combine . . . with . . .) VI

---

*See Appendix II: **DANS, EN, À,** p. 298.

joncher

1. _____ Qch de Qch (to strew, scatter . . . with . . .) VI

jongler

1. _____ avec Qch (to juggle . . .) V

jouer

1. _____ Qch (to play, *e.g.,* music; to bet, *e.g.,* money; to risk, *e.g.,* one's reputation) I

2. _____ Qn (to trick . . .) I

3. _____ à Qn (to play at being . . . Ex: *jouer à la paysanne,* to play at being a peasant. Note: the pronoun *Y* is used in substitutions. *Elle joue à la paysanne, elle y joue*; she plays at being a peasant, she plays at it) II

4. _____ à Qch (to play at . . . *e.g., à l'amour,* at love; to play a game, Ex: *jouer aux cartes,* to play cards) II

5. _____ de Qch (to play an instrument, *e.g., du piano,* the piano; *de la guitare,* the guitar) IV

6. se _____ de Qn ou Qch (to make fun of . . .; to take . . . lightly) IV

7. _____ avec Qn ou Qch (to play with . . .) V

8. _____ sur Qch (to speculate on . . .; to play on [words]) V

9. _____ *un tour* à Qn (to play a trick on . . .) VI

10. _____ à *Inf.* (to play at ---*ing*) VIII-A

jouir

1. _____ de Qn ou Qch (to enjoy . . .; to take pleasure in . . .) IV

juger

1. _____ Qn ou Qch (to judge . . .) I

2. _____ de Qch (to imagine . . . Ex: *Jugez de ma surprise,* imagine my surprise) IV

3. *À en juger par Qch* (judging by . . . Ex: *Il n'est pas très doué, à en juger par ses réponses,* he's not very smart, judging by his answers)

4. _____ sur Qch (to judge by, on . . . *e.g., sur les appa-rences*, on appearances) V

5. _____ Qn ou Qch sur Qch (to judge . . . by, on . . .) VI

jurer

1. _____ Qch (to swear . . .) I

2. _____ avec Qch (to clash with . . .) V

3. _____ sur Qch (to swear on, by . . .) V

4. _____ Qch à Qn (to swear . . . to . . .) VI

5. _____ de *Inf.* ou *Inf. passé* (to swear to . . ., to have . . .) IX-A

justifier

1. _____ Qn ou Qch (to justify . . .) I

2. _____ de Qch (to prove, give an account of . . .) IV

3. se _____ de Qch (to prove one's innocence of . . .) IV

4. _____ Qn de Qch (to prove . . . innocent of . . .) VI

L

lâcher

1. _____ Qn ou Qch (to release, let go of . . .; Coll: to drop . . . [*e.g.*, a friend]) I

2. _____ Qch à Qn (to let loose, throw . . . at . . .) VI

laisser

1. _____ Qn ou Qch (to leave, allow . . .) I

2. _____ Qch à Qn (to leave . . . to . . .; to bequeath . . . to . . .) VI

3. _____ Qn ou Qch à Qn (to leave . . . to . . .; to rely on someone for . . . Ex: *laisser les tâches ingrates à quelqu'un*, to leave the dirty work to someone) VI

4. _____ Qn à Qn ou Qch (to leave, abandon . . . to . . .) VI

5. _____ *Inf.* Qn ou Qch (to allow . . . to . . .) VII-B

6. ne _____ pas de *Inf.* (to continue to . . .; to not fail to . . .
Ex: *La situation politique ne laisse pas de m'inquiéter*, the political situation continues to worry me, is a source of worry to me) IX-A

lambrisser

1. _____ Qch (to panel . . .) I

2. _____ Qch de Qch (to panel . . . with . . .) VI

lamenter

1. se _____ sur Qn ou Qch (to lament . . .; to cry over . . .) V

2. se _____ de *Inf. passé* (to lament, bewail having . . .) IX-A

lancer

1. _____ Qn ou Qch (to throw, hurl, launch . . .) I

2. se _____ dans Qch (to take up . . .; to get involved in . . .
e.g., dans les affaires, in business) V

3. _____ Qch à Qn (to throw . . . at . . .) VI

4. _____ Qn ou Qch contre Qn ou Qch (to throw, hurl . . .
against . . .) VI

5. _____ Qn ou Qch dans Qch (to throw, launch . . . in,
into . . .) VI

languir

1. _____ de Qch (to languish with . . . *e.g., d'amour*, with
love) IV

2. _____ pour Qn (to long for . . .) V

3. _____ après Qch (to long for . . .) V

larder

1. _____ Qch (to lard . . .) I

2. _____ Qn ou Qch de Qch (to lard . . . with . . .; to riddle . . . with . . .) VI

lasser

1. _____ Qn ou Qch (to tire . . .) I

2. se _____ de Qn ou Qch (to grow tired of . . .) IV

3. se _____ à *Inf.* (to tire oneself by ---*ing*) VIII-A

4. _____ Qn à *Inf.* (to tire . . . ---*ing*) VIII-B
5. se _____ de *Inf.* (to grow bored with ---*ing*) IX-A

laver
1. _____ Qn ou Qch (to wash . . .) I
2. se _____ Qch (to wash one's . . . Ex: *se laver les mains,* to wash one's hands) I
3. se _____ de Qch (to cleanse oneself of . . .) IV
4. _____ Qn ou Qch de Qch (to cleanse . . . of . . .) VI
5. _____ Qch à Qn (to wash someone's . . . *e.g.,* face; *laver la tête à quelqu'un,* to chew someone out) VI

légiférer
1. _____ sur Qn ou Qch (to legislate on . . .) V

léguer
1. _____ Qch (to bequeath . . .) I
2. _____ Qch à Qn (to leave, bequeath . . . to . . .) VI

lésiner
1. _____ sur Qch (to be stingy with . . .) V

leurrer
1. _____ Qn ou Qch (to lure, entice . . .; to lead . . . on) I
2. se _____ (to deceive oneself) I
3. _____ Qn par Qch (to lead . . . on with . . . *e.g., par de fausses promesses,* with false promises) VI

lever
1. _____ Qn ou Qch (to raise, lift . . .) I
2. se _____ (to get up) I
3. se _____ de Qch (to get up from . . .) IV

libérer
1. _____ Qn ou Qch (to liberate, free . . .) I
2. _____ Qn ou Qch de Qn ou Qch (to liberate, free . . . from . . .) VI

lier
1. _____ Qn ou Qch (to tie, bind . . .) I
2. se _____ avec Qn (to become friendly, intimate with . . .) V
3. _____ Qn ou Qch à Qch (to tie, bind . . . to . . .) VI

liguer
1. _____ Qn ou Qch (to associate . . . in a league) I
2. _____ avec, contre Qn ou Qch (to conspire with, against . . .) V

limiter
1. _____ Qch (to limit . . .) I
2. se _____ à Qch (to limit, restrict oneself to . . .) III
3. se _____ à *Inf.* (to limit oneself to ---*ing*) VIII-A

lire
1. _____ Qch (to read . . .) I
2. _____ Qch *à haute voix, à voix basse* (to read . . . aloud, softly) I
3. _____ dans Qch (to read in, from . . .) V
4. _____ Qch à Qn (to read . . . to . . .) VI

lisérer
1. _____ Qch (to border, edge . . .) I
2. _____ Qch de Qch (to edge . . . with . . .) VI

livrer
1. _____ Qn ou Qch (to deliver, betray, surrender . . .) I
2. se _____ à Qn ou Qch (to surrender to . . .; to turn oneself in to . . .) III
3. _____ Qn ou Qch à Qn ou Qch (to deliver, hand over . . . to . . .) VI
4. _____ *passage* à Qn ou Qch (to make way for . . .) VI

localiser
1. _____ Qn ou Qch (to locate, localize . . .) I
2. se _____ dans Qch (to become localized in . . .) V
3. _____ Qn ou Qch dans Qch (to center, localize . . . in . . .) VI

loger
1. ———   Qn ou Qch (to lodge, give lodging to . . .; to ac-
            commodate, place, fit . . .) I
2. ———   à, dans [un endroit] (to lodge, reside in, on . . .
            e.g., à un hôtel, in a hotel; *dans un vieux quar-
            tier*, in an old neighborhood; *au 1ᵉʳ étage*, on
            the second floor) II, V
3. se ———   dans Qch (to become lodged, stuck in . . .) V
4. ———   Qn à Qch (to put . . . on, in . . . Ex: *On l'avait
            logé au troisième étage*, they had put him on the
            fourth floor) VI
5. ———   Qch dans Qch (to lodge, stick . . . in . . .) VI

lorgner
1. ———   Qn ou Qch (to peer at . . .; to have an eye on
            . . .) I

lotir
1. ———   Qch (to divide, parcel out . . .) I
2. ———   Qn de Qch (to allot something to someone) VI

loucher
1. ———   de Qch (to squint, be cross-eyed in . . . Ex:
            loucher de l'oeil gauche, to have a crossed left
            eye)
2. ———   vers, sur Qn ou Qch (Coll: to covet . . .; to eye
            . . . longingly) V

louer
1. ———   Qn ou Qch (to praise . . .) I
2. se ———   de Qn ou Qch (to be pleased, satisfied with . . .)
            IV
3. ———   Qn ou Qch de Qch (to praise . . . for . . .) VI
4. se ———   de *Inf. passé* (to congratulate oneself for having
            . . .) IX-A
5. ———   Qn de *Inf. passé* (to congratulate . . . for having
            . . .) IX-B

louer
1. ———— Qch (to rent . . .) I
2. ———— Qch à Qn (to rent . . . from, to . . .) VI

lutter
1. ———— avec, contre Qn ou Qch (to fight with, against . . .) V

M

macérer
1. ———— Qch (to macerate . . .) I
2. ———— Qch dans Qch (to macerate . . . in . . .) VI

mâcher
1. ———— Qch (to chew, champ at . . .) I
2. ———— Qch à Qn (to make . . . easy for . . .; *mâcher la besogne à quelqu'un*, to make someone's work easier for them; *mâcher les mots à quelqu'un*, to mince words with someone) VI

maigrir
1. ———— Qn (to make someone look thinner, Ex: *Cette robe la maigrit*, that dress makes her look thinner) I
2. ———— de Qch (to lose [weight], Ex: *Elle a maigri de cinq kilos*, she has lost five kilos) IV

maintenir
1. ———— Qch (to maintain . . .) I
2. se ——— contre Qch (to hold out against . . .) V
3. se ——— dans, en* Qch (to remain in . . . e.g., *dans ses fonctions*, in office; *en bonne santé*, in good health) V

---

*See Appendix II: **DANS, EN, À**, p. 298.

4. _____ Qn dans, en* Qch (to maintain, keep . . . in . . . *e.g.*, *dans la pénurie*, in poverty; *en servitude*, in servitude) VI

majorer

1. _____ Qch (to overestimate [a bill, a charge]) I
2. _____ Qch de Qch (to raise the price of . . . by . . .) VI

manger

1. _____ Qn ou Qch (to eat . . .) I
2. _____ Qn ou Qch de Qch (to eat up . . . with . . . *e.g.*, *de caresses*, with kisses; *des yeux*, with one's eyes) VI

manifester

1. _____ Qch (to demonstrate, show, reveal . . .) I
2. se _____ à Qn (to show, reveal oneself to . . .) III
3. _____ Qch à Qn (to demonstrate, reveal, show . . . to . . .) VI

manquer

1. _____ Qn ou Qch (to miss, *e.g.*, a train; to fumble, *e.g.*, a shot) I
2. _____ à Qn ou Qch (to be lacking to . . . Ex: *Le temps lui manque*, he, she is pressed for time; to be missed emotionally by . . . Ex: *Les enfants manquent aux parents*, the parents miss the children) II
3. _____ à Qch (to break, *e.g.*, *à sa parole*, one's word) II
4. _____ de Qch (to lack, be deficient in . . . Ex: *manquer de talent*, to lack talent) IV
5. ne _____ pas de *Inf.* (to be sure to, not fail to . . . Ex: *Il ne manquera pas de venir*, he will not fail to come) IX-A
6. _____ [de] *Inf.* (to nearly . . . Ex: *Il a manqué* [de] *mourir*, he nearly died) IX-A, VII-A

marbrer

1. _____ Qch (to marble . . .) I
2. _____ Qch de Qch (to marble . . . with . . .) VI

---

*See Appendix II: **DANS**, **EN**, **À**, p. 298.

marchander
1. ———— Qn (to haggle with . . .) I
2. ———— Qch (to haggle over . . .) I
3. ———— Qch avec Qn (to haggle over . . . with . . .) VI

marier
1. ———— Qn ou Qch (to give . . . in marriage; to perform a marriage for . . .; to blend, *e.g.*, colors) I
2. se ——— avec, à Qn (to marry . . .) V, III
3. ———— Qn ou Qch avec, à Qn ou Qch (to marry . . . to . . .; to join . . . with . . .) VI

mariner
1. ———— Qch (to marinate . . .) I
2. ———— Qch dans Qch (to marinate . . . in . . .) VI

marquer
1. ———— Qn ou Qch (to mark, indicate . . .; to score [points]) I
2. être marqué de Qch (to be marked, disfigured with, by . . .) IV
3. ———— Qch à Qch (to mark . . . with, in . . . *e.g., au crayon*, in pencil) VI
4. ———— Qn ou Qch de Qch (to mark, disfigure . . . with . . . *e.g., de taches*, with splotches) VI

marteler
1. ———— Qch (to hammer . . .) I
2. ———— *le cerveau à Qn* (to worry . . .) VI

masquer
1. ———— Qn ou Qch (to mask, conceal . . .) I
2. ———— Qch à Qn (to conceal . . . from . . .) VI

matcher
1. ———— Qn contre Qn (to match . . . against . . . [in a sports event]) VI

maugréer
1. ———— contre Qn ou Qch (to grumble at . . .) V

médire
1. ———— de Qn ou Qch (to speak ill of . . .) IV

méditer
1. ———— Qch (to ponder . . .; to have . . . in mind) I
2. ———— sur Qch (to reflect on . . .) V

méfier (se)
1. se ———— de Qn ou Qch (to be wary of . . .; to mistrust . . .) IV

méjuger
1. ———— de Qn ou Qch (to misjudge . . .) IV

mélanger
1. ———— Qch (to mix . . .) I
2. ———— Qch avec Qch (to mix . . . with . . .) VI

mêler
1. ———— Qch (to mix, mingle . . .) I
2. se ———— à, dans Qch (to mingle, participate in . . .) III, V
3. se ———— de Qch (to interfere in . . .; to get involved in . . .) IV
4. ———— Qch à, avec Qch (to mix . . . with . . .) VI
5. ———— Qn à, dans Qch (to implicate, involve . . . in . . .) VI

menacer
1. ———— Qn ou Qch (to menace . . .) I
2. ———— Qn de Qch (to threaten . . . with . . .) VI
3. ———— de *Inf.* (to threaten to . . .) IX-A

ménager
1. _____ Qch (to take care of . . .; to use . . . sparingly) I
2. se _____ (to take it easy) I
3. _____ Qch à Qn (to dole out . . . to . . .) VI

mener
1. _____ Qn ou Qch (to lead . . .) I
2. _____ à Qn ou Qch (to lead to . . .) III
3. _____ Qn *Inf.* (to take . . . to . . . Ex: *mener un prison-nier voir son avocat*, to take a prisoner to see his lawyer) VII-B

mentionner
1. _____ Qch (to mention . . .) I
2. _____ Qch à Qn (to mention . . . to . . .) VI

mentir
1. _____ à Qn (to lie to . . .) II
2. _____ sur Qch (to lie about . . .) V

méprendre (se)
1. se _____ sur Qn ou Qch (to be mistaken about . . .) V
2. se _____ quant à Qn ou Qch (to be mistaken regarding . . .) V

mépriser
1. _____ Qn ou Qch (to scorn . . .) I
2. _____ Qn de *Inf.* ou *Inf. passé* (to scorn . . . for ---*ing*, for having . . .) IX-B

mériter
1. _____ Qn ou Qch (to merit, deserve . . .) I
2. _____ de *Inf.* (to deserve to . . .) IX-A

mesurer
1. _____ Qn ou Qch (to measure . . .) I
2. se _____ avec, à Qn (to match oneself against . . .) V, III
3. _____ Qn ou Qch à Qn ou Qch (to measure . . . to, against . . .; to proportion . . . to . . .) VI

mésuser
1. _____ de Qch (to misuse . . .) IV

métamorphoser
1. _____ Qn ou Qch (to metamorphose, transform . . .) I
2. se _____ en Qn ou Qch (to turn, change into . . .) V
3. _____ Qn ou Qch en Qn ou Qch (to turn, change . . . into . . .) VI

mettre
1. _____ Qch (to put, place . . .; to put . . . down; to put on [clothes]) I
2. se _____ à Qch (to start, begin . . . Ex: *se mettre au travail*, to start work; *se mettre à table*, to sit down at the table; *se mettre au lit*, to get into bed) III
3. _____ Qn à Qch (to put . . . to . . . Ex: *mettre un prisonnier à mort*, to put a prisoner to death) VI
4. se _____ à *Inf.* (to begin to . . .) VIII-A
5. _____ Qch à *Inf.* (to set, put . . . out to . . . Ex: *mettre le linge à sécher*, to put the laundry out to dry) VIII-B

meubler
1. _____ Qch (to furnish . . .) I
2. _____ Qch de Qch (to furnish . . . with, in . . .) VI

meurtrir
1. _____ Qn ou Qch (to bruise . . .) I
2. _____ Qn *de coups* (to beat . . . black and blue) I

militer

1. _____ pour, contre, en faveur de Qn ou Qch (to militate for, against, in favor of . . .) V

miser

1. _____ Qch (to bet, wager . . .) I
2. _____ sur Qn ou Qch (to bet on . . .) V
3. _____ Qch sur Qn ou Qch (to bet . . . on . . .) VI

modeler

1. _____ Qn ou Qch (to model, mould, shape . . .) I
2. se _____ sur Qn ou Qch (to model oneself on, after . . .) V
3. _____ Qn ou Qch sur Qn ou Qch (to model . . . on, after . . .) VI

monter

1. _____ Qch (to take up . . . *e.g.*, a suitcase; to go up . . . *e.g.*, a staircase; to stage . . . *e.g.*, a play) I
2. se _____ [*la tête*] (to get excited) I
3. _____ à* Qch (to ride . . . *e.g.*, *à bicyclette*, a bicycle; *à cheval*, horseback; to climb . . . Ex: *monter à une échelle*, to climb a ladder) II
4. se _____ à Qch (to amount to . . . Ex: *L'addition se monte à vingt dollars*, the bill adds up to twenty dollars) III
5. _____ dans, en* Qch (to board, get on . . . Ex: *monter en voiture*; *dans le bus*, to get in the car, on the bus) V
6. _____ *sur la scène, sur les planches* (to go on the stage) V
7. se _____ en Qch (to outfit oneself in . . .; to stock up on . . .) V
8. _____ *la tête* à Qn [contre Qn] (to get someone upset [with someone]) VI
9. _____ *le coup* à Qn (Coll: to deceive someone) VI
10. _____ *Inf.* (to go upstairs in order to . . .) VII-A

*See Appendix II: **DANS, EN, À**, p. 298.

montrer
1. _____ Qn ou Qch (to show . . .) I
2. se _____ [+ adjectif] (to show oneself to be . . . *e.g.,* brave) I
3. _____ Qn ou Qch *du doigt* (to point out . . .) I
4. _____ Qn ou Qch à Qn (to show . . . to . . .) VI
5. _____ à Qn à *Inf.* (to show . . . how to . . .) VIII-B

moquer (se)
1. se _____ de Qn ou Qch (to make fun of . . .; to not care about . . .) IV
2. se _____ de *Inf.* (to not care about ---*ing*) IX-A

mordre
1. _____ Qn ou Qch (to bite . . .) I
2. se _____ Qch (to bite one's . . . Ex: *se mordre la langue,* to bite one's tongue) I
3. _____ à Qch (to take a bite of . . .) II
4. _____ dans Qch (to sink one's teeth into . . .) V
5. _____ sur Qch (to encroach on . . .) V

morigéner
1. _____ Qn (to lecture, scold . . .) I
2. _____ Qn de *Inf.* ou *Inf. passé* (to scold . . . for ---*ing*, for having . . .) IX-B

mouiller
1. _____ Qn ou Qch (to moisten, wet . . .) I
2. _____ Qn ou Qch de Qch (to moisten, wet . . . with . . .) VI

mouler
1. _____ Qch (to cast, mould . . .; to outline . . .) I
2. se _____ sur Qn ou Qch (to model oneself on, after . . .) V
3. _____ Qn ou Qch sur Qn ou Qch (to model . . . on, after . . .; to fashion . . . after . . .) VI

mourir

1. _____ de Qch (to die, be dying of . . . *e.g., de pneu-monie*, of pneumonia; *de peur*, of fright) IV
2. _____ [d'envie] de *Inf.* (to be dying to . . .) IX-A

munir

1. se _____ de Qch (to provide oneself with . . .) IV
2. _____ Qn ou Qch de Qch (to provide, furnish . . . with . . .) VI

murer

1. _____ Qch (to wall up, wall in . . .) I
2. se _____ (to isolate oneself) I
3. _____ Qch de Qch (to wall up . . . with . . .) VI

murmurer

1. _____ Qch (to murmer . . .) I
2. _____ contre Qn ou Qch (to complain about, protest against . . .) V
3. _____ Qch à Qn (to murmur . . . to . . .) VI
4. _____ Qch contre Qn ou Qch (to mutter . . . against . . .) VI

mutiner (se)

1. se _____ contre Qn ou Qch (to mutiny, rebel against . . .) V

N

nager

1. _____ dans Qch (to swim in . . . *e.g., dans le lac*, in the lake; Lit: to be swimming in . . . *e.g., dans le sang*, in blood; Coll: to be swimming in [one's clothes]) V

naître
1. _____ à Qch (Lit: to awaken to . . .; to experience . . . for the first time) II
2. _____ de Qn ou Qch (to be born of . . .; to result from . . . Ex: *un crime né du désespoir,* a crime born of despair) IV
3. être né pour Qch (to be born for . . . *e.g.,* success) V

nantir
1. _____ Qn (to coddle . . .; to give security to . . .) I
2. se _____ de Qch (to provide oneself with . . .) IV
3. _____ Qn de Qch (to provide . . . with . . .) VI

napper
1. _____ Qch (to cover . . . with a cloth; to nap . . . with a sauce) I
2. _____ Qch de Qch (to cover, nap . . . with . . .) VI

narrer
1. _____ Qch (to narrate . . .) I
2. _____ Qch à Qn (to narrate . . . to . . .) VI

négliger
1. _____ Qn ou Qch (to neglect . . .) I
2. _____ de *Inf.* (to fail to . . .) IX-A
3. *ne rien négliger pour Inf.* (to try every means to . . . Ex: *Il n'a rien négligé pour nous aider,* he did everything he could to help us) X

négocier
1. _____ Qch (to negotiate . . .) I
2. _____ avec Qn (to trade with . . .; to negotiate with . . .) V

nicher

1. ———— Qn ou Qch (to nest, lodge . . .) I
2. se ——— dans Qch (to nest, roost in . . .) V
3. ———— Qn ou Qch dans Qch (to put, nest, lodge . . . in . . .) VI

nommer

1. ———— Qn ou Qch (to name, appoint . . .) I
2. ———— Qn à Qch (to appoint . . . to . . .) VI

notifier

1. ———— Qch (to signify . . . Ex: *Le juge a notifié son approbation,* the judge indicated his approval) I
2. ———— Qch à Qn (to inform someone of something) VI

nouer

1. ———— Qch (to knot . . .) I
2. ———— Qch dans Qch (to knot, tie . . . in . . .) VI
3. ———— Qch avec Qn (to strike up, establish . . . with . . . Ex: *nouer conversation avec quelqu'un,* to strike up a conversation with someone) VI

nourrir

1. ———— Qn ou Qch (to feed, nourish . . .; to foster . . . *e.g.,* hopes) I
2. se ——— de Qch (to subsist on . . .; to sustain oneself with . . .) IV
3. ———— Qn ou Qch de Qch (to feed, nourish, foster . . . with, on . . .) VI

noyer

1. ———— Qn ou Qch (to drown . . .) I
2. être noyé de Qch (to be drowned in . . . *e.g.,* tears, sorrow) IV
3. se ——— dans Qch (to drown oneself in . . .) V
4. ———— Qn ou Qch dans Qch (to drown . . . in . . .) VI

nuancer
1. ———— Qch (to shade, color . . .) I
2. ———— Qch de Qch (to shade, color . . . with . . .) VI

nuire
1. ———— à Qn ou Qch (to harm . . .) II

O

obéir
1. ———— à Qn ou Qch (to obey . . .) II

objecter
1. ———— Qch (to raise . . . as an objection; to use . . . as an excuse) I
2. ———— Qch à Qn (to hold . . . against . . . Ex: *On lui a objecté sa jeunesse*, his youth was held against him) VI

obliger
1. ———— Qn (to be of service to . . .; to bind . . . legally) I
2. être obligé à Qn (to be grateful to . . .) II
3. ———— Qn ou Qch à Qch (to force something on . . .; to limit . . . to . . . Ex: *Sa faible santé l'oblige à une vie sédentaire*, his poor health limits him to a sedentary life) VI
4. s'———— à ou de *Inf.* (to make oneself . . .; to undertake to . . . *À* is more common; *de* is more literary) VIII-A, IX-A
5. ———— Qn à ou de *Inf.* (to oblige . . . to . . . *À* is more common; *de* is more literary) VIII-B, IX-B
6. être obligé de *Inf.* (to be obliged to . . .) IX-A

obliquer
1. ———— sur, vers Qch (to edge, slant towards . . .) V

obséder

1. _____ Qn (to obsess . . .) I
2. être obsédé de Qch (to be obsessed with . . .) IV
3. être obsédé par Qn ou Qch (to be obsessed by, driven mad by . . .) V

obstiner (s')

1. s'_____ à, dans Qch (to persist in . . .) III, V
2. s'_____ à *Inf.* (to persist in ---*ing*) VIII-A

obtenir

1. _____ Qch (to obtain . . .) I
2. _____ Qch de Qn (to obtain . . . from . . .) VI
3. _____ de *Inf.* (to succeed in ---*ing*; to arrange to . . . Ex: *Elle a obtenu de voir le président*, she succeeded in seeing the president) IX-A

obvier

1. _____ à Qch (to obviate . . .) II

occuper

1. _____ Qn ou Qch (to occupy, busy . . .) I
2. s'_____ de Qn ou Qch (to be interested in . . .; to take care of, see to . . .; to bother about . . .) IV
3. _____ Qn à *Inf.* (to busy, to put . . . to work ---*ing*) VIII-B
4. _____ Qch à *Inf.* (to spend . . . ---*ing*, Ex: *Il occupe ses heures de loisir à lire*, he spends his spare time reading) VIII-B

octroyer

1. _____ Qch (to grant, bestow . . .) I
2. _____ Qch à Qn (to bestow . . . on . . .; to grant . . . to . . .) VI

offenser

1. _____ Qn (to offend . . .; to give offense to . . .) I
2. s'_____ de Qch (to take offense at . . .) IV

offrir
  1. ———— Qch (to offer, give . . .) I
  2. s'———— à Qn ou Qch (to offer, volunteer oneself to . . .;
     to expose oneself to . . . *e.g.*, *à un danger*, to a
     danger; to make advances to . . .) III
  3. ———— Qch à Qn ou Qch (to offer, give . . . to . . .; to
     expose . . . to . . .) VI
  4. s'———— à *Inf.* (to offer, volunteer to . . .) VIII-A
  5. ———— de *Inf.* (to offer to . . .) IX-A

offusquer
  1. ———— Qn (to irritate, displease . . .) I
  2. s'———— de Qch (to be offended at, by . . .) IV

oindre
  1. ———— Qn (to anoint . . .) I
  2. ———— Qn de Qch (to anoint . . . with . . .) VI

ombrager
  1. ———— Qch (to shade, shadow . . .) I
  2. ———— Qn ou Qch de Qch (to shade, protect . . . from
     . . . *e.g.*, *du soleil*, from the sun) VI

omettre
  1. ———— Qn ou Qch (to omit . . .) I
  2. ———— de *Inf.* (to neglect to . . .) IX-A

opérer
  1. ———— Qn (to operate on . . .) I
  2. ———— Qch (to effect . . .) I
  3. ———— Qn de Qch (to operate on . . . for . . .) VI

opiniâtrer (s')
  1. s'———— dans Qch (to persist stubbornly in . . .) V
  2. s'———— à *Inf.* (to persist stubbornly in ---*ing*) VIII-A

opposer
1. _____ Qn ou Qch (to divide, separate, contrast . . .) I
2. s'_____ à Qn ou Qch (to oppose, resist . . .) III
3. _____ Qn ou Qch à Qn ou Qch (to set . . . against . . .; to contrast . . . with . . .; to offer . . . in opposition to . . . Ex: *Il ne trouva pas de réponse à opposer à mon argument,* he could find no answer to counter my argument) VI

opter
1. _____ entre Qch (to choose between . . .) V
2. _____ pour, contre Qch (to opt for, against . . .) V

ordonner
1. _____ Qch (to arrange . . .; to put . . . in order) I
2. _____ Qn (to ordain . . .) I
3. _____ Qch à Qn (to prescribe . . . for . . . Ex: *ordonner un remède à un malade,* to prescribe a remedy for a patient; to sentence someone to . . .; to mete out . . . to someone, Ex: *ordonner un travail à un ouvrier,* to give a worker a job) VI
4. _____ à Qn de *Inf.* (to order . . . to . . .) IX-B

orner
1. _____ Qn ou Qch (to adorn, decorate . . .) I
2. s'_____ de Qch (to adorn oneself with . . .) IV
3. _____ Qn ou Qch de Qch (to adorn, decorate . . . with . . .) VI

oser
1. _____ Qch (to dare . . .) I
2. _____ *Inf.* (to dare to . . .) VII-A

ôter
1. _____ Qch (to remove . . .) I
2. _____ Qn ou Qch à Qn (to take . . . away from . . .) VI
3. _____ Qn ou Qch de Qch (to remove . . . from . . .) VI

ouater
1. _____ Qch (to wad, pad . . .) I
2. _____ Qch de Qch (to wad, pad . . . with . . .) VI

oublier
1. _____ Qn ou Qch (to forget . . .) I
2. _____ de *Inf.* (to forget to . . .) IX-A

ouvrir
1. _____ Qch (to open . . .) I
2. s'_____ à Qn (to speak freely to . . .) III
3. _____ Qch à Qn (to open . . . for . . .) VI

P

pactiser
1. _____ avec Qn ou Qch (to deal with, make a pact with
. . . *e.g., avec l'ennemi*, with the enemy; to compromise with . . . *e.g., avec sa conscience*, with
one's conscience) V

pailleter
1. _____ Qch (to spangle . . .) I
2. _____ Qch de Qch (to spangle . . . with . . .) VI

palabrer
1. _____ avec Qn (to palaver with . . .) V

pâlir
1. _____ de Qch (to become pale, livid with . . . *e.g., de
colère*, with anger) IV

pallier
1. _____ Qch (to palliate . . .) I
2. _____ à Qch (to mitigate . . .) II

palpiter
1. ———— de Qch (to throb with . . . *e.g., d'émotion*, with emotion) IV

pâmer (se)
1. se ———— de Qch (to swoon, pass out with . . . *e.g., de rire*, with laughter; *d'admiration*, with admiration) IV

paraître
1. ———— [+ adjectif] à Qn (to seem . . . to . . . Ex: *La situation parut grave au général*, the situation seemed serious to the general) II
2. *Il paraît à Qn que* (it seems to . . . that . . .) II
3. ———— *Inf.* ou *Inf. passé* (to seem, appear to be ---*ing*, to have . . . Ex: *Il paraissait rêver*, he seemed to be dreaming) VII-A

pardonner
1. ———— Qch (to pardon, excuse . . .) I
2. ———— à Qn (to forgive, pardon . . .) II
3. ———— Qch à Qn (to forgive someone for something) VI
4. ———— à Qn de *Inf.* ou *Inf. passé* (to forgive . . . for ---*ing*, for having . . .) IX-B

parer
1. ———— Qn ou Qch (to adorn, decorate . . .) I
2. se ———— de Qch (to adorn oneself with . . .) IV
3. ———— Qn ou Qch de Qch (to adorn, decorate . . . with . . .) VI

parer
1. ———— Qch (to avoid, avert . . .) I
2. ———— à Qch (to guard against . . .) II

parier
1. _____ Qch (to bet, wager . . .) I
2. _____ à Qn que . . . (to bet someone that . . .) II
3. _____ sur, contre, pour Qn ou Qch (to bet on, against, for . . .) V
4. _____ avec Qn (to bet with . . .) V
5. _____ Qch sur, contre, pour Qn ou Qch (to bet . . . on, against, for . . .) VI

parler
1. _____ [une langue] (to speak . . . *e.g.*, French) I
2. _____ à Qn (to talk to . . .) II
3. _____ de Qn ou Qch (to talk about . . .) IV
4. _____ avec Qn (to talk with . . .) V
5. _____ pour, en faveur de, contre Qn ou Qch (to speak for, in favor of, against . . .) V
6. _____ sur Qn ou Qch (to speak about, on . . .) V
7. _____ de *Inf.* (to talk about *--ing*) IX-A

parsemer
1. être parsemé de Qch (to be strewn, sprinkled with . . .) IV
2. _____ Qn ou Qch de Qch (to strew, sprinkle . . . with . . .) VI

partager
1. _____ Qch (to divide, share . . .) I
2. _____ Qch à, entre Qn ou Qch (to divide, share . . . among . . .) VI
3. _____ Qch en Qch (to divide . . . into . . . Ex: *partager une pièce en deux*, to divide a room in half) VI
4. _____ Qch avec Qn (to share . . . with . . .) VI

participer
1. _____ à Qch (to take part in . . .) II
2. _____ de Qch (to have the characteristics of . . .) IV

partir
1. _____ de Qch (to leave from . . .) IV
2. _____ pour Qch (to leave for . . .) V
3. _____ *Inf.* (to leave in order to . . .) VII-A

parvenir
1. _____ à Qch (to reach, arrive at . . .) II
2. faire parvenir Qch à Qn (to send . . . to . . .; to forward . . . to . . .) VI
3. _____ à *Inf.* (to manage to . . . Ex: *Si tu le lui expliques bien, il parviendra à comprendre,* if you explain it to him well, he will manage to understand) VIII-A

passer
1. _____ Qch (to pass, surpass, pass by, cross . . .; to spend [time]; *passer un examen,* to take a test) I
2. se _____ (to take place, to happen) I
3. _____ à, dans* Qn ou Qch (to go over to, to defect to . . . Ex: *passer à l'ennemi,* to defect to the enemy; *passer dans l'opposition,* to go over to the opposition; to go on to . . . Ex: *Passons à autre chose,* let's go on to something else) II, V
4. se _____ de Qn ou Qch (to do without . . . Ex: *Je ne peux pas me passer d'elle,* I can't do without her) IV
5. _____ pour Qn ou Qch (to appear to be . . .; to pass for . . .) V
6. _____ par Qch (to pass through, by way of . . .) V
7. _____ sur Qch (to skip, pass over . . .) V
8. _____ chez Qn (to drop by someone's house) V
9. _____ Qch à Qn (to pass . . . to . . .) VI
10. _____ *Inf.* (to stop by to . . .) VII-A
11. _____ [un certain temps] à *Inf.* (to spend [time] ---*ing,* Ex: *J'ai passé l'hiver à faire du ski,* I spent the winter skiing) VIII-B
12. se _____ de *Inf.* (to do without ---*ing*) IX-A

_____
*See Appendix II: **DANS, EN, À,** p. 298.

passionner
1. _____ Qn (to impassion, arouse great interest in . . . Ex: *Ce film m'a passionné*, I was fascinated by the movie) I
2. être passionné de, pour Qn ou Qch (to be very interested in, enthusiastic about . . .) IV, V
3. se _____ pour Qch (to be very interested in . . .) V

pâtir
1. _____ de Qch (to suffer on account of . . .) IV

paver
1. _____ Qch (to pave . . .) I
2. _____ Qch de Qch (to pave . . . with . . .) VI

payer
1. _____ Qn ou Qch (to pay . . .; to pay for . . .) I
2. se _____ Qch (Coll: to give oneself . . .; to treat oneself to . . .) I
3. se _____ de Qch (to be satisfied with . . . Ex: *se payer de mots*, to be all talk) IV
4. _____ de Qch (to make a show of . . . Ex: *payer d'audace*, to put up a good front) IV
5. être payé pour Qch (to be paid, punished for . . .) V
6. _____ Qch à Qn (to pay . . . to . . .; to treat someone to something, Ex: *Il m'a payé un verre*, he bought me a drink) VI
7. _____ Qn de Qch (to pay . . . for . . .) VI
8. être payé pour *Inf.* (to be paid for ---*ing*, to . . .) X

pécher
1. _____ contre Qn ou Qch (to sin against . . .) V

peiner
1. _____ Qn (to grieve, distress . . .) I
2. être peiné de Qch (to be pained, distressed by, at . . .) IV
3. être peiné de *Inf.* (to be grieved, distressed to . . .) IX-A
4. *Il peine à Qn de Inf.* (it grieves, pains . . . to . . . Ex: *Il me peine de vous le dire*, it pains me to tell you) IX-B

pencher
1. ⸻ Qch (to tilt, bend . . .) I
2. se ⸻ sur Qn ou Qch (to bend over, towards . . .; to study closely, take an active interest in . . .) V
3. ⸻ pour Qn ou Qch (to lean towards, be inclined towards . . .) V

pendre
1. ⸻ Qn ou Qch (to hang . . .) I
2. ⸻ à Qch (to hang from . . .) II
3. être pendu à Qch (to be tied to, inseparable from . . .; to be hung from . . .) II
4. se ⸻ à Qn ou Qch (to hang on to, cling to . . .) III
5. ⸻ Qn ou Qch à Qch (to hang . . . from . . .) VI

pénétrer
1. ⸻ Qn ou Qch (to penetrate . . .) I
2. être pénétré de Qch (to be overcome with . . . *e.g.*, *de remords*, with remorse) IV
3. ⸻ dans Qch (to enter, break into . . .) V
4. ⸻ Qn ou Qch de Qch (to penetrate, pierce . . . with . . .; to imbue, inspire . . . with . . . Ex: *Il les a pénétrés de son enthousiasme*, he inspired them with his enthusiasm) VI

penser
1. ⸻ à Qn ou Qch (to think of, about . . .) III
2. ⸻ Qch de Qn ou Qch (to think . . . about . . .; in questions, to have an opinion about . . . Ex: *Que pensez-vous du nouveau professeur?* What do you think of the new professor?) VI
3. ⸻ *Inf.* (to intend to . . .; to think that . . . Ex: *Il pense pouvoir le faire*, he thinks that he can do it) VII-A
4. ⸻ à *Inf.* (to think about, consider ---*ing*) VIII-A

percer
1. _____ Qch (to pierce . . .) I
2. _____ Qch de Qch (to pierce . . . with . . .) VI

percuter
1. _____ Qch (to strike . . .; to crash into . . .) I
2. _____ contre Qn ou Qch (to explode against . . .; to crash into . . .) V

perfectionner
1. _____ Qch (to perfect . . .) I
2. se _____ dans Qch (to perfect oneself in . . .) V

périr
1. _____ de Qch (to die of . . . *e.g., d'inanition*, of starvation; to die from . . . *e.g., d'une blessure grave*, from a serious wound) IV

permettre
1. _____ Qch (to permit, allow . . .) I
2. _____ Qch à Qn (to permit someone something) VI
3. se _____ de *Inf.* (to take the liberty of ---*ing*) IX-A
4. _____ à Qn de *Inf.* (to allow . . . to . . .) IX-B

persévérer
1. _____ dans Qch (to persevere in . . .) V
2. _____ à *Inf.* (to persevere in ---*ing*) VIII-A

persister
1. _____ dans Qch (to persist in . . .) V
2. _____ à *Inf.* (to persist in ---*ing*) VIII-A

persuader
1. _____ Qn (to persuade, convince . . .) I
2. se _____ de Qch (to convince oneself of . . .) IV
3. _____ Qn de Qch (to convince . . . of . . .) VI
4. _____ à Qn de *Inf.* (to persuade . . . to . . .) IX-B

peser
1. _____ Qn ou Qch (to weigh . . .) I
2. _____ à Qn (to lie heavily on . . .; to trouble, be oppressive to . . . Ex: *Ses ennuis lui pèsent*, his problems are troubling him) II
3. _____ sur Qn ou Qch (to weigh upon . . .; to be a burden to . . .) V

pester
1. _____ contre Qn ou Qch (to rant and rave against . . .) V

pétrir
1. _____ Qch (to mold, knead . . .) I
2. être pétri de Qch (to be made of, filled with . . . e.g., *de rancune*, with bitterness; *d'orgueil*, with pride) IV

peupler
1. _____ Qch (to people, populate . . .) I
2. _____ Qch de Qn ou Qch (to people, populate . . . with . . .) VI

philosopher
1. _____ sur Qn ou Qch (to philosophize on . . .) V

picoter
1. être picoté de Qch (to be pock-marked with . . .) IV
2. être picoté par Qch (to be pricked, stung by . . .) V

pincer
1. _____ Qn ou Qch (to pinch . . .) I
2. _____ Qch à Qn (to pinch someone's . . . Ex: *pincer la joue à l'enfant*, to pinch the child's cheek) VI

piquer
1. _____ Qn ou Qch (to prick . . .; to offend . . .) I
2. se _____ de Qch (to pride oneself on . . .; to take offense at . . .) IV
3. se _____ de *Inf.* (to pride oneself on ---*ing*) IX-A

plaider
1. _____ Qch (to plead . . . *e.g.*, innocence) I
2. _____ contre, pour Qn ou Qch (to plead, argue in court against, for . . .) V

plaindre
1. _____ Qn ou Qch (to pity . . .) I
2. se _____ (to complain) I
3. se _____ à Qn (to complain to . . .) III
4. se _____ de Qn ou Qch (to complain about . . .) IV
5. se _____ de *Inf.* ou *Inf. passé* (to complain about ---*ing*, about having . . .) IX-A

plaire
1. _____ à Qn (to please, be pleasing to . . . Ex: *Cette maison me plaît beaucoup*, I like this house a lot) II
2. se _____ à un endroit (to like it in a place, *e.g., se plaire à la montagne*, to like it in the mountains) III
3. se _____ à *Inf.* (to enjoy, like ---*ing*; to amuse oneself by ---*ing*) VIII-A
4. *Il plaît à Qn de Inf.* (to like to . . .; to find . . . a pleasure, Ex: *Il me plaît beaucoup de sortir souvent*, I enjoy going out often) IX-B

plaisanter
1. _____ sur, de Qch (to joke about . . .) V, IV

planer
1. _____ sur Qn ou Qch (to hover over . . .) V

pleurer

1. ———— Qn ou Qch (to mourn, mourn for . . .; to cry . . . e.g., *des larmes de joie*, tears of joy) I
2. ———— de Qch (to weep for, with . . . e.g., *de honte*, with shame) IV
3. ———— sur Qch (to cry over . . .) V

plier

1. ———— Qn ou Qch (to fold, bend . . .) I
2. se —— à Qn ou Qch (to yield to . . .; to abide by . . .) III
3. ———— sous Qch (to bend under, give way to . . .) V
4. ———— Qn à Qch (to bend, break . . . to . . . Ex: *plier quelqu'un à la discipline*, to make someone be disciplined) VI

plonger

1. ———— dans Qch (to plunge into . . .) V
2. ———— Qn ou Qch dans Qch (to plunge, immerse . . . in . . .) VI

ployer

1. ———— devant Qn ou Qch (to give way before, under . . .) V

poivrer

1. ———— Qch (to pepper . . .) I
2. ———— Qch de Qch (to pepper . . . with . . .) VI

porter

1. ———— Qn ou Qch (to wear, carry . . .) I
2. se —— *bien, mal* (to be in good, bad health) I
3. se —— *à une extrémité* (to go to an extreme)
4. être porté sur Qch (to have a weakness for . . .) V
5. ———— sur Qch (to bear on, have bearing on . . .; to fall on . . . Ex: *La discussion porte sur la situation économique*, the economic situation is being discussed) V
6. ———— Qch à Qn (to carry . . . to . . .) VI

7. ⸺ Qn à Qch (to lead, incite . . . to . . .) VI
8. être porté à *Inf.* (to be inclined, disposed to . . .) VIII-A
9. ⸺ Qn à *Inf.* (to lead, cause . . . to . . .) VIII-B

poser

1. ⸺ Qch (to put, put down . . .; to ask [a question];
   to pose . . . *e.g.*, a problem) I
2. se ⸺ (to arise, Ex: *La question ne se pose pas*, the problem does not arise) I
3. ⸺ pour Qch (to pose for . . .) V
4. se ⸺ comme, en Qn ou Qch (to pose as . . .) V
5. se ⸺ sur Qn ou Qch (to alight on, rest on . . .) V
6. ⸺ Qch à Qn (to ask someone [a question]; to pose
   . . . for . . .) VI
7. ⸺ Qch sur, contre Qch (to put, rest . . . on, against
   . . .) VI

posséder

1. ⸺ Qn ou Qch (to possess . . .) I
2. être possédé de Qch (to be possessed by . . . *e.g.*, *d'un démon*,
   by a demon) IV

poudrer

1. ⸺ Qch (to powder . . .) I
2. ⸺ Qch de Qch (to powder . . . with . . .) VI

poudroyer

1. ⸺ Qch (to cover . . . with dust) I
2. ⸺ Qch de Qch (to dust . . . with . . .) VI

pourvoir

1. ⸺ à Qch (to provide for, see to . . . *e.g.*, *à ses besoins*, for one's needs) II
2. se ⸺ de Qch (to provide oneself with . . .) IV
3. ⸺ Qn de Qch (to provide . . . with . . .) VI

pousser
1. _____ Qn ou Qch (to push . . .; to utter . . . *e.g.*, a cry) I
2. _____ Qn à *Inf.* (to push, urge . . . to . . .) VIII-B

pouvoir
1. _____ *Inf.* (to be able to . . .) VII-A

pratiquer
1. _____ Qch (to practice [a profession]; to go in for . . .
   e.g., a sport) I
2. _____ Qch dans Qch (to cut, work . . . in . . . Ex:
   pratiquer un trou dans un mur, to cut a hole in
   a wall) VI

prêcher
1. _____ Qch (to preach . . .) I
2. _____ à Qn (to preach to . . .) II
3. _____ Qch à Qn (to preach . . . to . . .) VI

précipiter
1. _____ Qch (to throw, hurl . . .) I
2. se _____ dans Qch (to rush into . . .) V
3. se _____ sur Qn ou Qch (to throw oneself onto . . .; to rush
   at . . .) V
4. _____ Qn dans Qch (to rush, hurry . . . into . . .) VI

prédestiner
1. être prédestiné à Qch (to be predestined, born for . . .) II
2. être prédestiné à *Inf.* (to be predestined, born to . . .) VIII-A

prédire
1. _____ Qch (to predict . . .) I
2. _____ Qch à Qn (to predict . . . to, for . . .) VI

prédisposer
1. _____ Qn à Qn ou Qch (to predispose . . . towards . . .) VI
2. _____ Qn contre Qn ou Qch (to prejudice . . . against . . .) VI

prédominer
1. _____ sur Qch (to dominate . . .; to have the upper hand over . . .) V

préexister
1. _____ à Qn ou Qch (to be preexistent to . . .; to predate . . .) II

préférer
1. _____ Qn ou Qch (to prefer . . .) I
2. _____ Qn ou Qch à Qn ou Qch (to prefer . . . to . . .) VI
3. _____ *Inf.* (to prefer to . . .) VII-A

préjuger
1. _____ de Qch (to make a premature judgment on . . .) IV

préluder
1. _____ à Qch (to serve as a prelude to . . .; to precede . . .) II
2. _____ par Qch (to begin with . . .) V

préméditer
1. _____ Qch (to premeditate . . .) I
2. _____ de *Inf.* (to premeditate ---*ing*) IX-A

prémunir
1. se _____ contre Qch (to secure, protect oneself against . . .) V
2. _____ Qn ou Qch contre Qch (to caution, arm . . . against . . .) VI

prendre

1. _____ Qn ou Qch (to take . . .; to catch . . .) I
2. se (laisser) prendre à, dans Qch (to get caught by, in . . .
Ex: *se (laisser) prendre au piège*, to get caught
in a trap) III, V
3. s'en ___ à Qn [pour Qch] (to blame . . . [for . . .]) III
4. se _____ de Qch (to begin to have . . . Ex: *se prendre
d'amitié pour quelqu'un*, to begin to be friendly
with someone) IV
5. se _____ pour Qn ou Qch (to take oneself for . . .) V
6. être pris dans Qch (to be caught in . . .) V
7. _____ Qch à Qn (to take . . . from . . .) VI
8. _____ Qn ou Qch pour Qn ou Qch (to take, mistake . . .
for . . . *e.g., pour un voleur*, for a thief; *pour
un imbécile*, for an idiot) VI
9. _____ Qn ou Qch en Qch (to take a . . . to . . . Ex: *prendre quelqu'un en aversion*, to take a dislike to
someone) VI
10. _____ Qn comme, pour Qch (to take . . . as . . . *e.g.,
comme associé*, as a partner) VI
11. _____ *garde* de *Inf.* (to take care to . . .; Lit: to take
care not to . . .) IX-A
12. _____ *garde* de ne pas *Inf.* (to take care not to . . .)
IX-A

préparer

1. _____ Qn ou Qch (to prepare . . .) I
2. se ___ à Qch (to prepare oneself for . . ., *e.g., à la mort*,
for death) III
3. se ___ pour Qch (to get ready for . . . *e.g., pour le bal*,
for the dance) V
4. _____ Qn ou Qch à Qch (to prepare . . . for . . .) VI
5. _____ Qch à Qn (to prepare . . . for . . .; to have . . .
[*e.g.*, a surprise] in store for . . .) VI
6. être préparé à *Inf.* (to be prepared to . . .) VIII-A
7. _____ Qn ou Qch à *Inf.* (to prepare . . . to . . .) VIII-B

préoccuper
1. _____ Qn (to preoccupy . . .) I
2. se _____ de Qn ou Qch (to give one's attention to . . .; to be concerned about . . .) IV

préposer
1. _____ Qn à Qch (to appoint . . . to . . .; to put someone in charge of . . .) VI

prescrire
1. _____ Qch (to prescribe . . .) I
2. _____ Qch à Qn (to prescribe . . . to, for . . . Ex: *prescrire un remède à un malade*, to prescribe a remedy to, for a patient) VI
3. _____ à Qn de *Inf.* (to strongly advise . . . to . . .; to stipulate that someone . . .) IX-B

présenter
1. _____ Qn ou Qch (to present . . .) I
2. se _____ [à Qn] (to introduce oneself [to . . .]) III
3. se _____ à Qch (to report for . . . *e.g.*, *à un examen*, for a test) III
4. se _____ pour Qch (to apply for . . . *e.g.*, a job) V
5. _____ Qn à Qn (to introduce . . . to . . .) VI

préserver
1. _____ Qn ou Qch (to preserve . . .) I
2. se _____ de Qn ou Qch (to protect oneself from . . .) IV
3. _____ Qn ou Qch de Qn ou Qch (to protect . . . from . . .) VI

présider
1. _____ Qch (to chair . . .) I
2. _____ à Qch (to preside over . . .) II

pressentir

1. _____ Qch (to have a premonition of . . .; to foresee . . .) I
2. faire pressentir Qch à Qn (to give someone a hint of something) VI
3. _____ Qn sur Qch (to sound someone out on something) VI

presser

1. _____ Qn ou Qch (to press, hurry . . .) I
2. _____ Qn de Qch (to assail, ply . . . with . . .) VI
3. se _____ de *Inf.* (to hasten to . . .) IX-A
4. _____ Qn de *Inf.* (to urge . . . to . . .) IX-B

présumer

1. _____ Qn ou Qch (to presume . . . Ex: *présumer le pire*, to presume the worst; *présumer quelqu'un innocent*, to presume someone innocent) I
2. _____ de Qch (to overestimate . . . *e.g., de sa force*, one's strength) IV
3. _____ de *Inf.* (to presume to . . .) IX-A

prétendre

1. _____ Qch (to claim, affirm . . .) I
2. _____ à Qch (to lay claim to . . .; to pretend to . . . *e.g., au trône*, to the throne) II
3. _____ *Inf.* ou *Inf. passé* (to claim to . . ., to have . . .) VII-A

prêter

1. _____ Qch (to loan . . .) I
2. _____ à Qch (to give rise to . . .; to give occasion for . . . *e.g., à la censure*, to criticism; *prêter à rire*, to give rise to laughter; *prêter à sourire*, to make people smile) II

3. se _____ à Qch (to agree to . . .; to comply with, go along with . . . Ex: *Elle s'est prêtée à cette plaisanterie,* she went along with the joke) III

4. _____ Qch à Qn ou Qch (to loan . . . to . . .; to attribute . . . to . . .) VI

prévaloir

1. se _____ de Qch (to avail oneself of . . .; to pride oneself on . . .) IV

2. _____ sur, contre Qn ou Qch (to prevail over, against . . .) V

prévenir

1. _____ Qn ou Qch (to warn, notify . . .) I

2. _____ Qn de Qch (to notify, warn . . . about, of . . .) VI

3. _____ Qn contre Qn ou Qch (to prejudice . . . against . . .) VI

4. _____ Qn en faveur de Qn ou Qch (to bias . . . in favor of . . .) VI

prier

1. _____ Qn (to pray to . . .) I

2. _____ pour Qn ou Qch (to pray for . . .) V

3. _____ Qn à Qch (to invite . . . to . . .) VI

4. _____ Qn de *Inf.* (to beg, ask . . . to . . .) IX-B

primer

1. _____ Qn ou Qch (to take precedence over . . .; to excel over . . .) I

priver

1. se _____ de Qch (to deprive oneself of . . .; to abstain from . . .) IV

2. _____ Qn de Qch (to deprive . . . of . . .) VI

procéder
1. _____ à Qch (to proceed to . . .) II
2. _____ de Qch (to originate from . . .) IV
3. _____ avec Qch (to proceed with . . . *e.g., avec précaution*, with caution) V
4. _____ par Qch (to proceed by . . . *e.g., par élimination*, by elimination) V

procurer
1. se _____ Qch (to procure, acquire . . .) I
2. _____ Qch à Qn (to get, provide . . . for . . .) VI
3. se _____ Qch de Qn (to get . . . from . . .) VI

prodiguer
1. _____ Qch (to be lavish with . . .) I
2. se _____ (to be unsparing of oneself; to show off) I
3. se _____ pour Qn (to outdo oneself for . . .) V
4. _____ Qch à Qn (to shower someone with something) VI

profiler
1. se _____ sur, à Qch (to be outlined on . . .) V, III
2. se _____ contre Qch (to be outlined against . . .) V

profiter
1. _____ à Qn ou Qch (to be useful, profitable to . . .) II
2. _____ de Qn ou Qch (to take advantage of . .) IV

prohiber
1. _____ Qch (to prohibit . . .) I
2. _____ Qch à Qn (to prohibit, forbid someone something) VI
3. _____ à Qn de *Inf.* (to prohibit . . . from ---*ing*) IX-B

projeter
1. _____ Qch (to throw, cast . . . *e.g.*, a shadow; to plan . . .; to project . . .) I
2. _____ de *Inf.* (to plan to . . .) IX-A

prolonger
1. _____ Qch (to prolong . . .) I
2. _____ Qch de Qch (to lengthen . . . by . . .) VI

promettre
1. _____ Qch (to promise . . .) I
2. se _____ Qch (to count on . . .; to look forward to . . .) I
3. _____ Qn ou Qch à Qn (to promise . . . to . . .) VI
4. se _____ de *Inf.* (to resolve to . . .) IX-A
5. _____ [à Qn] de *Inf.* (to promise [someone] to . . .) IX-B

prononcer
1. _____ Qch (to pronounce . . .) I
2. _____ sur Qn ou Qch (to pass judgment on . . .) V
3. _____ Qch à Qn (to pronounce . . . to . . .) VI

proportionner
1. _____ Qch (to proportion, adjust . . .) I
2. _____ Qch à, avec Qch (to proportion, adjust . . . to . . .) VI

proposer
1. _____ Qn ou Qch (to propose, suggest . . .) I
2. se _____ Qch (to have . . . in mind) I
3. se _____ comme Qn ou Qch (to run for . . .; to offer one's services as . . . *e.g., comme interprète*, as an interpreter) V
4. _____ Qch à Qn (to propose . . . to . . .) VI
5. _____ Qn ou Qch comme Qch (to hold up . . . as . . . *e.g., comme modèle*, as a model) VI
6. _____ Qn ou Qch pour Qch (to suggest . . . for . . . *e.g., pour un poste*, for a job) VI
7. _____ de *Inf.* (to suggest ---*ing*) IX-A
8. se _____ de *Inf.* (to intend to . . .) IX-A
9. _____ à Qn de *Inf.* (to suggest to . . . that . . . Ex: *Je lui ai proposé de m'accompagner*, I suggested that he, she accompany me) IX-B

proscrire
1. _____ Qn ou Qch (to proscribe, outlaw . . .) I
2. _____ Qn ou Qch de Qch (to ostracize, outlaw, banish . . . from . . .) VI

prosterner
1. se _____ devant Qn ou Qch (to prostrate oneself before ...) V

protéger
1. _____ Qn ou Qch (to protect ...) I
2. se _____ de Qch (to guard against ...; to protect oneself from, against ...) IV
3. _____ Qn ou Qch contre Qn ou Qch (to protect ... from, against ...) VI

protester
1. _____ Qch (to protest ...) I
2. _____ de Qch (to affirm ... Ex: *protester de son innocence*, to affirm one's innocence) IV
3. _____ contre Qn ou Qch (to protest against ...) V

prouver
1. _____ Qch (to prove ...) I
2. _____ Qch à Qn (to prove ... to ...) VI

provenir
1. _____ de Qch (to come, originate from ...) IV

provoquer
1. _____ Qn ou Qch (to cause, provoke ...) I
2. _____ Qn à Qch (to incite, provoke ... to ...) VI
3. _____ Qn à *Inf.* (to induce, provoke ... to ...) VIII-B

puer
1. _____ Qch (to stink of ... Ex: *puer l'ail*, to stink of garlic) I

puiser
1. _____ Qch (to draw [water]) I
2. _____ Qch à, dans Qch (to draw ... from ... Ex: *puiser une cruche d'eau à la fontaine*, to draw a pitcher of water from the fountain) VI
3. _____ Qch chez Qn (to draw, derive one's ... from ... Ex: *puiser ses thèmes chez un auteur*, to take one's themes from an author) VI

punir

1. _____ Qn (to punish . . .) I
2. _____ Qn de, par Qch (to punish . . . with . . . *e.g., de mort*, with death) VI
3. _____ Qn pour, de Qch (to punish . . . for . . .) VI
4. Qn de *Inf. passé* (to punish . . . for having . . .) IX-B

purger

1. _____ Qn ou Qch (to purge, cleanse . . .) I
2. se _____ de Qch (to purge, rid oneself of . . .) IV
3. _____ Qn ou Qch de Qch (to purge, rid . . . of . . .) VI

purifier

1. _____ Qn ou Qch (to purify . . .) I
2. _____ Qn ou Qch de Qch (to cleanse, purify . . . of . . .) VI

Q

qualifier

1. _____ Qn ou Qch (to qualify, designate, call . . .) I
2. être qualifié [de] Qch (to be considered, called a . . .) IV, I
3. se _____ pour Qch (to qualify for . . .) V
4. _____ Qn ou Qch [de] Qch (to consider . . . a . . . Ex: *qualifier le vol de crime*, to consider theft a crime) VI
5. _____ Qn ou Qch pour Qch (to qualify . . . for . . .) VI

quémander

1. _____ Qch (to solicit . . .) I
2. _____ Qch de Qn (to solicit someone's . . .; to beg someone for something) VI

quereller

1. se _____ avec Qn (to quarrel with . . .) V

questionner
1. ——— Qn (to question . . .) I
2. ——— Qn de Qch (to question . . . about . . .) VI

R

rabâcher
1. ——— Qch (to harp on . . .) I
2. ——— Qch à Qn (to drum . . . into . . .) VI

rabattre
1. ——— Qch (to lower . . .; to pull . . . down; to turn . . . back) I
2. se —— sur Qch (to fall back on . . .; to have recourse to . . .) V

raccomoder
1. ——— Qch (to mend . . .) I
2. se —— avec Qn (to make up with . . .; to be reconciled with . . .) V
3. ——— Qn avec Qn (to reconcile . . . with . . .) VI

raccorder
1. ——— Qch (to join, coordinate . . .) I
2. se —— à Qch (to join, link up with . . .) III
3. ——— Qn ou Qch à, avec Qn ou Qch (to link, connect . . . with . . .) VI

raccrocher
1. ——— Qch (to hang up . . . again) I
2. se —— à Qn ou Qch (to clutch hold of . . .) III

racheter
1. ——— Qn ou Qch (to redeem . . .; to buy back . . .; to compensate for [a deficiency]) I
2. se —— (to redeem oneself) I
3. ——— Qn ou Qch à Qn (to ransom, buy back . . . from . . .) VI

raconter
1. _____ Qch (to relate, narrate . . .) I
2. _____ Qch à Qn (to relate, narrate . . . to . . .) VI

radier
1. _____ Qn ou Qch (to erase, cross off, eliminate . . .) I
2. _____ Qn ou Qch de Qch (to erase, cross off . . . from . . .) VI

raffiner
1. _____ Qch (to refine . . .) I
2. _____ sur Qch (to exaggerate, overdo . . .; to split hairs, Ex: *Il raffine sur l'étiquette,* he is overly fussy about etiquette) V

raffoler
1. _____ de Qn ou Qch (to adore, be crazy about . . .) IV

raidir
1. _____ Qn ou Qch (to stiffen . . .) I
2. se _____ contre Qn ou Qch (to brace oneself against . . .) V

raisonner
1. _____ Qch (to consider, study . . .) I
2. _____ Qn (to reason with . . .) I
3. _____ avec Qn (to have a discussion with . . .) V
4. _____ sur Qch (to speculate on, argue about . . .) V

rallier
1. _____ Qn (to win over . . .) I
2. se _____ à Qn ou Qch (to rally to . . .; to join . . .) III
3. _____ Qn à Qch (to win . . . over to . . .) VI

ramener
1. ———— Qn (to bring . . . back) I
2. se —— à Qch (to be reduced to . . .; to amount to . . .
   Ex: *Son argument se ramenait à une idée très simple*, his argument boiled down to a very simple idea) III
3. ———— Qn à Qch (to bring, take . . . back to . . . Ex: *ramener quelqu'un chez lui, à la maison*, to bring, take someone home; *ramener quelqu'un à la raison*, to bring someone back to his senses) VI

ramper
1. ———— devant Qn ou Qch (to grovel to . . .) V

rappeler
1. ———— Qn ou Qch (to call . . . back; to summon up . . .; to repeal . . .) I
2. se —— Qn ou Qch (to remember, recall . . .) I
3. ———— Qch à Qn (to remind someone of something) VI
4. ———— Qn à Qch (to call . . . back to . . . Ex: *rappeler quelqu'un à son devoir*, to remind someone of his duty) VI
5. se —— de *Inf.* ou *Inf. passé* (to remember to . . .; to remember having . . .) IX-A
6. ———— à Qn de *Inf.* (to remind . . . to . . .) IX-B

rapporter
1. ———— Qch (to relate, report . . .; to bring . . . back) I
2. se —— à Qch ou Qn (to relate to . . .; to have reference to . . . Ex: *Cette idée ne se rapporte pas au texte*, this idea has no relation to the text) III
3. s'en —— à Qn ou Qch (to leave it up to . . .; to rely on . . .) III
4. ———— Qch à Qch (to relate . . . to . . .; to refer . . . to . . . Ex: *Il faut rapporter la cause à l'effet*, one must relate the cause to the effect) VI

rapprocher
1. ——— Qn ou Qch (to compare . . .; to bring . . . together) I
2. se ——— de Qn ou Qch (to draw near to . . .; to resemble . . .) IV
3. ——— Qn ou Qch de Qn ou Qch (to bring . . . near to . . .; to make . . . approach . . . Ex: *rapprocher l'art à la vie*, to make art imitate life) VI

rassasier
1. ——— Qn ou Qch (to sate, satisfy . . .) I
2. se ——— de Qch (to have one's fill of . . .) IV
3. être rassasié de Qch (to have one's fill of . . .; to be fed up with . . .) IV
4. ——— Qn ou Qch de Qch (to satisfy, sate . . . with . . .) VI

rassurer
1. ——— Qn (to reassure . . .) I
2. se ——— sur Qch (to reassure oneself about . . .) V
3. ——— Qn sur Qch (to reassure . . . about . . .) VI

ratiboiser
1. ——— Qn (Coll: to swindle . . .; to clean . . . out) I
2. ——— Qch à Qn (Coll: to cheat, do someone out of something) VI

rattacher
1. ——— Qn ou Qch (to fasten, to reattach . . .) I
2. se ——— à Qch (to be connected with . . .) III
3. ——— Qn ou Qch à Qch (to fasten . . . to . . .; to connect . . . with . . .) VI

rattraper
1. ——— Qn ou Qch (to overtake . . .; to catch up with . . .; to make up for [a deficiency]) I
2. se ——— (to catch up) I
3. se ——— à Qch (to catch hold of . . .) III

ravaler

1. _____ Qn ou Qch (to cut down, debase . . .) I
2. _____ Qch (to choke down, swallow . . .) I
3. se _____ à Qch (to lower, debase oneself to . . .) III
4. _____ Qn ou Qch à Qch (to reduce . . . to . . .) VI

ravir

1. _____ Qn ou Qch (to delight . . .; to carry off . . .) I
2. être ravi de Qn ou Qch (to be delighted by, with . . .) IV
3. _____ Qn ou Qch à Qn (to steal . . . from . . .) VI
4. être ravi de *Inf.* (to be delighted to . . .) IX-A

ravitailler

1. _____ Qn ou Qch (to supply . . . [with food, munitions])
   I
2. se _____ en Qch (to stock up on . . . *e.g., en blé,* on
   wheat) V
3. _____ Qn ou Qch en Qch (to supply . . . with . . .) VI

rayer

1. _____ Qch (to rule, stripe, cross off . . .) I
2. _____ Qn ou Qch de Qch (to cross . . . off . . .; to remove . . . from . . .) VI

rayonner

1. _____ de Qch (Lit: to radiate with . . . *e.g., de joie,* with
   joy) IV

réaccoutumer

1. _____ Qn à Qch (to reaccustom . . . to . . .) VI

réagir

1. _____ à Qch (to react, respond to . . .) II
2. _____ contre Qch (to react against . . .) V
3. _____ sur Qch (to react with . . . [chemically]; to have
   a reciprocal influence on . . .) V

rebeller (se)
1. se _____ contre Qn ou Qch (to rebel against . . .) V

rebiffer (se)
1. se _____ contre Qn ou Qch (to bristle, bridle at . . .) V

rebuter
1. _____ Qn (to discourage, put off . .) I
2. être rebuté par Qch (to be dismayed, put off, disgusted by . . .) V
3. se _____ de *Inf.* (to be dismayed, disgusted at ---*ing*) IX-A

recevoir
1. _____ Qn ou Qch (to receive . . .; to admit . . . [to a school]) I
2. être reçu à Qch (to be admitted to . . . *e.g., à l'université*, to the university; to pass [an exam]) II
3. _____ Qch de Qn (to receive . . . from . . .) VI
4. _____ Qch dans Qch (to catch . . . in . . . Ex: *Le chien a reçu la balle dans sa bouche*, the dog caught the ball in his mouth) VI

réchapper
1. _____ de, à Qch (to escape from . . .; to make it through . . . Ex: *réchapper d'une maladie*, to recover from, make it through an illness) IV, II
2. en _____ (to make it through)

rechigner
1. _____ à Qch (to lack enthusiasm for . . .) II
2. _____ à *Inf.* (to be unwilling to . . .) VIII-A

réciter
1. _____ Qch (to recite . . .) I
2. _____ Qch à Qn (to recite . . . to . . .) VI

réclamer

1. _____ Qn ou Qch (to clamor for . . .; to require . . .
e.g., *beaucoup de patience*, much patience) I
2. se _____ de Qn (to appeal to . . .; to take . . . as an authority) IV
3. _____ contre Qn ou Qch (to protest against . . .) V
4. _____ Qch à Qn (to ask for, demand . . . from . . .) VI

recommander

1. _____ Qn ou Qch (to recommend . . .) I
2. se _____ à Qn (to commend oneself to . . .; to seek the protection of . . .) III
3. se _____ de Qn (to use, give . . . as a reference) IV
4. se _____ par Qch (to show one's merit by . . .) V
5. _____ Qn à Qn (to commend, recommend . . . to . . .) VI
6. _____ Qch à Qn (to recommend . . . to . . .; to enjoin someone to . . . *e.g., le secret*, to secrecy) VI
7. _____ à Qn de *Inf.* (to recommend that someone . . .) IX-B

recommencer

1. _____ Qch (to begin . . . again) I
2. _____ à ou de *Inf.* (to begin to . . . again) VIII-A, IX-A

récompenser

1. _____ Qn ou Qch (to reward . . .) I
2. _____ Qn de Qch (to reward . . . for . . .) VI

réconcilier

1. _____ Qn ou Qch (to reconcile, reconciliate . . .) I
2. se _____ avec, à Qn ou Qch (to make up with . . .; to reconcile oneself to . . .) V, III
3. _____ Qn ou Qch avec, à Qn ou Qch (to reconcile . . . with . . .) VI

reconnaître
1. _____ Qn ou Qch (to recognize . . .) I
2. se _____ (to recognize oneself; to know, make out where one is) I
3. se _____ *coupable* (to acknowledge one's guilt) I
4. _____ Qn à Qch (to recognize . . . by . . . Ex: *Je l'ai reconnue à sa voix*, I recognized her by her voice) VI
5. _____ Qch à Qn (to admit, recognize that someone possesses . . . Ex: *Il faut lui reconnaître du talent*, you must admit that he has talent) VI

recourir
1. _____ à Qn ou Qch (to have recourse to . . .) III

recouvrir
1. _____ Qn ou Qch (to cover . . . completely; to cover up . . .) I
2. se _____ de Qch (to cover oneself up with . . .; to mask oneself with . . .) IV
3. _____ Qn ou Qch de Qch (to cover up, mask . . . with . . .) VI

récrier (se)
1. se _____ de Qch (Lit: to cry out with, in . . . *e.g., d'admiration*, in admiration) IV
2. se _____ contre Qch (to cry out at . . .; to protest against . . .) V

récrire
1. _____ Qch (to rewrite . . .) I
2. _____ à Qn (to write to . . . again) II
3. _____ Qch à Qn (to write . . . to . . . again) VI

récriminer
1. _____ contre Qn ou Qch (to criticize . . . bitterly; to take recriminations against . . .) V

reculer
1. ———— devant Qn ou Qch (to shrink, retreat from . . .) V

redemander
1. ———— Qch (to ask for . . . again; to ask for more . . .; to ask for . . . back) I
2. ———— Qch à `Qn (to ask someone something again; to ask someone for something again; to ask someone to give something back; to ask someone for more . . .) VI

redevoir
1. ———— Qch (to owe a balance of . . .) I
2. ———— Qch à Qn (to owe a balance of . . . to . . .) VI

redire
1. ———— Qch (to tell . . . again) I
2. avoir, trouver [Qch] à redire à Qch (to find fault with . . .; to take exception to . . . Ex: *Je ne trouve rien à redire à sa façon d'agir*, I can find no fault with his actions) II
3. ———— Qch à Qn (to tell someone something again) VI

redoubler
1. ———— Qch (to redouble, increase . . .; to put a lining in . . .) I
2. ———— de Qch (to strengthen, increase . . . Ex: *redoubler de force, d'énergie*, to increase one's strength, one's zeal) IV

redouter
1. ———— Qn ou Qch (to dread . . .) I
2. ———— de *Inf.* (to dread ---*ing*) IX-A

réduire

1. ——— Qch (to reduce . . .) I
2. se ——— à Qch (to restrict oneself to . . .; to be reduced to . . .) III
3. se ——— en Qch (Of things: to turn into, be reduced to . . .) V
4. ——— Qch en Qch (to turn . . . into . . .; to reduce . . . to . . . Ex: *réduire une ville en ruines*, to reduce a city to ruins) VI
5. ——— Qn ou Qch à, en* Qch (to reduce, demote, drive . . . to . . . *e.g.*, *en esclavage*, to slavery; *au désespoir*, to despair) VI
6. ——— Qn à *Inf.* (to reduce, drive . . . to . . .) VIII-B

réexpédier

1. ——— Qch (to forward . . .; to return . . . to the sender) I
2. ——— Qch à Qn (to forward . . . to . . .) VI

référer

1. se ——— à Qn (to refer to . . . as an authority) III
2. se ——— à Qch (to refer to . . .) III
3. en ——— à Qn (to refer the matter to . . .) II
4. ——— Qch à Qch (to ascribe . . . to . . .) VI

refiler

1. ——— Qch à Qn (Coll: to palm off . . . on . . .) VI

réfléchir

1. ——— Qn ou Qch (to reflect . . .) I
2. ——— à, sur Qch (to meditate on . . .; to think about . . .) II, V

refouler

1. ——— Qn ou Qch (to repulse . . .; to drive, force, hold . . . back, Ex: *refouler l'ennemi*, to drive back the enemy; *refouler ses larmes*, to hold back one's tears) I

---

*See Appendix II: **DANS, EN, À**, p. 298.

refroidir
1. être refroidi par Qn ou Qch (to be turned off by . . .; to react negatively to . . .) V

réfugier (se)
1. se ⸻ à, dans, en* Qch (to take refuge in . . .) II, V
2. se ⸻ chez Qn (to take refuge with . . .) V

refuser
1. ⸻ Qn ou Qch (to refuse . . .) I
2. se ⸻ Qch (to deny oneself . . .) I
3. se ⸻ à Qch (to object to . . .; to refuse to accept . . .) III
4. ⸻ Qch à Qn (to deny . . . to . . . Ex: *refuser une permission à un soldat*, to deny a leave to a soldier) VI
5. se ⸻ à *Inf.* (to refuse to . . . [as a matter of principle]) VIII-A
6. ⸻ de *Inf.* (to refuse to . . .) IX-A

régaler
1. ⸻ Qn (to regale, entertain . . .) I
2. se ⸻ de Qch (to feast on . . .; to treat oneself to . . .) IV
3. ⸻ Qn de Qch (to treat . . . to . . .) VI

regarder
1. ⸻ Qn ou Qch (to look at . . .) I
2. ⸻ Qn (to concern . . . Ex: *cela ne vous regarde pas,* that's none of your business) I
3. ⸻ à Qch (to pay close attention to . . .; to consider . . . Ex: *regarder à ses dépenses*, to watch what one spends) II
4. se ⸻ comme Qch (to consider oneself . . .) V
5. ⸻ Qn ou Qch comme Qch (to consider . . . a . . .) VI
6. ⸻ *Inf.* Qn ou Qch (to watch someone or something . . . Ex: *regarder tomber la pluie*, to watch the rain fall) VII-B

See Appendix I: **PREPOSITIONS OF GEOGRAPHICAL LOCATION,** p. 289 and Appendix II: **DANS, EN, À,** p. 298.

regimber
1. _____ contre Qch (to balk, kick at, against . . .) V

régler
1. _____ Qch (to rule, regulate . . .; to settle, *e.g.*, a bill) I
2. se _____ sur Qn ou Qch (to go by . . .; to take . . . as an example) V
3. _____ Qch sur Qn ou Qch (to model . . . on . . .; to use someone or something as an example for . . .) VI
4. _____ *son compte* à Qn (Coll: to get even with . . .) VI

régner
1. _____ sur Qn ou Qch (to rule over . . .) V

regorger
1. _____ Qch (to regurgitate . . .) I
2. _____ de Qn ou Qch (to overflow with . . .; to be packed with . . .) IV

regretter
1. _____ Qn ou Qch (to regret, to miss . . .) I
2. _____ de *Inf.* ou *Inf. passé* (to be sorry to . . ., to have . . .) IX-A

réintégrer
1. _____ Qch (to regain possession of . . .) I
2. _____ Qn dans Qch (to reinstate . . . in . . .; to restore . . . to . . .) VI

rejaillir
1. _____ sur Qn ou Qch (to splash, splatter on . . .; to reflect on . . . Ex: *Son succès rejaillit sur sa famille*, her success was reflected on her family) V

rejeter
1. _____ Qn ou Qch (to reject . . .; to throw . . . back) I
2. _____ Qch sur Qn ou Qch (to cast . . . on . . .; to transfer . . . to . . . Ex: *rejeter la faute sur d'autres*, to cast the blame on others) VI

réjouir
1. _____ Qn ou Qch (to delight . . .; to cheer up . . .) I
2. se _____ à Qch (to be delighted at . . .) III
3. se _____ de Qch (to be delighted by . . .) IV
4. _____ Qn de Qch (to delight, cheer up . . . with . . .) VI
5. se _____ à *Inf.* (to be delighted to . . .) VIII-A
6. se _____ de *Inf.* (to be glad, thankful to . . .) IX-A

relater
1. _____ Qch (to relate, state . . .) I
2. _____ Qch à Qn (to relate, state . . . to . . .) VI

reléguer
1. _____ Qn ou Qch à Qch (to relegate . . . to . . .) VI

relever
1. _____ Qn ou Qch (to raise, pick up, heighten . . .) I
2. se _____ de Qch (to get over . . .; to recover from . . .) IV
3. _____ de Qch (to stem from . . .; to depend on . . .) IV
4. _____ Qn de Qch (to release . . . from . . . Ex: *relever un religieux de ses voeux*, to release a monk from his vows) VI
5. _____ Qch de Qch (to heighten, emphasize . . . with . . . Ex: *relever une étude sérieuse d'anecdotes amusantes*, to spark a serious study with amusing anecdotes) VI

relier
1. _____ Qn ou Qch (to bind, tie, connect . . .) I
2. _____ Qn ou Qch à, avec Qn ou Qch (to link, connect . . . with . . . Ex: *relier une oeuvre à la tradition*, to link a work with tradition) VI
3. _____ Qch en Qch (to bind . . . in . . . Ex: *relier un livre en cuir*, to bind a book in leather) VI

remarquer
1. _____ Qn ou Qch (to notice . . .) I
2. se faire remarquer (to draw attention to oneself) I
3. faire remarquer Qn ou Qch à Qn (to point out . . . to . . .)
VI

rembourser
1. _____ Qn ou Qch (to reimburse . . .) I
2. _____ Qch à Qn (to pay back . . . to . . .) VI
3. _____ Qn de Qch (to reimburse . . . for . . .) VI

remédier
1. _____ à Qch (to remedy, cure . . .) II

remercier
1. _____ Qn (to thank . . .) I
2. _____ Qn de, pour Qch (to thank . . . for . . . *e.g., de sa bonté*, for his kindness. *Pour* is often used for concrete objects, Ex: *remercier quelqu'un pour un cadeau*, to thank someone for a present) VI
3. _____ Qn de *Inf.* ou *Inf. passé* (to thank . . . for ---*ing*, for having . . .) IX-B

remettre
1. _____ Qn ou Qch (to put, set . . . back; to put on . . . again; to put off . . .) I
2. se _____ à Qch (to begin . . . again) III
3. s'en _____ à Qn [de Qch] (to rely on . . . [for . . .]) III
4. se _____ de Qch (to recover from . . .) IV
5. _____ Qch à Qn (to deliver, hand over . . . to . . .) VI
6. _____ Qch à Qch (to postpone . . . until . . . Ex: *remettre la conférence au lendemain*, to postpone the lecture until the next day) VI
7. se _____ à *Inf.* (to begin to . . . again) VIII-A

remonter

1. ———— Qn ou Qch (to take . . . upstairs again) I
2. ———— à Qch (to date back to . . .; to go back to . . . *e.g.*, *à la source*, to the source) II

remontrer

1. ———— Qch (to show . . . again) I
2. en ———— à Qn (to outdo . . .; to be superior to . . .) II

remplacer

1. ———— Qn ou Qch (to replace . . .; to substitute for . . .) I
2. ———— Qn ou Qch par Qn ou Qch (to replace . . . with, by . . .) VI

remplir

1. ———— Qch (to fill, fill up, in, out . . .) I
2. se ———— de Qch (to be filled with . . .) IV
3. ———— Qn ou Qch de Qch (to fill . . . with . .) VI

rémunérer

1. ———— Qn ou Qch (to remunerate . . .) I
2. ———— Qn de Qch (to remunerate . . . for . . .) VI

renâcler

1. ———— à, sur Qch (Coll: to sniff, snort at . . .; to disdain . . .) II, V

renaître

1. ———— à Qch (to be reborn to . . .; to feel . . . anew) II

renchérir

1. ———— Qch (to increase something's value) I
2. ———— sur Qn ou Qch (to outdo, outbid . . .; to improve on . . .) V

rencogner

1. ———— Qn (to drive . . . into a corner) I
2. se ———— dans Qch (to retreat into . . .; to ensconce oneself in . . . *e.g.*, *dans un fauteuil*, in an armchair) V

rendre
1. _____ Qn ou Qch (to return, give back . . .) I
2. _____ Qn ou Qch [+ adjectif] (to make . . . Ex: *rendre quelqu'un malade*, to make someone sick) I
3. se _____ *compte* de Qch (to realize . . .) IV
4. se _____ à Qn ou Qch (to yield, surrender to . . .) III
5. se _____ à Qch (to go to, report to . . .) III
6. _____ Qch à Qn (to return . . . to . . .) VI
7. _____ Qn ou Qch à Qch (to restore . . . to . . . *e.g., à la santé*, to health) VI

renfermer
1. _____ Qn ou Qch (to close up . . . again; to enclose . . .) I
2. se _____ dans Qch (to confine oneself to . . .; to withdraw into . . .) V
3. _____ Qn ou Qch dans Qch (to shut up . . . in . . .; to enclose . . . in . . .) VI

renfoncer
1. _____ Qch (to drive, knock . . . in further; to pull, push . . . down) I
2. se _____ dans Qch (to sink, settle into . . . *e.g., dans un coussin*, into a cushion) V

renoncer
1. _____ Qch (to renounce . . . *e.g.*, one's country) I
2. _____ à Qch (to renounce, waive, give up . . . Ex: *renoncer à ses droits*, to waive one's rights) II
3. _____ à *Inf.* (to forego, give up ---*ing*; to stop trying to . . .) VIII-A

renouer
1. _____ Qch (to tie up . . . again; to resume, renew . . .) I
2. _____ avec Qn ou Qch (to resume ties, relations with . . .) V

renseigner

1. ———— Qn (to inform . . .) I
2. se ———— sur Qn ou Qch (to find out about . . .) V
3. ———— Qn sur Qn ou Qch (to inform . . . about . . .) VI

rentrer

1. ———— Qch (to bring, take . . . in) I
2. ———— dans Qch (to fit into . . .) V
3. ———— *Inf.* (to come home, return in order to . . .) VII-A

renverser

1. ———— Qn ou Qch (to overthrow, overturn . . .; to lean
   . . . back) I
2. se ———— sur Qch (to fall back, lean back on . . .) V

renvoyer

1. ———— Qn ou Qch (to return . . .; to send . . . back; to
   fire [an employee]) I
2. ———— Qn ou Qch à Qn ou Qch (to send . . . back to . . .;
   to refer . . . to . . . Ex: *La note renvoie le lec-
   teur à l'appendice*, the note refers the reader to
   the appendix) VI

repaître

1. se ———— de Qch (Of animals: to eat one's fill of . . .; Lit:
   to feast on, fill oneself with . . . Ex: *se repaître
   de sang*, to feed on, revel in blood; *se repaître
   d'illusions*, to fill oneself with illusions) IV

répandre

1. ———— Qch (to pour out, shed, spread . . .) I
2. se ———— (to flow, spread out) I
3. se ———— en Qch (to overflow with . . .; to spew . . . Ex:
   se répandre en invectives, to hurl abuse; to be
   lavish with . . . Ex: *se répandre en éloges*, to
   give lavish praise) V

repartir
1. _____ de Qch (to depart from . . . again) IV
2. _____ pour Qch (to set off for . . . again) V

répartir
1. _____ Qch (to distribute, share . . .) I
2. _____ Qch en Qch (to separate, divide . . . into . . .) VI
3. _____ Qch entre Qn ou Qch (to distribute . . . among . . .) VI

repentir (se)
1. se _____ de Qch (to be sorry for, repent for . . .) IV
2. se _____ de *Inf. passé* (to repent for having . . .) IX-A

répéter
1. _____ Qch (to repeat . . .) I
2. se _____ (to repeat oneself; to reoccur) I
3. se _____ Qch (to repeat something to oneself) I
4. _____ Qch à Qn (to repeat . . . to . . .) VI

replier
1. _____ Qch (to fold up . . .) I
2. se _____ sur Qn ou Qch (to fold up into . . . Ex: *un couteau qui se replie sur le manche*, a knife that folds into the handle; to retreat to . . .; to withdraw into . . . Ex: *se replier sur soi-même*, to withdraw into oneself) V

répliquer
1. _____ à Qch (to respond to, answer . . .) II
2. _____ Qch à Qn (to retort . . . to . . . Usually used in questions, Ex: *Que pouvait-il répliquer à cet homme?* what could he answer that man) VI

replonger
1. _____ Qn ou Qch (to plunge, immerse . . . again) I
2. se _____ dans Qch (to immerse oneself in . . . again) V
3. _____ Qn ou Qch dans Qch (to plunge, immerse . . . in . . . again) VI

répondre

1. _____ Qch (to answer . . . *e.g.*, *la vérité*, the truth. Usually used in questions, Ex: *Qu'a-t-il répondu?* what did he answer?) I

2. _____ à Qn ou Qch (to answer . . . *e.g.*, *à une question*, a question; *au professeur*, the teacher) II

3. _____ à Qch (to correspond to . . ., to fit . . . Ex: *Le suspect ne répond pas au signalement*, the suspect does not fit the description) II

4. _____ de Qn ou Qch (to answer for . . .; to be responsible for . . .) IV

5. _____ par Qch (to answer by, in . . . *e.g.*, *par écrit*, in writing; *par télégramme*, by a telegram) V

6. _____ pour Qn (to answer for, in the place of . . .) V

7. _____ Qch à Qn (to answer . . . to . . .) VI

reporter

1. _____ Qch (to carry, take . . . back) I

2. se _____ à Qch (to refer to . . . Ex: *Reportons-nous au texte*, let us refer to the text) III

3. se _____ sur Qn ou Qch (to be given, transferred to [an undeserving object], Ex: *Tout son amour se reportait sur son chien*, he lavished all his love on his dog) V

4. _____ Qch à Qn ou Qch (to carry, take . . . back to . . .; to postpone . . . until . . .) VI

5. _____ Qch sur Qn ou Qch (to give, transfer . . . to . . .) VI

reposer

1. _____ Qch (to rest . . .) I

2. se _____ (to rest) I

3. se _____ Qch (to rest one's . . . Ex: *se reposer les pieds*, to rest one's feet) I

4. se _____ de Qch (to rest from . . .) IV

5. _____ sur Qch (to rest on, be based on . . .) V

6. se _____ sur Qn ou Qch [de Qch] (to rely on . . . [for . . .]) V

7. _____ Qch sur Qch (to lean, rest . . . against . . .; to base . . . on . . .) VI
8. se ____ de *Inf.* (to rest from ---*ing*) IX-A

reprendre

1. _____ Qch (to retake, recapture, resume . . .; to take . . . back) I
2. _____ Qn (to criticize . . .) I
3. se ____ (to recover one's wits; to correct oneself) I
4. se ____ à Qch (to take new interest in . . .; to take up . . . again) III
5. _____ de Qch (to help oneself to more . . .) IV
6. se ____ à *Inf.* (to begin to . . . again) VIII-A

représenter

1. _____ Qn ou Qch (to represent, depict . . .) I
2. se ____ Qch (to imagine . . .) I
3. _____ Qn ou Qch comme Qch (to describe, depict . . . as . . .) VI

reprocher

1. se ____ Qch (to blame oneself for . . .) I
2. _____ Qch à Qn ou Qch (to find something wrong with . . .; to begrudge someone something; to criticize someone or something for something, Ex: *On lui a reproché sa candeur*, his, her frankness was criticized) VI
3. se ____ de *Inf.* ou *Inf. passé* (to blame oneself for ---*ing*, for having . . .) IX-A
4. _____ à Qn de *Inf.* ou *Inf. passé* (to criticize, blame . . . for ---*ing*, for having . . .) IX-B

répugner

1. _____ Qn (to repulse, revolt . . .) I
2. _____ à Qn (to be repugnant, revolting to . . .) II
3. _____ à Qch (to be revolted by . . .; to find . . . distasteful) II
4. _____ à *Inf.* (to be loath to . . .) VIII-A
5. *Il répugne à Qn de Inf.* (to be loath to . . . Ex: *Il me répugne de faire cela*, I am loath to do that) IX-B

réputer
1. être réputé [pour] Qch (to be known as, considered to be
   . . . *e.g.*, *le meilleur*, the best) V, I
2. être réputé *Inf.* ou *Inf. passé* (to be considered, reputed to
   . . ., to have . . .) VII-A

réserver
1. _____ Qch (to reserve . . .) I
2. se _____ pour Qn ou Qch (to wait for, save oneself for
   . . .) V
3. être réservé sur Qch (to be discreet about . . .) V
4. _____ Qn ou Qch à, pour Qn (to reserve . . . for . . .; to
   hold . . . in store for . . . Ex: *La nuit réservait
   des dangers aux voyageurs*, the night held dangers in store for the travelers) VI
5. se _____ [le droit] de *Inf.* (to reserve the right to . . .) IX-A

résider
1. _____ à, dans, en* [un endroit] (to reside in . . . *e.g.*, *à
   Paris*, in Paris; *en France*, in France) II, V
2. _____ dans, en** Qch (Figurative: to lie, reside in . . .
   Ex: *La difficulté réside en ceci*, the problem
   lies in this; *le danger réside dans l'extrême hau-
   teur*, the danger lies in the extreme height) V

résigner
1. _____ Qch (to give up . . .) I
2. se _____ à Qn ou Qch (to resign oneself to, submit to . . .)
   III
3. se _____ à *Inf.* (to resign oneself to ---*ing*) VIII-A

résister
1. _____ à Qn ou Qch (to resist, withstand . . .) II

*See Appendix I: **PREPOSITIONS OF GEOGRAPHICAL LOCA-
TION**, p. 289.

See Appendix II: **DANS, EN, À, p. 298.

résoudre
1. _____ Qch (to solve, resolve . . .) I
2. se _____ en Qch (to dissolve, turn into . . .) V
3. être résolu en Qch (Of things: to be dissolved, turned into . . .) V
4. _____ Qch en Qch (to dissolve, reduce, transform . . . into . . . Ex: *résoudre la vapeur en eau*, to turn steam into water) VI
5. se _____ à *Inf.* (to make up one's mind to . . .) VIII-A
6. être résolu à, de *Inf.* (to be resolved to . . .) VIII-A, IX-A
7. _____ Qn à *Inf.* (to persuade . . . to . . .) VIII-B
8. _____ de *Inf.* (to resolve to . . .) IX-A

resplendir
1. _____ de Qch (to glow, shine with . . . *e.g., de santé,* with health) IV

ressembler
1. _____ à Qn ou Qch (to resemble . . .) II

ressentir
1. _____ Qch (to feel . . . *e.g., du chagrin,* sorrow) I
2. se _____ de Qch (to feel . . . deeply; to feel the effect of . . .) IV

ressortir
1. _____ Qch (to bring out . . . again) I
2. faire ressortir Qch (to emphasize, bring out . . . Ex: *Cette robe fait ressortir la couleur de ses yeux*, that dress brings out the color of her eyes) I
3. _____ à Qn ou Qch (to come under the jurisdiction of . . .; to be derived from . . .) II
4. _____ de Qch (to be the result of . . .; to result from . . .) IV

ressouvenir
1. se _____ de Qn ou Qch (to have a faint memory of . . .) IV
2. faire ressouvenir Qn de Qn ou Qch (to remind . . . of . . .) VI
3. se _____ de *Inf. passé* (to remember having . . .) IX-A

rester
1. *Il reste Qch ou Qn* (to be left, remain, Ex: *Il reste une bouteille*, there is one bottle left) I
2. en _____ à Qch (to remain at . . .; to go no further than . . . Ex: *Nous en sommes restés aux préliminaires*, we didn't get past the preliminaries) II
3. _____ de Qn ou Qch (to remain, be left of . . . Ex: *C'est tout ce qui reste de sa fortune*, that's all that's left of his, her fortune) IV
4. *Il reste Qch à Qn ou Qch* (to have . . . left, Ex: *Il ne lui reste que cinq dollars*, he, she only has five dollars left) VI
5. _____ (à, pour) *Inf.* (to stay, remain to, in order to . . . Ex: *Il reste à dîner avec nous*, he is staying to have dinner with us. Omission of preposition is more colloquial) VIII-A, X, VII-A
6. _____ à *Inf.* (to remain, keep on ---*ing*, to continue to . . . Ex: *Après son repas, il restait à fumer en regardant passer les gens*, after his meal, he sat smoking as he watched the people go by) VIII-A
7. _____ à *Inf.* (to be left, to remain to . . . Ex: *La vaisselle reste à faire*, the dishes still have to be done) VIII-A
8. *Il reste à Qn à Inf.* (to still have to . . . . Ex: *Il me reste à finir mon travail*, I still have to finish my work) VIII-B
9. *Il reste Qch à Inf.* (there are still, there remain . . . to . . . Ex: *Il reste deux villages à traverser*, there are still two villages to pass through) VIII-B
10. *Il reste à Qn Qch à Inf.* (to still have . . . to . . . Ex: *Il nous reste deux devoirs à faire*, we still have two assignments to do) VIII-B

restituer

1. _____ Qch (to restore, return, make restitution of . . .) I
2. _____ Qch à Qn (to return, make restitution of . . . to . . .) VI

restreindre

1. _____ Qn ou Qch (to restrain, limit . . .) I
2. se _____ à Qch (Of things: to be limited to . . .) III
3. _____ Qch à Qch (to limit . . . to . . .) VI

résulter

[Only in Third Person]

1. _____ de Qch (to result from . . .) IV

résumer

1. _____ Qch (to summarize, sum up . . .) I
2. se _____ à Qch (Coll: to boil down to . . .) III

retarder

1. _____ Qn ou Qch (to delay . . .) I
2. _____ de [un certain temps] (Of clocks: to be . . . slow, Ex: *Ma montre retarde de cinq minutes*, my watch is five minutes slow) IV

retenir

1. _____ Qn ou Qch (to keep, hold . . .; to keep, hold . . . back, in, up, Ex: *retenir ses larmes*, to hold back one's tears; to reserve . . . *e.g.*, a table; to remember . . . *e.g.*, a number) I
2. se _____ à Qch (to catch hold of . . .) III
3. _____ Qch sur, de Qch (to retain, withhold . . . from . . . Ex: *On a retenu dix dollars sur ses gages*, ten dollars were withheld from his wages) VI
4. _____ Qn à, pour *Inf.* (to keep, detain . . . to . . . Ex: *Nous avons retenu le professeur à dîner*, we asked the professor to stay for dinner) VIII-B, X
5. se _____ de *Inf.* (to refrain from, keep oneself from ---*ing*) IX-A
6. _____ Qn ou Qch de *Inf.* (to prevent, keep . . . from ---*ing*) IX-B

retentir

1. _____ de Qch (to ring out, peal with . . . Ex: *La maison retentit de leurs rires*, the house rang out with their laughter) IV

retirer

1. _____ Qch (to withdraw . . .; to take . . . off, out) I
2. se _____ de Qch (to leave . . .; to withdraw from . . .) IV
3. _____ Qch à Qn (to take . . . away from . . .; to take . . . back from . . .) VI
4. _____ Qn ou Qch de Qch (to take . . . out of, away from . . . Ex: *retirer un lapin d'un chapeau*, to take a rabbit out of a hat; *retirer un enfant de l'école*, to take a child out of school; *retirer de l'argent de la banque*, to withdraw money from the bank) VI

retomber

1. _____ dans Qch (to relapse into . . . *e.g., de mauvaises habitudes*, bad habits; to sink back into . . . *e.g., dans l'oubli*, into oblivion) V
2. _____ sur Qch (to fall back, down onto . . .) V
3. _____ sur Qn ou Qch (to fall to, be the responsibility of . . . Ex: *Le blâme retombera sur lui*, the blame will fall on him) V

retourner

1. _____ Qch (to turn . . . over, inside out; to return . . . *e.g.*, a gift) I
2. se _____ (to turn around, over) I
3. _____ à Qch (to return to . . .; to revert to . . .) II
4. se _____ contre Qn ou Qch (to turn against . . .) V
5. _____ Qch à Qn (to return, counter someone's . . . Ex: *retourner sa critique à quelqu'un*, to counter someone's criticism) VI
6. _____ Qch à Qn ou Qch (to return . . . to . . . Ex: *retourner un cadeau au magasin*, to take a gift back to the store) VI
7. _____ Qch contre Qn ou Qch (to turn . . . against . . .) VI
8. _____ Inf. (to return, to go back in order to . . .) VII-A

retrancher

1. _____ Qch (to cut . . . out; to expurgate, eliminate . . .) I
2. se _____ derrière Qn ou Qch (to take refuge behind . . .) V
3. se _____ dans Qch (to entrench oneself in . . . Ex: *Il s'est retranché dans cette attitude hostile*, he stubbornly maintained that hostile attitude) V
4. _____ Qch de Qch (to expurgate . . . from . . .; to cut . . . out, off from . . . Ex: *Le maire a retranché quelques remarques de son discours*, the mayor cut out several remarks from his speech) VI
5. _____ Qch sur Qch (to deduct . . . from . . .; to withhold . . . from . . .) VI

retremper

1. _____ Qn ou Qch (to dip, wet . . . again) I
2. se _____ à Qch (to draw renewed vigor from . . .) III
3. se _____ dans Qch (to immerse oneself in . . . again) V
4. _____ Qn ou Qch dans Qch (to dip, immerse . . . in . . . again) VI

réunir

1. _____ Qn ou Qch (to convene . . .; to join, unite, re-unite . . .) I
2. se _____ (to meet, Ex: *se réunir une fois par mois*, to meet once a month) I
3. se _____ contre Qn ou Qch (to join together against . . .) V
4. se _____ avec Qn (to gather, meet with . . .) V
5. se _____ en Qch (to join together, unite in . . .) V
6. _____ Qch à Qch (to attach, join . . . to, with . . .) VI
7. se _____ pour *Inf.* to gather, join together to . . .) X

réussir

1. _____ Qch (to complete . . . successfully, Ex: *J'ai réussi mon expérience*, my experiment was a success) I
2. _____ à Qch (to succeed at . . . Ex: *réussir à un examen*, to pass a test) II
3. _____ à Qn (to turn out well for . . . Ex: *Tout lui réussit*, everything turns out well for him, her) II

4. _____ dans Qch (to be successful in . . . *e.g., dans son travail,* in one's work) V

5. _____ à *Inf.* (to succeed in *---ing*; to manage to . . .) VIII-A

revaloir

1. _____ Qch à Qn (to pay someone back in kind for something, Ex: *Je vous revaudrai ces paroles-là,* I'll get even with you for those words!) VI

réveiller

1. _____ Qn ou Qch (to awaken . . .) I

2. se _____ de Qch (to awaken from . . . *e.g., d'un rêve,* from a dream) IV

3. _____ Qn de Qch (to awaken . . . from . . .) VI

révéler

1. _____ Qch (to reveal . . .) I

2. _____ Qch à Qn (to reveal . . . to . . .) VI

revenir

1. _____ à Qch (to come back to . . .; to amount to . . . Ex: *Le repas revient à six dollars,* the meal comes to six dollars; *cela revient au même,* that amounts to the same thing) II

2. en _____ à Qch (to revert to, go back to . . . Ex: *Il en revient toujours à ses manières-là,* he always reverts to that way of behavior) II

3. _____ à Qn (to return, come back to . . .) II

4. _____ de Qch (to come back from . . . *e.g., de Paris,* from Paris; to get over, recover from . . . Ex: *revenir de sa peur,* to get over one's fright; to be disabused of . . . *e.g., de ses illusions,* of one's illusions) IV

5. _____ sur Qch (to retrace . . . Ex: *revenir sur ses pas,* to retrace one's steps; to go back on . . . *e.g., sur sa parole,* on one's word; to harp on . . . Ex: *revenir sur le même sujet,* to harp on the same subject) V

6. _____ *Inf.* (to come back in order to . . .) VII-A

rêver
1. _____ Qch (to dream . . .) I
2. _____ à Qn ou Qch (to muse about, daydream about . . .) III
3. _____ de Qn ou Qch (to dream about . . .) IV
4. _____ de *Inf.* (to dream of ---*ing*) IX-A

revêtir
1. _____ Qn ou Qch (to clothe, cover . . .; to put on . . .) I
2. se _____ de Qch (to put on . . .; to clothe oneself in . . .) IV
3. _____ Qn ou Qch de Qch (to clothe . . . in . . .; to cover . . . with . . .) VI

révolter
1. _____ Qn ou Qch (to revolt, disgust . . .) I
2. se _____ contre Qn ou Qch (to rebel, revolt against . . .) V

rigoler
1. _____ de Qn ou Qch (Coll: to joke, kid about . . .) IV

rimer
1. _____ Qch (to versify . . .; to set . . . to verse) I
2. _____ à Qch (to jibe, be in accord with . . . Ex: *Cela ne rime à rien*, that doesn't make any sense) II
3. _____ avec Qch (to rhyme with . . .) V

riposter
1. _____ Qch (to retort . . .) I
2. _____ à Qn ou Qch (to give a sharp answer to . . .) II
3. _____ Qch à Qn (to retort . . . to . . .) VI

rire
1. _____ à Qn ou Qch (Lit: to greet . . . with a smile; to smile on . . .) II
2. _____ de Qn ou Qch (to laugh at . . .) IV

risquer
1. _____ Qch (to risk . . .) I
2. se _____ à Qch (to take a chance at . . . *e.g., au jeu*, at gambling) III
3. se _____ dans Qch (to venture in, into . . .) V
4. se _____ à *Inf.* (to venture to, dare to . . .) VIII-A
5. _____ de *Inf.* (to have a chance of ---*ing*, Ex: *Il risque de tomber*, he might fall; *La situation risque de devenir grave*, the situation may well become serious) IX-A

rivaliser
1. _____ avec Qn ou Qch (to rival . . .) V
2. _____ avec Qn ou Qch de Qch (to rival . . . in . . . *e.g., d'élégance*, in elegance) V

rogner
1. _____ Qch (to clip, pare . . .) I
2. se _____ Qch (to clip, pare one's . . . *e.g., les ongles*, one's nails) I
3. _____ *les ailes* à Qn (to clip someone's wings) VI

rompre
1. _____ Qch (to break, break off . . .) I
2. se _____ à Qch (to get used to, broken in to . . .) III
3. être rompu à Qch (to be used to, broken in to . . .) II
4. être rompu de Qch (to be worn out with . . . *e.g., de fatigue*, with fatigue) IV
5. _____ avec Qn ou Qch (to break off with, break up with . . .) V
6. _____ *la tête, les oreilles* à Qn (Coll: to make a deafening noise, to talk someone's ears off) II
7. _____ Qn à Qch (to break in . . . to . . . Ex: *rompre un ouvrier au travail*, to break in a worker to a job) VI

ronger
1. _____ Qch (to gnaw . . .) I
2. se _____ de Qch (to torment oneself with . . . *e.g.*, *de ja-lousie*, with jealousy) IV
3. être rongé de Qch (to be consumed, eaten away with . . . *e.g.*, *de regret*, with regret; to be riddled with . . . *e.g.*, *de trous*, with holes) IV
4. être rongé par Qn ou Qch (to be gnawed, eaten away by . . . *e.g.*, *par les rats*, by rats) V

rougir
1. _____ Qch (to redden . . .) I
2. _____ de Qch (to flush, blush with . . . *e.g.*, *de honte*, with shame; to be embarrassed by . . ., to be ashamed of . . . *e.g.*, *de ses vêtements râpés*, of one's shabby clothing) IV

rouler
1. _____ Qn (Coll: to swindle, trick . . .) I
2. _____ Qch (to roll, turn over . . .) I
3. _____ sur Qch (to roll along . . .; to run to . . . Ex: *La conversation roulait sur la politique*, the conversation turned to politics; *rouler sur l'or*, to be rolling in money) V
4. se _____ dans, en* Qch (to roll up in, into . . . *e.g.*, *dans une couverture*, in a blanket; *en boule*, into a ball) V
5. _____ Qn ou Qch dans, en* Qch (to roll . . . in, into . . .) VI

ruer
1. se _____ à, vers Qn ou Qch (to rush to, towards . . .) III, V
2. se _____ sur Qn ou Qch (to hurl, fling oneself at, on . . .; to rush at . . .) V

*See Appendix II: **DANS, EN, À,** p. 298.

ruisseler
1. ———— de Qch (to stream with . . . *e.g.*, *de sueur*, with perspiration) IV

ruminer
1. ———— Qch (to ruminate on . . .) I

ruser
1. ———— avec Qn (to be wily, crafty with . . .) V

S

sacrifier
1. ———— Qn ou Qch (to sacrifice . . .) I
2. ———— à Qch (to conform to . . ., *e.g.*, *à la mode*, to fashion) II
3. se ———— à Qn ou Qch (to sacrifice oneself to . . .) III
4. se ———— pour Qn ou Qch (to sacrifice oneself for . . .) V
5. ———— Qn ou Qch à Qn ou Qch (to sacrifice . . . to . . .) VI

saigner
1. ———— Qn (to bleed . . .) I
2. ———— de Qch (to bleed from . . . Ex: *Il saigne du nez*, his nose is bleeding) IV
3. se ———— [*aux quatre veines*] pour Qn ou Qch (to bleed oneself [dry] for . . .) V

saisir
1. ———— Qn ou Qch (to seize . . .) I
2. se ———— de Qn ou Qch (to seize upon, grab hold of . . .) IV
3. ———— Qn ou Qch à Qch (to grab . . . by . . . *e.g.*, *au bras*, by the arm; *au collet*, by the collar) VI

sanctionner
1. _____ Qch (to sanction . . .) I
2. être sanctionné par Qch (to be sanctioned by . . .) V

satisfaire
1. _____ Qn ou Qch (to satisfy, content . . .) I
2. _____ à Qch (to carry out . . ., *e.g.,* one's duties; to meet
   . . . *e.g.,* demands) II
3. être satisfait de Qn ou Qch (to be satisfied with . . .) IV
4. être satisfait de *Inf.* ou *Inf. passé* (to be glad, satisfied to
   . . ., to have . . .) IX-A

saturer
1. _____ Qn ou Qch (to saturate . . .) I
2. se _____ de Qch (to become saturated with . . .) IV
3. _____ Qn ou Qch de Qch (to saturate . . . with . . .) VI

saupoudrer
1. _____ Qn ou Qch (to sprinkle . . .) I
2. _____ Qn ou Qch de Qch (to sprinkle . . . with . . .
   Usually culinary, Ex: *saupoudrer un bifteck de
   sel et de poivre*, to sprinkle a steak with salt and
   pepper) VI

sauter
1. _____ Qch (to skip . . .) I
2. faire sauter Qch (to fry . . .; to blow up, explode . . .) I
3. _____ à Qn ou Qch (to jump, leap at . . .; to skip to
   . . .) II
4. _____ de Qch (to jump with, for . . . *e.g., de joie,* for
   joy) IV
5. _____ sur, par, dans Qn ou Qch (to jump on, through,
   in . . .) V

sauver

1. _____ Qn ou Qch (to save . . .) I
2. se _____ (to run away, to get away) I
3. se _____ de Qn ou Qch (to make one's escape from . . .; to run away from . . .) IV
4. _____ Qn ou Qch de Qn ou Qch (to save . . . from . . .) VI
5. _____ Qch pour Qn ou Qch (to save . . . for . . .) VI
6. _____ Qn de *Inf.* (to save . . . from ---*ing*) IX-B

savoir

1. _____ Qch (to know . . .) I
2. faire savoir Qch à Qn (to inform someone of something, Ex: *Il ne m'a pas fait savoir ses projets*, he hasn't informed me of his plans) VI
3. _____ *Inf.* (to know how to . . .) VII-A

scandaliser

1. _____ Qn (to scandalize . . .) I
2. se _____ de Qch (to become shocked at, by . . .) IV
3. être scandalisé de Qch (to be shocked at . . .) IV
4. être scandalisé par Qch (to be shocked by . . .) V

sceller

1. _____ Qch (to seal . . .) I
2. _____ Qch de Qch (to seal . . . with . . .) VI

sculpter

1. _____ Qch (to sculpt, carve . . .) I
2. _____ Qch dans Qch (to carve . . . in, out of . . .) VI

seconder

1. _____ Qn ou Qch (to second . . .; to assist . . .) I
2. être secondé par Qn (to be seconded by . . .) V

sembler
1. _____ [+ adjectif] à Qn (to seem . . . to . . . Ex: *Cela lui semble normal*, that seems normal to him, her) II
2. *Il semble à Qn que* (it seems to . . . that . . . Ex: *Il me semble qu'elle a raison*, it seems to me that she's right) II
3. _____ *Inf.* ou *Inf. passé* (to seem to . . ., to have . . .) VII-A

semer
1. _____ Qch (to sow . . .) I
2. _____ Qch de Qch (to sow . . . with . . .) VI

sentir
1. _____ Qn ou Qch (to feel, smell . . .) I
2. _____ Qch (to smell of . . . Ex: *sentir la pipe*, to smell of pipe smoke; to taste of . . .) I
3. se _____ *Inf.* (to feel oneself ---*ing*, Ex: *se sentir glisser*, to feel oneself slipping) VII-A
4. _____ *Inf.* Qn ou Qch (to feel someone or something . . . Ex: *J'ai senti s'arrêter la voiture*, I felt the car stop) VII-B

seoir
[Only in third person]
1. _____ à Qn (to suit, become . . . Ex: *Cette robe lui sied*, that dress becomes her) II
2. *Il sied à Qn de Inf.* (it is fitting for . . . to . . .) IX-B

séparer
1. _____ Qn ou Qch (to separate . . .) I
2. se _____ de, d'avec Qn ou Qch (to leave, separate from . . . *e.g.*, *de son mari*, from one's husband) IV, V
3. être séparé de, d'avec Qn (to be separated from . . .) IV, V
4. _____ Qn ou Qch de, d'avec Qn ou Qch (to separate . . . from . . .) VI

seriner
1. _____ Qch (to grind out . . . *e.g.,* a melody) I
2. _____ Qch à Qn (to drum . . . into . . .) VI

servir
1. _____ Qn ou Qch (to serve . . .) I
2. se _____ (to help oneself) I
3. _____ à Qch (to be useful for . . .) II
4. _____ à Qn [pour Qch ou *Inf.*] (to be useful to . . . [for . . ., for --*ing*]) II
5. _____ de Qn ou Qch [à Qn] (to serve, act as . . . [for . . .]) IV
6. se _____ de Qn ou Qch (to use, make use of . . .) IV
7. _____ à *Inf.* (to be used for ---*ing*, to . . . Ex: *Un couteau sert à couper*, a knife is used for cutting, to cut) VIII-A
8. *À quoi* [*ça*] *sert de Inf.* ou *Inf. passé* (What is the use of ---*ing*, of having . . .; what good does it do to, to have . . . Ex: *À quoi sert d'attendre?* What is the use of waiting? Use of *ça* is colloquial) IX-A

sévir
1. _____ contre Qn ou Qch (to deal severely with . . .; to punish . . .) V

sevrer
1. _____ Qn (to wean . . .) I
2. se _____ de Qch (to wean, deprive oneself of . . .) IV
3. _____ Qn de Qch (to wean, deprive . . . of . . .) VI

siéger
1. _____ à Qch (to sit in, on . . . *e.g.*, *au Congrès*, in Congress; *à la Cour suprême*, on the Supreme Court) II

signaler
1. _____ Qn ou Qch (to point out . . .; to signal . . .) I
2. se _____ par Qch (to distinguish oneself, be distinguished by . . .) V
3. _____ Qn oh Qch à Qn ou Qch (to point . . . out to . . .; to draw . . . [*e.g.*, someone's attention] to . . .) VI

signifier
1. ———— Qch (to signify . . .) I
2. ———— Qch à Qn (to indicate . . . to . . .; to inform someone of something) VI

sillonner
1. ———— Qch (to furrow . . .) I
2. ———— Qch de Qch (to furrow . . . with . . .) VI

soigner
1. ———— Qn ou Qch (to take care of . . .; to look after
. . .; to polish, be careful of . . . *e.g.*, one's
style) I

solidariser
1. se ——— avec Qn ou Qch (to join together with . . .; to
support . . .) V

solliciter
1. ———— Qn ou Qch (to solicit, apply for . . .; Lit: to attract, invite . . . *e.g.*, attention) I
2. être sollicité par Qn pour Qch (to be solicited by . . . for
. . . *e.g.*, a contribution) V
3. ———— Qn pour Qch (to ask . . . for . . .) VI
4. ———— Qn de *Inf.* (to ask, urge . . . to . . .) IX-B

sombrer
1. ———— sous, dans Qch (to sink under, into . . .) V
2. ———— dans Qch (Figurative: to sink into . . . *e.g.*, *dans
la folie*, into madness) V

sommer
1. ———— Qn (to summon . . .) I
2. ———— Qn de, à *Inf.* (to call on . . . to . . .; to summon
. . . to . . .) IX-B, VIII-B

songer
1. ———— à Qn ou Qch (to think, muse about . . .) III
2. ———— à *Inf.* (to think of, about ---*ing*) VIII-A

sonner
1. _____ Qch (to ring, sound . . . *e.g.*, a bell) I
2. _____ de Qch (to play [a horn], Ex: *sonner du clairon*, to play the bugle) IV

sortir
1. _____ Qn ou Qch (to take . . . out) I
2. _____ de Qch (to go out of . . .; to come from . . . Ex: *sortir d'une bonne famille*, to come from a good family; *sortir du peuple*, to come from the people) IV
3. se _____ de Qch (to get out of . . . *e.g.*, a bad situation) IV
4. _____ Qch de Qch (to take . . . out of . . .) VI
5. _____ *Inf.* (to go out in order to . . .) VII-A

soucier
1. se _____ de Qn ou Qch (to care about, trouble oneself about . . .) IV
2. ne pas se soucier de *Inf.* (to not care about, not bother to . . . Ex: *Il ne se soucie pas de répondre*, he doesn't bother to answer) IX-A

souder
1. _____ Qch (to solder . . .) I
2. _____ Qch avec Qch (to solder . . . to . . .) VI

souffler
1. _____ Qch to utter, breathe . . . *e.g.*, a word; to snuff [a candle]) I
2. _____ dans, sur Qch (to blow, breathe on, in . . . *e.g.*, *sur sa soupe*, on one's soup; *dans, sur ses mains*, on one's hands [to warm them]) V
3. _____ Qn ou Qch à Qn (to suggest, whisper . . . to . . .; to steal . . . from . . .) VI

souffrir
1. _____ Qn ou Qch (to suffer, put up with . . .; to bear . . .) I

2. _____ de Qch (to suffer from . . . *e.g., du froid,* from the cold; to have a pain in . . . Ex: *souffrir du dos,* to have a backache) IV

3. _____ de *Inf.* (to suffer from, at ---*ing*) IX-A

souhaiter

1. _____ Qch (to wish for, desire . . .) I

2. _____ Qch à Qn (to wish someone something, Ex: *Je vous souhaite une bonne année,* I wish you a happy new year) VI

3. _____ *Inf.* (to hope to . . . Ex: *Nous souhaitons aller en France l'année prochaine,* we hope to go to France next year) VII-A

souiller

1. _____ Qn ou Qch (to soil, dirty, sully . . .) I

2. _____ Qn ou Qch de Qch (to soil, dirty, sully . . . with . . .) VI

soulager

1. _____ Qn ou Qch (to relieve, ease, comfort . . .) I

2. se _____ (to ease one's mind; to relieve oneself) I

3. se _____ de Qch (to ease, relieve one's . . . Ex: *se soulager de sa douleur,* to ease one's pain) IV

4. _____ Qn ou Qch de Qch (to ease someone's . . .; to relieve . . . of . . . *e.g., de sa peine,* of his grief) VI

5. se _____ de *Inf.* ou *Inf. passé* (to be relieved at, eased by ---*ing*, by having . . .) IX-A

soûler

1. _____ Qn (Coll: to get . . . drunk) I

2. se _____ (Coll: to get drunk) I

3. se _____ de Qch (to gorge on . . .; to glut oneself with . . .; to become drunk with . . . *e.g., de pouvoir,* with power) IV

4. _____ Qn de Qch (to intoxicate . . . with . . .) VI

soulever
1. _____ Qn ou Qch (to raise, lift . . .) I
2. se _____ contre Qn ou Qch (to rise up in rebellion against
   . . .) V
3. _____ Qn contre Qn ou Qch (to arouse . . . against . . .)
   VI

soumettre
1. _____ Qch (to submit . . .; to control . . .) I
2. se _____ (to yield) I
3. être soumis à Qn ou Qch (to be subject to, under the control
   of . . .) II
4. se _____ à Qn ou Qch (to yield to : . .; to comply with
   . . .) III
5. _____ Qn ou Qch à Qn ou Qch (to submit, subject . . .
   to . . .) VI

soupçonner
1. _____ Qn ou Qch (to suspect . . .) I
2. _____ Qn de Qch (to suspect . . . of . . .) VI
3. _____ Qn de *Inf.* ou *Inf. passé* (to suspect . . . of ---*ing*,
   of having . . .) IX-B

soupirer
1. _____ après, pour Qn ou Qch (to desire . . .; to yearn,
   long for . . .) V

sourire
1. _____ à Qn ou Qch (to smile at, on . . .) II
2. _____ de Qn ou Qch (to be amused by . . .) IV

souscrire
1. _____ Qch (to sign, draw . . . *e.g.*, a check; to under-
   write . . . *e.g.*, a loan) I
2. _____ à Qch (to contribute to . . .; to consent to, subscribe to . . . *e.g.*, an opinion, a belief) II

soustraire
1. _____ Qch (to subtract, remove . . .; to take . . . away) I
2. se _____ à Qch (to avoid, elude . . .) III
3. _____ Qn ou Qch à, de Qch (to shield, protect . . . from . . .) VI
4. _____ Qch à Qn ou Qch (to remove, steal . . . from . . .) VI

soutirer
1. _____ Qch (to tap, draw off . . .) I
2. _____ Qch à Qn (to get, wheedle . . . out of . . .) VI

souvenir
1. se _____ de Qn ou Qch (to remember . . .) IV
2. *Il souvient à Qn de Qn ou Qch* (Lit: to recall . . . Ex: *Il me souvient d'un incident assez drôle*, I recall a rather funny incident) II
3. faire souvenir Qn de Qn ou Qch (to remind . . . of . . .) VI
4. se _____ de *Inf.* ou *Inf. passé* (to remember to . . .; to remember ---*ing*, having . . .) IX-A

spécialiser (se)
1. se _____ dans Qch (to specialize in . . .) V

spéculer
1. _____ sur Qch (to speculate in, on . . .) V

statuer
1. _____ sur Qch (to pronounce judgment on . . .; to settle . . . *e.g.*, a dispute) V

stigmatiser
1. _____ Qn ou Qch (to brand, stigmatize . . .) I
2. _____ Qn ou Qch de Qch (to brand, stigmatize . . . with, as . . .) VI

stupéfier
1. ———— Qn (to stupefy . . .) I
2. être stupéfié par Qch (to be stupefied, astounded by . . .) V

subdiviser
1. ———— Qch (to subdivide . . .; to split up . . .) I
2. ———— Qch en Qch (to subdivide, split . . . in . . .) VI

subir
1. ———— Qn (to be forced to accept . . .; to bear with, endure . . .) I
2. ———— Qch (to undergo . . . *e.g.*, an operation; to come under . . . *e.g.*, an influence; to suffer . . . *e.g.*, a loss) I
3. faire subir Qch à Qn (to inflict . . . on . . .; to make someone undergo . . . Ex: *faire subir un examen au candidat*, to make the candidate take a test) VI

submerger
1. ———— Qn ou Qch (to submerge . . .) I
2. être submergé de Qch (to be submerged, swamped with . . .) IV
3. ———— Qn ou Qch de Qch (to submerge, swamp . . . with . . .) VI

subordonner
1. ———— Qn ou Qch (to subordinate . . .) I
2. se ———— à Qn ou Qch (to subordinate oneself to . . .) III
3. ———— Qn ou Qch à Qn ou Qch (to subordinate . . . to . . .) VI

subsister
1. ———— de Qch (to subsist on . . .) IV

substituer
1. se ———— à Qn (to substitute for . . .; to take someone's place) III
2. ———— Qn ou Qch à Qn ou Qch (to substitute . . . for . . .) VI

subvenir

1. _____ à Qch (to provide for . . .; to subsidize . . . Ex:
*L'Etat subvient aux frais universitaires et sco-
laires*, the state subsidizes tuition fees) II

succéder

1. se _____ (to follow one another, Ex: *Les années se succè-
dent*, the years follow one another) I
2. _____ à Qn ou Qch (to succeed, follow after . . .) II

succomber

1. _____ à Qch (to yield to, be overcome by . . . *e.g.*, sleep,
temptation) II
2. _____ sous Qch (to succomb to, sink under . . . *e.g.*, a
weight) V

suffire

1. _____ à Qch (to be adequate, equal to . . . *e.g.*, *à ses
besoins*, to one's needs) II
2. *Il suffit de Qch pour Inf.* (. . . is, are sufficient to . . . Ex: *Il
suffit de quelques mots pour la faire pleurer*, a
few words are enough to make her cry) IV
3. _____ à, pour *Inf.* (to be adequate, suffice to . . .) VIII-
A, X
4. *Il suffit de Inf.* (it is sufficient to . . .) IX-A
5. *Il suffit à Qn de Inf.* (to be satisfied with ---*ing*, Ex: *Il suf-
fisait aux enfants de regarder*, the children were
satisfied with watching) IX-B

suffoquer

1. _____ Qn ou Qch (to suffocate, smother . . .) I
2. _____ de Qch (to choke with . . . *e.g.*, *de colère*, with
anger) IV

suggérer

1. _____ Qch (to suggest . . .) I
2. _____ Qch à Qn (to suggest . . . to . . .) VI
3. _____ à Qn de *Inf.* (to suggest that someone . . .) IX-B

suivre
1. _____ Qn ou Qch (to follow . . .) I
2. être suivi de Qn ou Qch (to be followed by . . . Ex: *La voiture du président fut suivie d'un long cortège*, the President's car was followed by a long cortege; *la cérémonie fut suivie d'une réception*, the ceremony was followed by a reception) IV
3. être suivi par Qn ou Qch (to be followed by . . . Indicates greater physical pursuit than #2, Ex: *Le suspect fut suivi par un détective*, the suspect was followed by a detective) V
4. _____ Qn ou Qch *des yeux, du regard* (to follow, look after . . . with one's eyes) I

superposer
1. _____ Qch (to superimpose . . .) I
2. _____ Qch à Qch (to superimpose . . . on . . .) VI

suppléer
1. _____ Qch (to supply . . .; to fill in, make up [a lack]) I
2. _____ Qn (to replace, take the place of . . .) I
3. _____ à Qch [par Qch] (to compensate for . . . [with . . .]) II

supplier
1. _____ Qn (to beg, entreat . . .) I
2. _____ Qn de *Inf.* (to beg, entreat . . . to . . .) IX-B

supprimer
1. _____ Qch (to suppress, put down . . .) I
2. _____ Qn (Coll: to kill, rub out . . .) I
3. _____ Qch à Qn (to deprive someone of something; to take . . . away from . . .) VI
4. _____ Qch de Qch (to eliminate, delete . . . from . . .) VI

surabonder
1. _____ de, en Qch (to overflow with, be glutted with . . ., to have an excess of . . . Ex: *surabonder de blé*, to have an excess of wheat; *surabonder en éloges*, to overflow with praise) IV, V

surcharger
1. _____ Qn ou Qch (to overload, overwork . . .) I
2. se _____ de Qch (to overburden oneself with . . .) IV
3. _____ Qn ou Qch de Qch (to overburden . . . with . . .)
VI

surenchérir
1. _____ sur Qn (to bid higher than . . .; to outbid . . .) V

surpasser
1. _____ Qn ou Qch (to surpass . . .) I
2. se _____ (to outdo oneself) I
3. _____ Qn ou Qch en Qch (to surpass . . . in . . .; to be
superior to . . . in . . . Ex: *surpasser quelqu'un
en beauté, en intelligence*, to be prettier, smarter
than someone) VI

surprendre
1. _____ Qn ou Qch (to surprise . . .; to catch . . . unaware; to come across . . . unexpectedly) I
2. être surpris de Qch (to be surprised at, by . . .) IV
3. _____ Qn à *Inf.* (to catch someone ---*ing*) VIII-B
4. être surpris de *Inf.* (to be surprised to . . .) IX-A

surseoir
1. _____ à Qch (to delay, stay, postpone . . .) II

survivre
1. _____ à Qn ou Qch (to survive, outlive . . .) II

survoler
1. _____ Qch (to fly over . . .; to skip over . . .) I

suspecter
1. _____ Qn ou Qch (to suspect, doubt . . .) I
2. _____ Qn ou Qch de Qch (to suspect . . . of . . .) VI
3. _____ Qn ou Qch de *Inf.* ou *Inf. passé* (to suspect . . . of
---*ing*, of having . . .) IX-B

suspendre
1. _____ Qn ou Qch (to suspend, hang . . .) I
2. se ____ à Qch (to hang by, onto, from . . .) III
3. être suspendu sur Qch (to hang over . . . *e.g.*, the edge) V
4. _____ Qn ou Qch à Qch (to hang . . . from, on . . .) VI
5. _____ Qn ou Qch par Qch (to hang . . ., suspend . . . by . . .) VI

sympathiser
1. _____ avec Qn (to get along well with . . .) V

–T–

tabasser
1. _____ Qn (Coll: to beat up . . .) I

tabler
1. _____ sur Qch (to count on, reckon on . . .) V

tâcher
1. _____ de *Inf.* (to try, strive to . . .) IX-A

taire
1. _____ Qch (to hush up, suppress . . .; to keep silent about . . .) I
2. faire taire Qn (to silence . . .) I
3. se ____ (to keep silent) I
4. se ____ sur Qch (to say nothing about . . .) V
5. _____ Qch à Qn (to keep, conceal . . . from . . .) VI

taper
1. _____ Qch (to beat, tap . . .; to type . . .) I
2. _____ *des pieds* (to stamp one's feet)
3. _____ sur Qn ou Qch (Coll: to beat up . . .; to beat down on . . .) V

tarder
1. _____ à *Inf.* (to delay, to be late in ---*ing*, Ex: *Ne tardez pas à venir*, don't put off coming) VIII-A
2. *Il tarde à Qn de Inf.* (to be anxious to . . . Ex: *Il lui tarde de commencer*, he, she is anxious to begin) IX-B

targuer (se)
1. se _____ de Qch (to pride oneself on . . .) IV
2. se _____ de *Inf.* ou *Inf. passé* (to pride oneself on ---*ing*, on having . . .) IX-A

tarir
1. _____ Qch (to dry up . . .) I
2. se _____ (to run dry) I
3. ne _____ pas sur Qch (to be forever talking about . . .) V

tâter
1. _____ Qn ou Qch (to touch, feel . . .; to feel out . . .) I
2. _____ de Qch (to experience . . .; to try one's hand at . . .) IV
3. _____ *le pouls* à Qn (to take someone's pulse) VI

taxer
1. _____ Qch (to tax . . .; to set, regulate . . . *e.g.*, a price) I
2. _____ Qn ou Qch de Qch (to call . . . [a] . . . Ex: *taxer quelqu'un de menteur*, to call someone a liar; *taxer la protestation de trahison*, to call protest treason; to accuse . . . of . . . *e.g.*, *de négligence*, of negligence) VI

teindre
1. _____ Qch (to dye, stain . . .) I
2. être teint de Qch (to be stained, colored with . . .) IV
3. se _____ de Qch (to take on a tinge of . . .) IV
4. _____ Qch en [+ couleur] to dye something . . . Ex: *teindre quelque chose en bleu*, to dye something blue) VI
5. _____ Qch de Qch (to dye, stain . . . with . . .) VI

teinter
1. _____ Qch (to tint . . .) I
2. être teinté de Qch (to be tinted with . . .) IV
3. se _____ de Qch (to have, take on a tint of . . .) IV
4. _____ Qch de Qch (to tint . . . with . . .) VI

télégraphier
1. _____ Qch (to telegraph, wire, cable . . .) I
2. _____ à Qn (to send a telegraph, wire, cable to . . .) II
3. _____ Qch à Qn (to telegraph, wire, cable . . . to . . .) VI
4. _____ à Qn de *Inf*. (to telegraph, wire, cable . . . to . . .) IX-B

téléphoner
1. _____ à Qn (to telephone, call . . .) II
2. _____ Qch à Qn (to tell someone something over the telephone, Ex: *J'ai téléphoné les résultats à Pierre*, I called Pierre with the results) VI
3. _____ à Qn de *Inf*. (to tell someone by telephone to . . .) IX B

témoigner
1. _____ Qch (to show, manifest . . . Ex: *témoigner sa surprise*, to show one's surprise) I
2. _____ de Qch (to affirm, bear witness to . . ., to give evidence of . . . Ex: *Elle témoigna de sa fidélité*, she affirmed her loyalty) IV
3. _____ en faveur de, contre Qn (to testify, give evidence in favor of, against . . .) V

tempêter
1. _____ contre Qn ou Qch (to storm, rage against . . .) V

tendre
1. _____ Qch (to stretch . . .; to stretch out, hold out . . .) I
2. _____ à Qch (to strive for, towards . . . *e.g.*, *à la perfection*, for perfection) II
3. _____ Qch à Qn (to hold out . . . to . . .) VI
4. _____ *un piège* à Qn (to set a trap for . . .) VI
5. _____ à *Inf*. (to tend to . . .) VIII-A

tenir

1. _____ Qn ou Qch (to hold . . .; to keep . . . *e.g.*, a promise) I
2. se _____ (to remain, to be, Ex: *se tenir debout*, to be standing) I
3. _____ à Qn ou Qch (to be fond of . . . Ex: *Je tiens beaucoup à ce portrait*, I'm very fond of this portrait; With a thing as subject: to be caused by . . . Ex: *Sa mauvaise santé tient à son régime*, his poor health is a result of his diet) III
4. se _____ à Qch (to hang on to . . .; to keep to, abide by . . . Ex: *se tenir aux règles*, to abide by the rules) III
5. s'en _____ à Qch (to limit oneself to . . .) III
6. ne _____ qu'à Qn ou Qch (to be entirely up to . . .; to rest entirely on . . . Ex: *Ma vie ne tient qu'à lui*, my life is entirely in his hands) III
7. _____ de Qn (to take after . . .) IV
8. _____ de Qch (to be of the same nature as . . .) IV
9. _____ contre Qn ou Qch (to resist, hold out against . . .) V
10. en _____ pour Qn (to have a crush on . . .) V
11. _____ Qch de Qn (to have learned . . . from . . .; to have received . . . from . . .; to be indebted to someone for something) VI
12. _____ Qn ou Qch pour Qn ou Qch (to consider . . . a . . .; to take . . . for . . .) VI
13. _____ Qn ou Qch par Qch (to hold . . . by . . . *e.g.*, *par la main*, by the hand) VI
14. _____ à *Inf.* (to be set on --- *ing*, to be eager to . . .) VIII-A
15. être tenu de *Inf.* (to be obliged, expected to . . .) IX-A

tenter

1. _____ Qn (to tempt . . .) I
2. _____ Qch (to undertake, attempt . . .) I
3. _____ de *Inf.* (to attempt to, try to . . .) IX-A
4. être tenté de *Inf.* (to be tempted to . . .) IX-A

terminer
1. _____ Qch (to end, finish, conclude . . .) I
2. se _____ en, par* Qch (to finish, end in . . . Ex: *Quels mots se terminent par un "x"?* What words end in "x"? *Une comédie qui se termine en tragédie,* a comedy that ends in tragedy) V
3. _____ Qch par *Inf.* (to conclude, end . . . by ---*ing*) X

tirer
1. _____ Qn ou Qch (to pull . . .; to draw . . . *e.g.,* a sword) I
2. _____ à [*sa*] *fin* (to be ending, drawing to a close)
3. se _____ de Qch (to extricate oneself from . . .) IV
4. _____ sur, contre Qn ou Qch (to shoot at . . .; to fire on . . .) V
5. _____ vers, sur Qch (to border on . . . Ex: *Un bleu qui tire sur le vert,* a blue that borders on green) V
6. _____ Qn ou Qch de Qn ou Qch (to take . . . from, out of . . .; to draw, derive . . . from . . .; to drag . . . from, out of . . .; to save . . . from . . . Ex: *tirer quelqu'un du danger,* to save someone from danger) VI

tomber
1. faire tomber Qn ou Qch (to knock, push . . . over; to cause . . . to fall) I
2. laisser tomber Qch (to drop . . .) I
3. laisser tomber Qn (Coll: to stand . . . up; to stop seeing . . .) I
4. _____ de Qch (to fall from . . . *e.g., du ciel,* from the sky; to drop with . . . *e.g., de fatigue,* with fatigue) IV
5. _____ dans, en* Qch (to fall in, into . . . Ex: *tomber en disgrâce,* to fall into disgrace; *tomber dans l'oubli,* to sink into oblivion; *tomber dans un trou,* to fall into a hole) V
6. _____ sur Qn ou Qch (to attack . . .; to come across . . .) V

*See Appendix II: **DANS, EN, À**, p. 298.

tonner
1. _____ contre Qn (to thunder, inveigh against . . .) V

toquer (se)
1. se ___ de Qn (Coll: to have a crush on . . .) IV

tordre
1. _____ Qch (to twist . . .) I
2. se ___ Qch (to twist one's . . . Ex: *se tordre la cheville*, to twist one's ankle) I
3. se ___ de Qch (to double up with . . . *e.g., de rire*, with laughter; *de douleur*, with pain) IV
4. _____ Qch à Qn (to twist someone's . . . Ex: *tordre le bras à quelqu'un*, to twist someone's arm) VI

toucher
1. _____ Qn ou Qch (to touch . . .; of money: to receive or cash . . .) I
2. _____ à Qch (to tamper, meddle with . . .; to approach, draw near to, approximate . . .; to handle . . . *e.g.*, merchandise; to dabble in . . . Ex: *toucher à la peinture,* to dabble in painting) II
3. être touché de Qch (to be touched, moved by . . .) IV

tourmenter
1. _____ Qn ou Qch (to torment, harass, worry . . .) I
2. se ___ de Qch (to worry, fret about . . .) IV
3. être tourmenté par Qn ou Qch (to be tormented by . . .) V
4. _____ Qn ou Qch de Qch (to torment, harass . . . with . . .) VI
5. se ___ pour *Inf.* (to take the trouble to, bother to . . .) X

tourner

1. _____   Qch (to turn, revolve . . .) I
2. _____   *un film* (to shoot a movie) I
3. _____   autour de Qn ou Qch (to linger, pace around . . .; to revolve around . . .) V
4. _____   sur Qch (to depend on . . . Ex: *Tout tourne sur sa réponse*, everything depends on his, her answer) V
5. se _____   vers, contre Qn ou Qch (to turn towards, against . . .) V
6. _____   Qch en Qch (to turn . . . into . . .) VI
7. _____   Qch autour de Qch (to wind . . . around . . .) VI

traduire

1. _____   Qn ou Qch (to translate . . .) I
2. _____   de Qch (to translate from . . . *e.g., de l'anglais,* from [the] English) IV
3. se _____   par Qch (to become manifest by . . . Ex: *Son désir se traduisit par son regard*, his longing was evident in his expression) V
4. _____   Qn ou Qch en Qch (to translate . . . into . . .; *traduire quelqu'un en justice*, to prosecute someone) VI

trafiquer

1. _____   Qch (to trade, do business in . . .; to tamper with, doctor . . .) I
2. _____   de Qch (to make money on . . .; to sell . . . *e.g.,* one's honor; to traffic in . . . *e.g., de drogues,* in drugs) IV

traiter

1. _____   Qn ou Qch (to treat, deal with . . .) I
2. _____   de Qch (to deal with [a subject]) IV
3. _____   avec Qn (to negotiate with . . .) V
4. _____   Qn de Qch (to call . . . a . . . *e.g.,* a coward) VI

tramer
1. ——— Qch (to weave, to plot . . .) I
2. ——— Qch contre Qn ou Qch (to plot . . . against . . .) VI

trancher
1. ——— Qch (to cut, slice . . .; to settle . . . *e.g.*, an argument) I
2. ——— avec Qch (to contrast strongly with . . .) V
3. ——— sur Qch (to stand out against, from . . .) V
4. ——— Qch à Qn (to cut off someone's . . . *e.g.*, someone's head) VI

tranquilliser
1. ——— Qn (to calm, reassure . . .) I
2. ——— Qn sur Qn ou Qch (to reassure . . . about . . .) VI

transférer
1. ——— Qn ou Qch (to transfer . . .) I
2. ——— Qch à Qn (to transfer . . . to . . .; to sign over . . . to . . .) VI

transformer
1. ——— Qn ou Qch (to transform . . .) I
2. se ——— en Qn ou Qch (to turn into . . .) V
3. ——— Qn ou Qch en Qn ou Qch (to turn, transform . . . into . . .) VI

transiger
1. ——— avec Qn ou Qch (to compromise with . . .; to make concessions to . . .) V

transmettre
1. ——— Qch (to transmit . . .) I
2. ——— Qch à Qn (to transmit . . . to . . .) VI

transmuer

1. _____ Qch en Qch (to transmute . . . into . . .) VI

transpirer

1. _____ de Qch (to perspire, Ex: *Il transpire des mains,* his hands perspire) IV
2. _____ sur Qch (to sweat over . . .; to work hard on . . .) V

travailler

1. _____ Qn ou Qch (to work . . .; to cultivate . . . *e.g.,* the earth; to work on, study . . . *e.g.,* a role) I
2. _____ à Qch (to work for, towards . . .) II
3. _____ pour Qn ou Qch (to work for . . .) V
4. _____ à *Inf.* (to strive to . . .) VIII-A

travestir

1. se _____ en Qn ou Qch (to disguise oneself, dress up as . . .) V
2. _____ Qn ou Qch en Qn ou Qch (to disguise, dress up . . . as . . .) VI

trébucher

1. _____ sur, contre Qch (to stumble over, against . . .) V

trembler

1. _____ de Qch (to tremble with . . . *e.g., de peur,* with fear) IV
2. _____ de *Inf.* ou *Inf. passé* (to tremble at the thought of ---*ing*; to fear that . . . Ex: *Je tremble de lui avoir déplu,* I fear that I displeased him) IX-A

tremper

1. _____ Qch (to dilute, soak, dip . . .) I
2. _____ dans Qch (to be involved in . . .; to have a hand in . . .) V
3. se _____ dans Qch (to be steeped in . . .) V
4. _____ Qch dans Qch (to dip, dunk . . . in . . .) VI

trépigner
1. _____ de Qch (to stamp, dance with . . . *e.g., de rage*, with rage) IV

trinquer
1. _____ à Qch (to drink to . . .) II
2. _____ avec Qn (to have a drink with . . .; to drink a toast with . . .) V

triompher
1. _____ de Qn ou Qch (to triumph over . . .; to get the better of, overcome . . .) IV

tromper
1. _____ Qn (to deceive . . .) I
2. _____ Qch (to disappoint . . . *e.g.*, one's expectations) I
3. se _____ (to be mistaken) I
4. se _____ de Qch (to be mistaken about . . . Ex: *se tromper d'adresse*, to have the wrong address) IV
5. _____ Qn sur Qch (to mislead, deceive . . . about . . .) VI

troquer
1. _____ Qn ou Qch (to trade, barter, swap . . .) I
2. _____ Qn ou Qch contre Qn ou Qch (to swap, exchange . . . for . . .) VI

trouver
1. _____ Qn ou Qch (to find . . .) I
2. se _____ (to be located) I
3. _____ Qch à Qn ou Qch (to consider someone or something to have . . . Ex: *Je ne lui trouve aucun talent*, I don't think he, she has any talent) VI
4. _____ à *Inf.* (to manage to . . . Ex: *Elle trouve à nourrir ses enfants*, she finds a way to feed her children) VIII-A

tuer
1. _____ Qn ou Qch (to kill . . .) I
2. se _____ à, de Qch (to kill oneself with . . . Ex: *se tuer au, de travail*, to kill oneself with work) III, IV
3. se _____ à *Inf.* (to kill, exhaust oneself *---ing*) VIII-A

U

unir

1. _____ Qn ou Qch (to unite . . .) I
2. s'_____ à Qn ou Qch (to unite with, join with . . .) III
3. _____ Qn ou Qch à, avec Qn ou Qch (to unite . . . with . . .) VI

user

1. _____ Qch (to wear out, use up . . .) I
2. s'_____ (to wear oneself out; to become worn out) I
3. _____ de Qch (to use, make use of . . . *e.g.*, one's power; to avail oneself of . . . *e.g.*, one's rights) IV
4. s'_____ à *Inf.* (to wear oneself out ---*ing*) VIII-A

usurper

1. _____ Qch (to usurp . . .) I
2. _____ sur Qn ou Qch (to encroach on . . .) V

V

vacciner

1. _____ Qn contre Qch (to immunize . . . against . . .) VI

valoir

1. _____ Qch (to be worth . . .) I
2. _____ Qn (to be as good as, worth as much as . . .) I
3. faire valoir Qch (to make the most of . . .; to set . . . to advantage, Ex: *Elle fait valoir ses beaux cheveux*, she makes the most of her pretty hair) I
4. _____ Qch à Qn (to result in, lead to . . . for . . . Ex: *cette action lui a valu un avancement*, that action got him a promotion) VI
5. *Il vaut mieux Inf.* (it is better, a better idea to . . .) VII-A

vanter
1. _____ Qn ou Qch (to praise . . .) I
2. se ____ (to brag, boast) I
3. se ____ de Qch (to boast of, about . . .) IV
4. _____ Qn ou Qch à Qn (to praise . . . to . . .) VI
5. se ____ de *Inf.* ou *Inf. passé* (to claim boastfully to be able to . . ., of having . . .) IX-A

vaquer
1. _____ à Qch (to attend to . . .) II

veiller
1. _____ Qn (to sit up with, keep watch over . . .) I
2. _____ à Qch (to look after, keep an eye on . . . Ex: *veiller à ses intérêts*, to look out for one's interests) II
3. _____ sur Qn ou Qch (to take care of, look after the welfare of . . .) V

vendre
1. _____ Qn (to betray . . .) I
2. _____ Qch (to sell . . .) I
3. _____ Qn ou Qch à Qn (to sell, betray . . . to . . .) VI

venger
1. _____ Qn ou Qch (to avenge . . .) I
2. se ____ de Qch (to take vengeance for . . .) IV
3. se ____ de Qn (to get even with . . .) IV
4. se ____ sur Qn de Qch (to take vengeance on . . . for . . .) V
5. _____ Qn de Qch (to avenge . . . for . . .) VI

venir
1. en ____ à Qch (to come to . . . *e.g., aux coups*, to blows; to be reduced to . . . *e.g., au vol*, to theft) II

2. ———— de Qn ou Qch (to come from . . .) IV

3. ———— *Inf.* (to come in order to . . . Ex: *Elle vient voir les photos,* she is coming to see the pictures) VII

4. ———— à *Inf.* (to happen to . . . Ex. *Si je venais à mourir,* if I happened to die) VIII-A

5. en ——— à *Inf.* (to end up by ---ing, Ex: *Il en est venu à mendier,* he ended up by begging) VIII-A

6. ———— de *Inf.* (to have just . . . Ex: *Nous venons de manger,* we have just eaten) IX-A

verbaliser

1. ———— sur Qch (Of police: to write out a report, a summons on, about . . .) V

2. ———— contre Qn (to testify, issue a summons against . . .) V

verser

1. ———— Qch (to pour, spill . . .) I

2. ———— dans Qch (to verge on, fall into . . . Ex: *Cet auteur verse dans le sublime,* that author verges on the sublime) V

3. se ——— dans Qch (to flow into . . .) V

4. ———— Qch dans Qch (to pour . . . into . . .) VI

5. ———— Qch sur Qn ou Qch (to pour, spill . . . on . . .) VI

vêtir

1. ———— Qn ou Qch (to dress, clothe . . .) I

2. ———— Qn ou Qch de Qch (to dress, clothe . . . in . . .) VI

vexer

1. ———— Qn (to vex, annoy . . .) I

2. se ——— de Qch (to get annoyed, vexed at . . .) IV

3. être vexé de Qch (to be annoyed, vexed at, by . . .) IV

4. se ——— de *Inf.* ou *Inf. passé* (to be annoyed, vexed at ---ing, at having . . .) IX-A

vider

1. ———— Qn ou Qch (to empty, drain . . .) I

2. se ——— dans Qch (to empty into . . .) V

3. _____ Qn ou Qch de Qch (to empty, drain . . . of . . .) VI

4. _____ Qch dans, sur Qn ou Qch (to empty, pour . . . into, onto . . .) VI

virer

1. _____ à Qch (to curve, turn to . . . Ex: *virer à droite*, to turn, curve to the right; *virer au tragique*, to turn to tragedy) II

viser

1. _____ Qn ou Qch (to take aim at . . .) I

2. _____ à Qch (to aim for . . . *e.g.*, *à la perfection*, for perfection) II

3. _____ à *Inf.* (to aspire to . . .; to set one's sights on ---*ing*) VIII-A

vivre

1. _____ de Qch (to live on, by . . .) IV

vociférer

1. _____ Qch contre Qn ou Qch (to shout, yell . . . at . . .) VI

voiler

1. _____ Qn ou Qch (to veil, hide . . .) I

2. _____ Qch à Qn (to veil, hide . . . from . . .) VI

3. _____ Qn ou Qch de Qch (to veil, obscure . . . with . . .) VI

voir

1. _____ Qn ou Qch (to see . . .) I

2. _____ *Inf.* Qn ou Qch (to see someone or something . . . Ex: *J'ai vu arriver le train*, I saw the train arrive) VII-B

3. _____ à *Inf.* (to see to, to take care to . . . Ex: *Voyez à tout préparer*, see to it that everything is ready) VIII-A

voler
1. _____ Qn (to rob . . .) I
2. _____ Qch (to steal . . .) I
3. _____ Qch à Qn (to steal . . . from . . .) VI

voter
1. _____ Qch (to pass . . . *e.g.*, a law; to carry . . . *e.g.*, a motion; to vote . . . *e.g.*, appropriations) I
2. _____ pour, contre Qn ou Qch (to vote for, against . . .) V

vouer
1. se _____ à Qn ou Qch (to dedicate oneself to . . .) III
2. _____ Qn ou Qch à Qn ou Qch (to dedicate, consecrate . . . to . . .) VI

vouloir
1. _____ Qn ou Qch (to want, desire . . .) I
2. s'en _____ (to be angry with oneself) I
3. en _____ à Qn [de Qch] (to be angry with . . ., to have a grudge against . . . [about . . .]) II
4. _____ de Qn ou Qch (to want some of something, Ex: *Veux-tu de ces bonbons?* do you want any of this candy?; to want something to do with . . . Ex: *Ils ne veulent pas de lui*, they want nothing to do with him) IV
5. _____ Qch de Qn (to want . . . from . . .) VI
6. _____ *Inf.* (to want to . . .) VII-A
7. s'en _____ de *Inf. passé* (to be angry with oneself for having . . .) IX-A
8. en _____ à Qn de *Inf.* ou *Inf. passé* (to be angry with . . . for ---*ing*, for having . .) IX-B

APPENDIX I

Prepositions of Geographical Location

- - - - - - - - - - - - - - - - - - -

A. Prepositions used with names of Cities and Countries

Various prepositions are used, with or without a definite article, with verbs of coming (e.g., *venir*), going (e.g., *aller*), being (e.g., *être*), or doing (e.g., *habiter*), depending on whether the object of the preposition is a feminine country, a masculine country, or a city.

Feminine countries end in *e*, for example, *la France, l'Italie, l'Argentine.* (Exceptions: *le Mexique, le Cambodge*). Masculine countries end in a consonant or a vowel other than *e*, for example, *l'Irak, le Canada, les États-Unis.*

	Feminine Countries	Masculine Countries	Cities
Place In Which	en	au, aux	à
Place To Which	en	au, aux	à
Place From Which	de, d'	du, des	de

Examples:

Place In Which

Tu habites *en* Italie?	Do you live *in* Italy?
Elle a vu beaucoup de choses *au* Canada.	She saw a lot *in* Canada.
Nous avons passé six semaines *à* Rome.	We spent six weeks *in* Rome.

Place To Which

Il est allé *en* France l'été passé.	He went *to* France last summer.
Nous irons *au* Brésil pour le Mardi gras.	We will go *to* Brazil for the Mardi gras.
Je dois aller *à* Chicago la semaine prochaine.	I have to go *to* Chicago next week.

Place From Which

Je suis arrivé *de* France hier.	I arrived *from* France yesterday.
Il faut traverser la frontière pour aller *du* Canada aux États-Unis.	You have to cross the border to go *from* Canada to the United States.
Êtes-vous venu *de* Paris?	Did you come *from* Paris?

Note 1: Masculine countries beginning with a vowel follow the rules for feminine countries, e.g., *Je vais* **en** *Iran.* I am going *to* Iran; *Je viens* **d'***Irak.* I am coming *from* Iraq.

Three masculine countries can take either *en* or *au.* One can say: *en Danemark* or *au Danemark*; *en Portugal* or *au Portugal*; *en Luxembourg* or *au Luxembourg.*

Note 2: When a definite article is part of the city's name, e.g., *Le Havre, La Nouvelle-Orléans*, the article is kept and a contraction is made with the preposition when necessary. The contraction is not capitalized.

Je viens *du* Havre.	I am coming *from* Le Havre.
Elle a débarqué *au* Havre.	She landed *at* Le Havre.
Nous habitons *à La* Nouvelle-Orléans.	We live *in* New Orleans.

Note 3: When the name of a city or country is modified, e.g., *le vieux Paris, la France méridionale*, the preposition *dans* is used with the definite article in place of *en.*

J'aurais aimé vivre *dans le* vieux Paris.	I would have liked to live *in* (*the*) old Paris.
Il a passé l'été *dans la* France méridionale.	He spent the summer *in* southern France.

B. Prepositions used with names of Continents

Continents that are modified (e.g., *l'Amérique du Sud*, *l'Afrique du Nord*) take a preposition plus a definite article. Continents that are not modified take no definite article. *For example*:

Elle a passé plusieurs années *dans l'*Amérique du Sud.	She spent several years *in* South America.
Il a beaucoup voyagé *en* Asie.	He has traveled extensively *in* Asia.
Le bateau vient *d'*Afrique.	The boat is coming *from* Africa.

	Modified Continent	Unmodified Continent
Place In Which	dans l'*	en
Place To Which	dans l'*	en
Place From Which	de l'	d'

*In spoken French, *en* is often used instead of *dans l'*.

C. Prepositions used with names of Provinces and States

French Provinces

Note that feminine provinces (i.e., those ending in *e*) follow the rules for feminine countries.

	Feminine Provinces	*Masculine Provinces*
Place In Which	en	dans le, l'
Place To Which	en	dans le, 1'
Place From Which	de, d'	du, de l'

Examples:

Nous avons bu de la bière *en* Alsace.

We drank beer *in* Alsace.

As-tu cherché des truffes *dans le* Périgord?

Did you hunt for truffles *in* Perigord?

Ils sont allés en voiture *de* Normandie *en* Bretagne.

They drove *from* Normandy *to* Brittany.

Note: In spoken French, masculine provinces can be used with the same prepositions as feminine provinces:

J'ai passé mes vacances *en* Poitou.

I spent my vacation *in* Poitou.

American States

Some American states have French forms. Most of these forms are feminine:

la Californie
la Floride
la Georgie
la Louisiane

la Pennsylvanie
la Virginie
la Virginie occidentale

States which are feminine in French follow the rules for feminine countries.

Two states have French forms and are masculine:

le Maine
le Nouveau Mexique

The other states have no French form, e.g., *le Nebraska*. These states are masculine.

	*Feminine States**	*Masculine States*
Place In Which	en	au**, dans le, l' (dans l'état de)
Place To Which	en	au**, dans le, l' (dans l'état de)
Place From Which	de	du, de l' (de l'état de)

*Even though they are feminine, the two states *la Caroline du Nord* and *la Caroline du Sud* take the same prepositions as masculine states.

**Note that *au* is used with a masculine state beginning with a consonant (*e.g.*, *Texas*). However, for masculine states beginning with a vowel, *à l'* is NOT used. Either *dans l'* or *dans l'état d'* is used.

Examples:

Je suis né *en* Virginie.	I was born *in* Virginia.
La ville de New York se trouve *dans l*'état de New York.	New York City is located *in* New York State.

Pour aller *du* Colorado *en* Californie, il faut traverser les Montagnes Rocheuses.	To go *from* Colorado *to* California, you have to cross the Rocky Mountains.

D. Prepositions used with Street Names

Street names are frequently used *without* a preposition in French where the preposition *on* would be used in English.

J'habite rue Cambon.	I live *on* Cambon Street.
Il travaille boulevard St-Michel.	He works *on* St-Michel Boulevard.

There are French prepositions, however, which correspond to the English preposition *on*. The preposition varies according to the type of thoroughfare and is used with a definite article.

Examples:

Il habite *dans la* rue Cambon.	He lives *on* Cambon Street.
Il habite *dans l'*avenue Foch.	He lives *on* Foch Avenue.
Il habite *sur le* boulevard St-Michel.	He lives *on* St-Michel Boulevard.
Il habite *sur la* route nationale N7.	He lives *on* Highway N7.

The prepositions *de* or *à* are used along with a definite article with verbs of coming from or going to a street name.

Vas-tu *à la* Cinquième avenue?	Are you going *to* Fifth Avenue?
Il est venu *du* boulevard Raspail.	He came *from* Raspail Boulevard.

E. Prepositions used with names of Islands

The use of prepositions with names of islands is somewhat complex. The preposition varies according to the gender, size, and geographic location of the island. There are five major categories:

1. *Masculine Islands* (e.g., *Cuba, Madagascar*)

2. *Large Feminine Islands* (e.g., *la Sardaigne, l'Islande, la Corse, la Sicile*)

3. *Small Feminine Islands Near Europe* (e.g., *Chypre, Malte*)

4. *Small Feminine Islands Far From Europe* (e.g., *la Martinique, la Réunion, la Guadeloupe*)

5. *Very Small Islands* (usually with the word *île* in their name, e.g., *l'île de la Cité, l'île Maurice, l'île d'Yeu*)

	Masculine	Large* Feminine	Small Feminine Near	Small Feminine Far	Very Small
Place In Which	à	en	à	à la, l'	dans l'
Place To Which	à	en	à	à la, l'	dans l'
Place From Which	de, d'	de, d'	de, d'	de la, l'	de l'

*Exception: *la Terre-Neuve*, Newfoundland. This large feminine island takes the same prepositions as masculine islands.

Examples:

On cultive le sucre *à* Cuba.

Sugar is grown *in* Cuba.

Beaucoup de Français passent leurs vacances *en* Corse.

Many French people spend their vacation *in* Corsica.

La guerre a éclaté *à* Chypre.

War has broken out *on* Cyprus.

Ils ont fait une croisière *à la* Martinique.

They took a cruise *to* Martinique.

Ce restaurant se trouve *dans* l'Île de la Cité, en face de Notre-Dame.

That restaurant is *on the* Île de la Cité, across from Notre Dame.

Dans, En, À

A. When to Use DANS, EN and À

The prepositions *dans* and *à* (like most other prepositions, e.g., *par*, *sur*, etc.) are generally used when the noun is preceded by a definite article, an indefinite article, a demonstrative adjective, or a possessive adjective.*

Examples:

Il a passé deux années *dans la* prison d'Alcatraz.	He spent two years *at* Alcatraz.
Nous avons dîné *dans un* restaurant français.	We ate dinner *in a* French restaurant.
Marie étudie *dans sa* chambre.	Marie is studying *in her* room.
Il s'est jeté *à l'*eau.	He jumped *into the* water.
On l'avait logé *à un* très mauvais hôtel.	They put him up *at a* very bad hotel.

---

*With the exception of geographical place names: See Appendix I.

The preposition *en* is generally used when the noun is NOT preceded by a definite article, an indefinite article, a demonstrative adjective, or a possessive adjective.

Examples:

On l'a jeté *en* prison.

They threw him *in* jail.

Ils ont fait des courses *en* ville.

They did some shopping *in* town.

Je suis venu *en* classe sans avoir préparé ma leçon.

I came *to* class without having prepared my lesson.

Exceptions: The following expressions take *en* with a definite article:

en l'absence de	in the absence of
en l'honneur de	in honor of
en l'espace de	in the space of
en l'air	in the air
en l'an	in the year

B. Differences in Meaning Between DANS, EN and À

The preposition *dans* often has a more physical or precise meaning than the prepositions *à* or *en*. *Dans* frequently has the sense of *inside* or *into*. Compare the following sentences:

Elle est montée *dans* la
voiture.

She got *into* the car.

Nous sommes venus *en*
voiture.

We came *by* car.

Je ne veux pas entrer *dans*
ce bar.

I don't want to go *into* this
bar.

On a applaudi quand il est
entré *en* scène.

They applauded when he
came *on* stage.

Elle est entrée *au* couvent
à l'âge de dix-huit ans.

She entered the convent at
the age of eighteen.

Ne faites pas tant de bruit
dans la maison!

Don't make so much noise
in the house!

Est-ce que ta mère est *à* la
maison?

Is your mother *at* home?

On a mis les bouteilles au
frais *dans* la rivière.

They put the bottles to
cool *in* the river.

Ne reste pas *au* soleil;
mets-toi *à* l'ombre.

Don't stay *in* the sun; go
sit *in* the shade.

C. The Use of DANS, EN and À with Vehicles of Transportation

1. To go somewhere by . . .

   On va quelque part:

en autobus	à bicyclette
en auto(mobile)	à cheval
en avion	à moto(cyclette)
en bateau	à pied
en scooter	
en taxi	par le train
en vélo	
en voiture	

2. To get on, get in . . .

   On monte:

   dans un autobus
   dans un avion
   à bord d'un bateau, sur un bateau
   dans un taxi
   dans un train
   dans une voiture

3. To be in, be on . . .

   On est:

   dans un autobus

dans un avion
à bord d'un bateau, sur un bateau
dans un taxi
dans un train
dans une voiture

Listen to the real sounds of France

Most language learning tapes present French as if it were something that existed in a vacuum. The *Ensemble* is different! The brief dramatizations use the sounds of France. The sketches are based on real situations and the recordings were made in France—in the streets, in cafes and shops, in people's houses —and so the voices you hear are those of ordinary French people going about their everyday activities. Practice your new language by listening to authentic French.

Tape 1—Programs 1-12, $5.20; Tape 2—Programs 13-24, $5.20

The *Ensemble* texts include transcripts for those conversations on tape, plus explanations of grammatical points and exercises to practice what you've learned.

Book 1—Programs 1-12, $2.00; Book 2—Programs 13-24, $2.00

Available at your local bookseller or
order direct adding 10% postage plus applicable sales tax.

French grammar

on one card by J. A. Cremona, Edited by J. L. M. Trim

I. NOUNS AND QUALIFYING ADJECTIVES

A. GENDER

B. NUMBER

C. AGREEMENT OF ADJECTIVE

D. POSITION OF ADJECTIVE

II. ARTICLES

A. DEFINITE ARTICLE

B. INDEFINITE ARTICLE

C. PARTITIVE ARTICLE

III. PERSONAL PRONOUNS

A. CONJUNCTIVE PRONOUNS

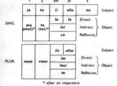

B. DISJUNCTIVE PRONOUNS

C. ADVERBIAL PRONOUNS (EN AND Y)

IV. OTHER ADJECTIVES AND PRONOUNS

A. RELATIVE PRONOUNS

B. DEMONSTRATIVE ADJECTIVES AND PRONOUNS

C. POSSESSIVE ADJECTIVES AND PRONOUNS

D. INDEFINITE ADJECTIVES AND PRONOUNS

E. INTERROGATIVE ADJECTIVES AND PRONOUNS

FRENCH BILINGUAL DICTIONARY

A BEGINNER'S GUIDE IN WORDS AND PICTURES

The Apple

La Pomme

Typical entry:

acheter [a-SHTAY] : to buy

j'achète	nous achetons
tu achètes	vous achetez
il, elle achète	ils, elles achètent

Le garcon achète une balle.
The boy is buying a ball.

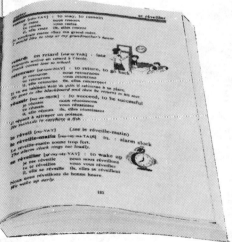

By Gladys C. Lipton,
Asst. to Dir., Bureau of Foreign Languages, Board of Education of the City of New York

- 1300 word entries spotlighting the most commonly used words—a dictionary especially for beginners
- English-French Finder List which permits instant translations of primary words
- special reference tables—bilingual number tables, measurements, grammatical terms, classroom expressions, and more

Each word entry is followed by a pronunciation key and includes a sentence example using the word. Idiomatic expressions are cross-listed and the overall format of the book is simple.

$3.95 paper

A workbook in French composition

Beginning to Write in French

A programmed
workbook designed to
develop skill in
writing simple French.

Over 200 basic
regents idioms and
verbal expressions.

Over 100 common verbs.

40 units, 13 tests.

Each unit contains
5 idioms related
in thought.

Exercises in
parallel writing,
controlled, and free
composition.

Practice in
writing answers to
simple questions
asked orally in French.
by Christopher Kendris

Barron's
Educational Series

From
1001 Pitfalls in French

Hebreu ou Grec?
Quand un Français ne comprend rien à ce qu'il lit ou entend, il dit: "C'est de l'hébreu" au lieu de "C'est du grec" comme nous.

$2.95

1001 PITFALLS IN FRENCH

A style guide and general reference for quick answers to common but troublesome difficulties in learning and using French. Alphabetical order of topics eliminates searching through pages of grammar texts for an answer to a specific question. Common pitfalls in vocabulary nuances, grammar, usage and style are illustrated by contrastive examples to help the student understand and avoid future mistakes. Topics controlled by questionnaire responses from hundreds of French teachers, including their favorite "faux amis." Current French usage is emphasized. Fully indexed.